IN DEFENSE OF THE CONSTITUTION

A Liberty*Press*
Edition

George W. Carey teaches American government and American political theory at Georgetown University, where he is Professor of Government. His works include *The Federalist: Design for a Constitutional Republic* (1989) and *The Basic Symbols of the American Political Tradition* (1970, with the late Willmoore Kendall), both of which explore in depth the fundamental values and underlying principles of the American political order. Professor Carey is also the coeditor of two books: *A Second Federalist: Congress Creates a Government* (1967, with Charles S. Hyneman), and the first student edition of *The Federalist* (1990, with James McClellan). He has served on the Council of the National Endowment for the Humanities (1982–88), and since 1970 he has edited *The Political Science Reviewer,* an annual journal devoted to article-length reviews of leading works in political science and related disciplines.

George W. Carey

IN DEFENSE OF

—— THE ——

CONSTITUTION

REVISED AND EXPANDED

EDITION

Liberty Fund
Indianapolis
1995

This is a Liberty*Press* Edition published by Liberty Fund, Inc., a foundation established to encourage study of the ideal of a society of free and responsible individuals.

The cuneiform inscription that serves as our logo and as the design motif for our endpapers is the earliest-known written appearance of the word ''freedom'' (*amagi*), or ''liberty.'' It is taken from a clay document written about 2300 B.C. in the Sumerian city-state of Lagash.

Originally published by the Center for Judicial Studies, © 1989.

Revised and Expanded Edition © 1995 by Liberty Fund, Inc. All rights reserved. Printed in the United States of America.

Liberty Fund, Inc.
8335 Allison Pointe Trail, Suite 300
Indianapolis, Indiana 46250-1687
(317) 842-0880

Library of Congress Cataloging-in-Publication Data

Carey, George Wescott, 1933-
   In defense of the Constitution / George W. Carey.—Rev. and
expanded ed.
      p.   cm.
   Includes bibliographical references.
   ISBN 0-86597-137-4 (hard : acid-free paper).—ISBN 0-86597-138-2
(pbk. : acid-free paper)
   1. United States—Constitutional history.   I. Title
KF4541.C36   1994
342.73′029—dc20
[347.30229]   94-38245
                                       CIP

10 9 8 7 6 5 4 3 2 1

Contents

Acknowledgements

I would like to express my appreciation to the following individuals and organizations for making this work possible. James B. Williams, Michael Jackson, Roland Gunn, and Pamela Sullivan, over the years, have read and critically commented on one or more of the selections that follow. Needless to say, I have benefitted from their criticisms. David A. Bovenizer is due special thanks for lending his deft editorial hand to the completion of this book.

The substance of the chapters that follow first appeared in article form in various journals, although I have significantly revised some of them. I would like to thank Donald P. Kommers, editor, *Review of Politics*, for permission to incorporate "Publius—A Split Personality?" (January 1984); George Panichas, editor, *Modern Age*, for "Majority Rule and the Extended Republic Theory of James Madison" (Winter 1976) and "The Supreme Court, Judicial Review, and Federalist Seventy-Eight" (Fall 1974); the American Political Science Association for "Separation of Powers and the Madisonian Model: A Reply to the Critics" (*American Political Science Review*, March 1978); James McClellan, editor, *Benchmark*, for "James Madison and the Principle of Federalism" (January–April 1987) and "Liberty and the Fifth Amendment: Original Intent" (Fall 1990); and James P. McFadden, editor, *Human Life Review*, for "Abortion and the American Political Crisis" (Winter 1977).

The generosity of the Earhart Foundation, Ann Arbor, Michigan, and the Institute for Educational Affairs, Washington, D.C., provided me with the opportunity to complete major sections of this work. I am deeply grateful.

Finally, I owe a special debt to James McClellan. In his capacities both as Director of the Center for Judicial Studies and now as Publications Director for Liberty Fund, he has been a source of inspiration and encouragement.

January 1995

George W. Carey
Georgetown University

Note to the Reader

Throughout this book all references to *The Federalist* are to the student edition edited by George W. Carey and James McClellan (Dubuque: Kendall/Hunt, 1990). The parenthetical citations in the text refer to essay number and page except when the essay number is evident from the discussion.

The following abbreviations have been used in the parenthetical citations in the text of chapter 1, "Publius—A Split Personality?" SP refers to Alpheus T. Mason's article, "The Federalist—A Split Personality," *American Historical Review* 57 (1952); TF, to Gottfried Dietze's *The Federalist: A Classic on Federalism and Free Government* (Baltimore: Johns Hopkins Press, 1960); and DP, to Douglass Adair's article, "The Authorship of the Disputed Federalist Papers," reprinted in *Fame and the Founding Fathers: Essays by Douglass Adair*, ed. Trevor Colbourn (New York: W. W. Norton, 1974).

IN DEFENSE OF THE CONSTITUTION

Introduction

While the essays that follow are addressed to different aspects of our constitutional order and operations, there is an underlying unity to them. The principal source of this unity takes the form of a reaction to a revisionist school of thought, now dominant in academia, that has sought in various ways to disparage our Founding Fathers and their handiwork. Because so much of what I say in the following selections presupposes an understanding of the development and major tenets of this school of thought, I will examine it and the consequences that have flowed from its "teachings" at the outset.

For several decades now, since the early 1900s to be exact, the Constitution has come under increasingly severe and sustained attack for what is alleged to be its "undemocratic" character. The initial attacks were "shocking" in the sense that they challenged the prevailing orthodoxy that served to place the Founders and the Constitution above reproach. Today, by contrast, the gist of these early attacks constitutes commonplace observations—advanced normally in the guise of undisputed facts—found in many colleges and high school government and history texts concerning the motives and purposes of our Founding Fathers and the nature of the system they bequeathed to us.

While, as we shall see, there are differences between the early revisionists and their modern counterparts, the most notable being a belated but welcome acceptance of a strong national government, there is at least one common theme that weaves through their critiques: namely, the Constitution is an "undemocratic" document. In this respect, the critiques are, so to speak, double-edged; that is, not only is the Constitution found wanting from the perspective of the majority rule principle, it is viewed as an instrumentality that thwarts the realization of "democratic" ends such as those presumably embodied in the second paragraph of the Declaration of Independence. Thus, the revisionists' democracy is of two kinds: one concerned with the means or methods of decision making, the other with goals or ends.

Now what is often overlooked is that these two conceptions of democracy are not entirely compatible. For instance, a majority may vote for policies that contravene the presumed democratic ends. To some extent, the liberal revisionists have been able to avoid facing the theoretical difficulties posed by this incompatibility by assuming, sometimes tacitly, that majorities do cherish these democratic ends, but that our institutions and processes either thwart or distort their will. Accordingly, they have long held that, once the Constitution has been democratized, majorities will actively pursue and ultimately realize these democratic ends. For the New Left, neo-Marxists, and other social dissidents, of course, to reach this coincidence of ends and means requires a good deal more than mere institutional "reform," since institutions are only the reflection of dominant social and economic forces. For them the problem is overcoming the hurdles—social, economic, educational, and the like—that prevent majorities from perceiving their true interests, an undertaking that would necessarily involve comprehensive social engineering.

What seems increasingly clear in recent decades is that the revisionists, off at the end, have given primacy to ends over means; that is, their commitment to majority rule is secondary to their commitment to democratic ends which, to a great extent, come down to egalitarianism mixed with virtually unbridled liberty. Indeed, their commitment to majority rule seems to be contingent on whether they like what the majority wills. One reason for this, we may surmise, is that it is now painfully obvious to most revisionists that majorities can (that is, from the revisionists' point of view) be a "beast," that they are not as "enlightened" as some of the earlier revisionists seemed to assume.

Without going into the whys and wherefores—for this is a matter I will take up in due course—what has emerged from these revisionists' reservations concerning republicanism and their quest for the realization of democratic ends is what can appropriately be termed a new "constitutional morality"; that is, they advocate and justify a way of looking at the proper operations and relationships of our constitutional institutions and processes that is inimical to the older morality wrought by the Framers and articulated in *The Federalist*. This new morality, it should be noted, is truly revolutionary because it represents, as the following essays will endeavor to show, a repudiation of the basic principles upon which our constitutional system was founded. In this connection, we should also observe that this new morality, though revolutionary, is often not perceived for what it is, primarily because of the evasive tactics of revisionists that I will spell out later.

My conclusions, I believe, are borne out by looking at the enormous power the courts have assumed within our system, an assumption of power that, according to one constitutional authority, rests on a conviction "almost universal among academics . . . that the American people are not to be trusted with self-government and are much in need of restraint by their moral and intellectual betters." Such a view, he quite rightly holds, "is an insult to our national heritage."[1] But even this depiction of the Court's new role is understated. As the late Charles S. Hyneman was one of the first to perceive,[2] the Court by the mid-1950s had already reached

---

[1]Lino Graglia, "Was the Constitution a Good Idea?" *Human Life Review* 10 (Fall 1984), 88–89.

[2]*The Supreme Court on Trial* (New York: Atherton Press, 1963). This is a much neglected work that was the first, to my knowledge, to point out the full implications of the Court's desegregation decisions.

a new plateau of power well beyond that attained by the Court of the mid-1930s that had prompted Roosevelt's Court packing plan. The 1930s Court had merely "vetoed" certain of Roosevelt's New Deal programs, whereas the modern Court has actually concocted "constitutionally" mandated remedies for perceived social ills.

Hyneman wondered aloud whether the Court would be so bold as to take upon itself the task of correcting the presumed "political failures" of the elective branches. The answer was soon forthcoming in a series of reapportionment decisions in the 1960s based on the formula, "one man, one vote"—a "standard" of republicanism that, in the words of Philip Kurland, "never existed in the past . . . was clearly rejected by the framers of the national constitution for the national government and . . . remains a standard unjustified by the Court itself."[3] Instances of equally blatant judicial behavior and reasoning abound. No serious student of the Court today, no matter what his ideological or political persuasion, denies that the Court in many instances simply legislates. What is more, many controversial pieces of such "legislation" are based upon constitutional interpretation that places them "above" ordinary laws passed by Congress. All of this, I daresay, is something relatively new under our constitutional sun—a state of affairs alien to the abiding principles of the Constitution as it emerged from Philadelphia.

That the Court provides perhaps the most visible example that can be offered to illustrate the altered character of our regime should not blind us to other, equally significant, departures from the constitutional morality of the Framers that inhere in this state of affairs. For instance, for the Court to legislate in the fashion it does without being called to account indicates that we have either forgotten or discarded the Framers' concern about maintaining the separation of powers. Moreover, implicit in the expanded conception of judicial power and authority is a distrust, not only of the Founders' "solution" to the problem of curbing unjust majorities, but of our representative institutions as well. Beyond this, we are led to speculate why it is that the Court—not, say, the Congress—seems to be the centerpiece of this new morality. This can be taken as further evidence that beneath this morality resides a primary concern, not with guaranteeing republican government understood as rule by the people, but with securing "rights" and substantive ends that conform with preconceived patterns of "justice"—rights and ends that might not be recognized as such by the more politically accountable branches. In sum, the exalted position of the Court, though noteworthy in its own right, is the outgrowth of fundamental changes in position and attitude toward basic principles—e.g., republicanism, the separation of powers—woven into our constitutional fabric.

This much said by way of general introduction, two observations are called for that will serve to refine and sharpen the theoretical concerns that prompted the following essays. First, my assessment and that of many others, if

---

[3]"Government by Judiciary," *Modern Age* 20 (Fall 1976), 366.

correct, would mean that we are in a constitutional crisis of sorts. This crisis can be pictured in terms of a new and antagonistic morality encroaching upon the old, an encroachment that has caused, and will continue to cause, bitter divisions in the nation. These divisions do and will revolve not only around the substance of given decisions but around the legitimacy of the manner or processes by which they are made. Such is the case because the new morality, if nothing else, involves a significant reshuffling of decision-making authority among the branches of government.

I am well aware that there are legitimate rejoinders to this position. A very persuasive one is simply that there is nothing really unique about our present constitutional differences: that, in fact, our system has never really been free from controversy over what must be regarded as constitutional questions of the first order. In the very first decade of its operation, for instance, disputes arose over the relative authority of the state and national governments, the extent of Congressional power vis-à-vis the executive authority, and, *inter alia*, the role of the Supreme Court.

One answer to this rejoinder that, I believe, helps us to comprehend the nature of our present difficulties can be put as follows: these early controversies, as well as those of similar nature we have experienced throughout our history, normally involved disagreements about the proper applications or operations of a given constitutional principle, not the principle itself. In this respect, evidence abounds that the Founders fully anticipated such disputes arising once the system was set in motion. However, rather than trying to provide any hard and fast answers to forestall such disputes—an impossibility on the face of it—they left their resolution to be worked out under the forms and processes provided in the Constitution. For example, and very much to this point, Madison, in writing about the separation of powers fused into the Constitution, does not even attempt to delineate with precision the relative boundaries of the three branches. Rather, he relies upon the operations of the system itself, wherein "those who administer each department [are given] the necessary constitutional means and personal motives to resist the encroachment of the others," (51:26)[4] to secure these ends. In other words, the Framers seemed to feel that the Constitution, once set in motion, would be a self-adjusting or self-correcting mechanism. In these terms, our present predicament is of a different order: it involves, not an adjustment *through* the system in the fashion described by Madison, but a fundamental change in the system itself.

The distinction that I draw here is far from being simply academic. Certainly no one would deny that we confronted a constitutional crisis at the time of our Civil War. To be sure, at its center was an irreconcilable difference over what is the most fundamental of all constitutional concerns—the nature of the union

---

[4]*The Federalist*, ed. George W. Carey and James McClellan (Dubuque: Kendall/Hunt, 1990). All subsequent parenthetical citations to *The Federalist* in the text are to this edition. When the essay number is not evident from the discussion, it will be placed before the page number.

established by the Constitution. Nevertheless, its character was not unlike that which we confront in the disputes over our constitutional order today. In both cases, we see differences over constitutional principles, the resolution of which cannot help but have a "ripple effect" on the fundamental character of the regime. Suppose, to illustrate this point dramatically, the view of the union as a contract or compact between the states had prevailed at some point in our history prior to the Civil War. Clearly, the entire character of our union—the relative powers of national and state governments, to say nothing of the role and function of the Supreme Court—would be drastically different from what it is today. Indeed, it might well be that the states would not be politically unified to any significant degree.

My second point relates to the nature of the new morality. To this juncture I have been using the expression "new constitutional morality" in a manner to suggest that it constitutes a body of principles as reasoned, coherent, and complementary as the older morality. But this is not quite the case. On certain matters relating to both means and ends, this morality is clear enough. We know, for instance, that its scope is far ranging; that it would call for the abandonment or drastic reformulation of principles long associated with our constitutional tradition. But save for heroic, though unsuccessful, efforts to reconcile judicial supremacy with republicanism, the proponents of the new morality have not to any great extent systematically explored the questions and problems that logically flow from its principles.[5] Not the least of these, trivial though it may seem at first glance, relates to the tacit assumption that a legal education equips the judges to exercise their newly acquired authority wisely.

Of course, there are concerns of a more strategic nature. One of the most important of these in my estimation is this: given the fact that the new morality is ill at ease, so to speak, under the existing and presumably antiquated constitutional forms and principles, why is it that its proponents do not seek constitutional changes that would serve to reconcile theory and practice? One obvious answer, in my opinion, is that the proponents of the new morality know very well that they could not secure the necessary changes that, in fact, would probably necessitate an entirely new constitution. Outside the groves of academe, that is, the American people still very much revere the Philadelphia Constitution, and they certainly would not look kindly upon any proposal whose declared purpose is to dismantle it. From the Machiavellian point of view, then, these proponents can be viewed as having adopted a strategy that will allow them to achieve their ends, or many of them at any rate, through the path of least resistance.

---

[5]In my view, the most ambitious of these has been John Hart Ely's *Democracy and Distrust* (Cambridge: Harvard University Press, 1980). For an excellent analysis of Ely's position and why Ely does not reconcile republicanism with his particular form of judicial oversight, see Stanley C. Brubaker, "Fear of Judging: Ely's Theory of Judicial Review," *Political Science Reviewer* 12 (1982).

Clearly, however, this strategy can be successful only as long as it is not widely perceived for what it is—a fact that, I believe, goes a long way towards accounting for the character of our contemporary "debate" on this matter. This is to say, as most opponents of the new morality would no doubt argue, the strategy has not been widely perceived in its proper context so that the real issue at stake—i.e., should we overhaul the Constitution or not—remains "hidden" from the people.[6] Be that as it may, it can be said that, whether by design or not, the reasoning and lines of argument advanced in its defense go a long way towards insuring that the issue remains hidden. In this regard, for example, we find aspects of the older tradition co-opted and employed on behalf of the new. Thus, somewhat ironically, we find arguments on behalf of an independent judiciary, which do make sense in the context of the older morality, transposed to support the notion of judicial supremacy. At another level, we are told that ours is a "living" and "flexible" Constitution and that the Framers would surely want us to adapt it to the changing circumstances of the modern world, which, of course, seems reasonable enough but leaves us with a host of questions regarding what particular provisions of the Constitution should or should not be treated as "living" and "flexible." Or we may be told, depending on the particular circumstances, that it is difficult, if not impossible, to determine the Framers' intent so that the Courts are obliged to use their best lights to interpret the Constitution in keeping with its "spirit" or, if not that, within the bounds of "contemporaneous consensus." In other words, the justifications are linked, however tenuously, to the older constitutional morality in such a way as to direct our attention and critical thinking away from the central issue and over to matters that, by their very nature, are incapable of definitive resolution. I cannot help but note, for example, that the findings of Raoul Berger's monumental study[7] of the intended scope of the Fourteenth Amendment, no small matter given the key role of this amendment in reshaping the American political landscape by judicial fiat, can so easily be dismissed by new morality advocates on various grounds—e.g., the Courts of the modern era are interpreting the Fourteenth Amendment in the "spirit" intended by its drafters—which are, by their nature, virtually impossible to come to grips with.

These observations lead to questions of a different order whose answers are, at least in part, to be found in the sustained attacks on the Constitution that have encouraged the development of this new morality. That is to say, the new morality did not achieve its present status and acceptance overnight, particularly among academics. What are its attractions? How can it be justified? What are its objectives?

---

[6]For an interesting discussion "around" this point see Joseph Sobran, "A Naive View," *Human Life Review* 9 (Winter 1983). Writes Sobran: "Even conservative members of the Court, including preeminently the most serious of them, William Rehnquist, have not raised the fundamental question whether we have fundamentally corrupted the original system" (14).

[7]*Government by Judiciary: The Transformation of the Fourteenth Amendment* (Cambridge: Harvard University Press, 1977).

We can, I believe, trace its origins back to shortly after the turn of the century with the publication of James Allen Smith's *The Spirit of American Government.*[8] Smith's work was revolutionary primarily because it challenged the then prevailing belief that the Constitution embodied democratic principles. For this reason, it is generally recognized as the first of the "revisionist" works that have proven so instrumental in providing the foundations for the new morality.

Smith contended that "ordinary text books" and "popular works" that dealt with the Constitution did not deal sufficiently with the "political philosophy upon which it rests" so that "the American people," he felt, were ill-informed about the "fundamental nature of their system of government."[9] "Democracy—government by the people, or directly responsible to them—was not," he argued, "the object which the framers of the American Constitution had in view, but the very thing which they sought to avoid."[10] He found it "difficult" to believe that anyone at all familiar with the proceedings of the Philadelphia Convention or the character and background of the Framers could think otherwise. For his part, he found the "evidence . . . overwhelming" that the Framers placed "no faith in the wisdom or political capacity of the people." Rather, in his words, they sought to entrench the "wealthy and conservative classes."[11]

Smith provided still another perspective for looking at the Constitution and the purposes of the Founders, namely, that the Constitution was a reactionary document designed to reverse the democratic impulses unleashed during the Revolution. In this vein, he wrote, "our form of government after the Declaration of Independence"—i.e., the Articles—was clearly democratic in character because the "English system of checks and balances was discarded" and "all important powers of government were vested in the legislature."[12] All this, he took pains to emphasize, was undone with the adoption of the Philadelphia Constitution.

Certain of Smith's views have been extensively modified or even abandoned over the decades. Revisionist thought, for example, eventually came to reject the value of political decentralization that Smith, true to Jeffersonian principles, regarded as essential for truly popular rule. And history has proved him wrong in his conviction that the Supreme Court would constitute a permanent barrier for majorities intent upon securing economic "justice." In recent decades, for reasons that will become apparent in due course, the Court has come to be viewed from a perspective that simultaneously renders it central to the new morality and compatible with the overarching values associated with revisionism. Nevertheless, two major elements of Smith's thought are very much with us today. The

---

[8]*The Spirit of American Government* (New York: The Macmillan Company, 1907). This work has been reprinted by the Harvard University Press (1965) with an excellent critical "Introduction" by Cushing Strout. All citations are to the Harvard edition.

[9]*The Spirit of American Government*, 30.

[10]Ibid., 29–30. ˙

[11]Ibid., 32.

[12]Ibid., 27.

first of these is that the Constitution is basically an undemocratic document designed by men who feared the levelling tendencies of popular majorities. The second, which to a great extent flows from the first, holds that the Constitution represents a betrayal of the values associated with the Declaration of Independence or, if not that precisely, those associated with "social justice."

Both these themes were refined and developed some twenty years later in Vernon Parrington's widely heralded two-volume work, *Main Currents in American Thought*,[13] which he dedicated to his former teacher James Allen Smith. Parrington pictured the theoretical climate prior to the Constitution against the backdrop of "French radicalism" and "English liberalism." "The root of French radicalism," according to Parrington, "was anarchistic, and its idea was an agrarian society of freeholders. It would sweep away the long accumulated mass of prescriptive rights, the dead hand of the past, and encourage free men to create a new society that should have as its sole end and justification, the common well-being."[14] He regarded Rousseau as the chief spokesman for the "passionate social idealism" that characterized "French romantic philosophy" whose main elements were, in Parrington's words, "that a juster, more wholesome social order should take the place of the existing obsolete system; that reason and not interests should determine social institutions; that the ultimate ends to be sought were universal liberty, equality, and fraternity." For Parrington, "English liberalism," originally set forth by Harrington and subsequently refined by Locke and Adam Smith, embraced principles essentially alien to these. Moreover, he believed, the freedom and liberty it sought was of a markedly different kind: its "great concern," in his view, was that government "should . . . assist and not hamper industry and trade" and that "political policies should follow and serve commercial interests."[15]

Parrington did not disguise his feelings towards these two schools of thought. While he noted that both were "characterized" by a "pronounced individualism," he went on to remark that the French individualism "was humanitarian, appealing to reason and seeking social justice," whereas the English "was self-seeking, founded on the right of exploitation, and looking toward capitalism." But, he continued, "the French humanitarian conceptions of equality and fraternity found little response in [the] middle-class, competitive world" of the era.[16] Thus, the main question at the time of founding, as Parrington viewed it, came down to whether the confederation under the Articles ought to be replaced by a stronger, more "coercive" national government. And he was outspoken in his belief that the adoption of the Constitution was brought about "by a skillful minority in face of a hostile majority." Outside the South, he contended, this minority represented the "large property interest" or "powerful money groups"

---

[13]*Main Currents in American Thought*, 2 vols. (New York: Harcourt, Brace, and Company, 1927).
[14]*Main Currents*, 1, *The Colonial Mind*: 1620–1800, 276.
[15]Ibid., 275–76.
[16]Ibid., 277.

that had since "pre-Revolutionary days . . . greatly increased" both their "re-sources and . . . prestige as a result of war financing and speculation in currency and lands." This monied group, in Parrington's scenario, found a willing ally for a stronger national government among the "planter aristocracy" of the South.[17]

In Parrington's account, as we might expect, the real loser in all of this maneu-vering turned out to be the "small property holders" who lacked "disciplined cohesion." As he would have it, "astute politicians" like Alexander Hamilton blamed the post-war depression on "too much agrarianism" which, in turn, they attributed to "too much democracy." Their argument that "prosperity" was not possible until such time that "a competent national government was set up on a substantial basis" was, in Parrington's estimation, "a sharp setback" for the "ideal of popular democratic rule." Indeed, he contended, the "aristocratic prej-udices of the colonial mind" were exploited by "skillful propaganda": "Democ-racy was pictured as no other than mob rule, and its ultimate purpose the denial of all property rights. Populistic measures were fiercely denounced as the natural fruit of democratic control."[18]

Parrington's views on the Constitution and the founding period are the most comprehensive we have of one wing of revisionist thought. To be sure, Charles A. Beard's *An Economic Interpretation of the Constitution of the United States*[19] had covered a good deal of the same general terrain some fifteen years earlier. And Beard's thirteen-count indictment of the Framers certainly raised more eye-brows than did Smith's charges, no doubt, in large part because Beard presumably had mustered the evidence to prove that the Framers were "with but few excep-tions, immediately, directly, and personally interested in, and derived economic advantages from, the establishment of the new system."[20] Moreover, Beard's work added a good deal of credibility to what can be termed the "conspiracy theory" of our founding. To this end, for example, he pointed out that there was no popular vote, either direct or indirect, "on the proposition to call" the Phila-delphia Convention; that "a large propertyless mass" was "excluded" from any role in "framing the Constitution"; and, *inter alia*, that because of apathy and suffrage qualifications, "not more than one-sixth of the adult males" voted to ratify the Constitution.[21] However, it was Parrington who wrapped Smith's con-cerns about the direction of our political tradition together with Beard's allegedly "hard" data concerning the Framers' economic motivations into a coherent whole.

No account of revisionist thinking that has contributed to the new morality would be satisfactory or complete without surveying the "progressive" thought

---

[17]Ibid., 277–78.

[18]Ibid., 279.

[19]*An Economic Interpretation of the Constitution of the United States of America* (New York: The Macmillan Company, 1913).

[20]Ibid., 324.

[21]Ibid., 324–25.

of Herbert Croly, particularly that set forth in his *Promise of American Life*[22] which appeared only four years after Smith's initial assault on our constitutional heritage. Croly, like Smith, was aware that his view on the Constitution might well seem heretical. Indeed, for Croly, the existing "strong, almost dominant tendency to regard the existing Constitution with superstitious awe, and to shrink with horror from modifying it even in the smallest detail" served to hold the genuine "American spirit" in "great bondage."[23] Moreover, his vision of our "national promise" in many ways paralleled Parrington's conception of the "French humanism" that had been rejected in favor of "English liberalism" at the time of our founding. For instance, Croly was extremely critical of the "traditional American confidence in individual freedom" which he believed "had resulted in a morally and socially undesirable distribution of wealth." The self-acquisitiveness that had produced this state of affairs, he argued, needed to be supplanted by a new morality calling "for the subordination of the individual to the demands of a dominant and constructive national purpose." What Croly sought was "a higher type of associated life" in which "desirable competition" would be encouraged by minimizing the "mercenary motive" and placing a premium on "excellence of work."[24] Beyond this, he sought to attain or approach as nearly as possible the Rousseauistic ideal of "individual disinterestedness" wherein each citizen would be willing "to sacrifice his recognized private interest to the welfare of his countrymen."[25]

There are differences of varying degrees between the views of Croly and those of Smith and Parrington that, in the main, stem from Croly's realization that the achievement of the "American national promise" could only be brought about through a strong national government. For this reason, it would seem, Croly did not look upon the founding period in the same black-and-white terms as Smith. For instance, he viewed the adoption of the Constitution not as the result of any conspiracy or political chicanery but as the outcome of the "conversion of public opinion" through "powerful and convincing arguments." It was achieved, in his words, "chiefly by virtue of capable, energetic and patriotic leadership." What is more, he had kind words for Hamilton and the early Federalists for realizing the potential of the new government and for advancing the national welfare: "A vigorous, positive, constructive national policy was outlined and carried substantially into effect—a policy that implied a faith in the powers of an efficient government to advance the national interest, and which justified the faith by actually meeting the critical problems of the time with a series of wise legislative measures.[26] Where Hamilton failed, in Croly's estimation, was "in seeking to base the perpetuation of the Union upon the interested motives of a minority of well-to-do

---

[22]*The Promise of American Life* (New York: The Macmillan Company, 1911).
[23]Ibid., 278.
[24]Ibid., 415.
[25]Ibid., 418.
[26]Ibid., 38.

citizens'' rather than entrusting ''its welfare to the good-will of the whole people.'' And this Croly attributed to Hamilton's ''English conception of a nation state, based on domination of special privileged orders and interests.''[27]

As we might expect from his appraisal of Hamilton, Croly was highly critical of Jefferson, whose conception of democracy he describes as ''meager, narrow, and self-contradictory'' because of its ''extreme individualism.'' While Croly held that Jefferson ''understood his fellow countrymen better and trusted them more'' than Hamilton, his conception of democracy was flawed because it carried with it the implication ''that society and individuals could be made better without actually planning the improvement or building up an organization for the purpose.'' In sum, from Croly's point of view, Jeffersonian democracy called for a negative, ''hands off'' government, one ill-equipped to promote a ''higher type of associated life.''[28]

Croly's critique of the Constitution and what he took to be the Framers' motives is not totally dissimilar to that of Smith, Parrington, or Beard. But, again, he is not nearly so harsh. The Federalists, he acknowledged, ''demanded a government adequate to protect property rights,'' but, in his view, ''they were not seeking any exceptional privileges.''[29] The chief end of the Constitution, he held, was to secure ''liberty from any possible dangers,'' and, for this reason, he maintained, it ''was framed, not as the expression of a democratic creed, but partly as a legal fortress against the possible errors and failings of democracy.'' The ''system of checks and balances'' and the separation of powers were, in his judgment, ''calculated to thwart the popular will'' but only when that will threatened ''the essentials of a stable political and social order.''[30] In sum, he was not overly concerned about the ''undemocratic'' character of the Constitution. Indeed, he wrote that, for ''all its faults,'' it ''proved capable of becoming both the organ of an efficient national government and the fundamental law of a potentially democratic state.''[31] In this last analysis, from Croly's perspective, the basic flaw of the Constitution was that it lacked the power that ''every popular government should possess,'' that is, after due deliberation, the capacity to take ''any action, which, in the opinion of a decisive majority of the people, is demanded by the public welfare.''[32]

The views of Croly, Smith, Beard, and Parrington have been modified over the years. However, what we see in these modifications are principally variations on two basic themes. The first of these, which emerges most clearly in the writings of Smith, Beard, and Parrington, is that the Constitution is not a democratic document, and that it was drafted to protect the interests of economic and

---

[27]Ibid., 41.
[28]Ibid., 43.
[29]Ibid., 32.
[30]Ibid., 33.
[31]Ibid., 34.
[32]Ibid., 35.

social minorities from the ravages of majority rule.[33] Modern political scientists who dwell on this theme are apt to put it somewhat differently. They would say that the constitutional rules—both the formal and the informal, which have developed over the years—are skewed to benefit certain interests at the expense of others in ways consonant with the general aims of the Framers.[34] That is, in their view, the more affluent and better organized interests in society enjoy a distinct advantage over groups less well organized and affluent: the rich and well-to-do, in other words, still run the show. This at least is the impression conveyed, expressly or implicitly, in the vast majority of American government college texts.

In this connection it is not surprising to note that by 1950 a majority of the leading college textbooks in American history had come to embrace the proposition that "the Fathers were intent on protecting the property of the few at the expense of the many." Moreover, the conception of the Constitution as a "reactionary" document, that is, as one rejecting the noble and progressive doctrines of the Declaration of Independence, had also gained widespread acceptance by this point in time.[35] As one close student put this: "The Declaration is portrayed as the ultimate expression of Revolutionary ideals, to wit, egalitarianism, popular majority rule, and human rights; the Constitution is cast in the role of a counter-revolutionary reaction in support of monied privilege, minority rule, and property rights."[36] In this respect, the revisionists' views seem to have won the day over those of the "traditionalists." Whereas Smith and Croly may have been fighting a lonely battle in their time, today the traditionalists' views are seldom heard, much less defended, in the academy.

The second basic theme relates to Croly's major concern, namely, the conception of democracy associated with and to some extent embodied in the Constitution leads to a protective, limited, and relatively inactive government. Now this is a far more complicated theme than the first because its expression has subsequently taken many forms. Croly, more activist-oriented and less wedded to Jeffersonian theory than either Smith or Parrington, provides us with a greater insight into the basic difficulty that seems to have prompted a good deal of revisionist thought in the first place: namely, the lack of an instrumentality to achieve the desired ends that, in recent decades, have come to be those derived from the second paragraph of the Declaration. To put this more accurately, Croly had no substantial complaint with the Constitution as an instrumentality; rather, as we have seen, he was distressed with the Jeffersonian theory that guided its use. For

---

[33]Perhaps the best known of the modern statements to this effect is to be found in chapter one of Robert A. Dahl's *A Preface to Democratic Theory* (Chicago: University of Chicago Press, 1956).

[34]James MacGregor Burns has popularized this view, which is widely held in the political science profession. See, for example, his *Uncommon Sense* (New York: W. W. Norton, 1974), 76.

[35]Douglass Adair, "The Tenth Federalist Revisited," in *Fame and the Founding Fathers: Essays by Douglass Adair*, ed. Trevor Colbourn (New York: W. W. Norton, 1974), 76.

[36]Richard F. Gibbs, "The Spirit of '89: Conservatism and Bicentenary," *The University Bookman* 14 (Spring 1974), 54.

him, the basic difficulty with the system could be overcome with the acceptance of the Hamiltonian conception of union. For this reason, Croly is regarded by some as the "theoretical" father of the New Deal, which certainly seemed to follow his prescriptions by adopting Hamiltonian means while simultaneously paying due homage to Jeffersonian ends.[37]

The initial success of the New Deal in inaugurating policies that had long been dormant on the liberal agenda certainly lent credence to Croly's views. However, while there is virtual unanimity that the Hamiltonian conception is necessary for the achievement of a comprehensive program such as that embodied in Croly's "national promise," few today would regard it as sufficient. This is to say, according to modern critics, the system seems to move in "fits and starts," reacting in piecemeal fashion to problems and then only when they become acute.[38] From the critic's point of view, it seems incapable of formulating comprehensive and sustained programs that can produce either the changes or the results necessary for the realization of "liberal" ideals.

While a variety of reasons have been offered for this state of affairs, most of them bring us back around, in one fashion or another, to the first revisionist theme: that the structure and principles of the system simply militate against such programs. For one thing, authority is dispersed among formal and informal institutions and procedures. For another, this decentralization not only provides an outlet for the numberless interests that have naturally arisen in our free society, it even encourages the growth of new ones. Given those conditions, then, it is not hard to see why the development of a consensus on interrelated, long-term, national goals and policies such as that envisioned by Croly is extremely time-consuming, difficult, or, in some cases, simply impossible. This, at least, seems to be the view of many, if not most, reform-minded political scientists who over the decades have sought to join Woodrow Wilson's notion of a cabinet government with the British "model" of disciplined, responsible, and programmatic political parties.[39] Their reforms are designed, in other words, to channel our pluralism through the medium of our parties, while simultaneously overcoming the centrifugal forces of federalism and separation of powers.

To reform our parties, to "nationalize" them by pulling up their roots which are now firmly implanted at the state and local levels, and to overcome the friction between the branches would require an overhaul of the entire system. This means,

---

[37]On Croly and the New Deal see Samuel H. Beer, "Liberalism and the National Idea" in *Left, Right and Center*, ed. Robert S. Goldwin (Chicago: Rand McNally, 1965).

[38]This is another complaint of James MacGregor Burns's that is widely echoed in the political science profession. See his *The Deadlock of Democracy* (Englewood Cliffs, N.J.: Prentice-Hall, 1963).

[39]For a recent and comprehensive call for reforms along these lines see *Reforming American Government*, ed. Donald L. Robinson (Boulder and London: Westview Press, 1985). For an excellent article that examines such reforms and their underlying ideology see: Evron M. Kirkpatrick, "Toward a More Responsible Two-Party System: Political Science, Policy Science, or Pseudo-Science?" *American Political Science Review* 65 (December 1971).

in effect, that the American constitutional order will never outwardly conform to what can be called the "liberal" model. Nevertheless, under its present form, it may operate in the same way as the liberal model presumably would. A "strong" president like Roosevelt II, for example, can overcome for a short period the inherent centrifugal forces and tendencies of the system. But the operative words here are "a short period," because what seems clear is that such unity comes about only occasionally and then only as a result of a national crisis. Put otherwise, the openings or opportunities for ambitious programs designed to fulfill our "national promise" are infrequent and short-lived. What is more, sustaining, modifying, or expanding such programs is extremely difficult once the "window of opportunity" has been "shut."

With these observations before us it is not difficult to see why the new morality poses such a formidable threat to the older morality that has guided our constitutional development for the better part of two hundred years. In significant political and social areas, the Court can provide the central direction necessary for reshaping American society. To reemphasize the point I made at the outset, the Court under this new morality is not confined to saying "no" to the actions of the political arms of our system; rather, it can itself undertake positive and comprehensive action to achieve what it interprets to be constitutionally mandated conditions or goals. Moreover, and this again according to the tenets of the new morality, it can do so as the final arbiter of the meaning and language of the Constitution, that is, with an authority that neither the Congress nor the President can ever claim. In sum, this judicial supremacy that lies at the heart of the new constitutional morality undercuts virtually every constitutional principle in providing an ingenious shortcut to the attainment of the ideals that the revisionists thought could not be achieved under the forms of the Philadelphia Constitution. And, as I have noted, its proponents can claim, spuriously, but nevertheless with sufficient effectiveness to confuse the issue in the public arena, that it is nothing more than the logical outgrowth of the principles embodied in the older morality.

The foregoing discussion and analysis form a backdrop against which the following essays should be read. These essays, in turn, are directed at one or more of the four fundamental principles of the American political system: republicanism, the separation of powers, federalism, and limited government. I have used this approach for a number of reasons, the most important of which are that it not only embraces the full range of concerns and debates over the nature of the American system such as those discussed above, but it also helps us to focus on the significant, rather than secondary, issues. Additionally, it offers a framework that readily allows one to see interrelationships between constitutional principles. For those so inclined, it is also convenient for drawing comparisons with other political systems.

Finally, by way of introduction, I should note that my analysis of the Philadelphia Constitution with respect to these principles relies heavily, though not entirely, on *The Federalist* and, in particular, on the contributions of Hamilton and Madison written under the pseudonym "Publius." This should be the least controversial aspect of this undertaking because there is a consensus among both friend and foe of the Philadelphia Constitution that *The Federalist* represents by far the most comprehensive defense and explication of the Constitution that we have. Put another way, *The Federalist* lends a coherence and theoretical understanding to the Philadelphia deliberations that no other single document can even approach. So much, at least, is acknowledged by the revisionists and critics of the Constitution who have, over the decades, increasingly seen fit to direct their attacks against the Constitution by tackling *The Federalist*.

1

Publius—A Split Personality?

INTRODUCTORY NOTE

It may seem odd that I begin with an essay that touches upon what would, at first glance, seem to be an arcane academic quarrel concerning the authorship of certain essays in *The Federalist*. After all, how can such a dispute possibly bear upon our understanding of the Constitution and the intentions of the Framers? The answer is a bit involved, but, as I will show, the relationship is undeniably an important one.

This dispute over the authorship of these essays has now entirely subsided. But, until its resolution in relatively recent times, it provoked some anger and hard feeling among scholars as their debate over the relative merits of the competing claims of authorship took on a partisan character. In the course of these debates, as we might expect, the substance of the essays assumed importance on the unarticulated assumption that there were theoretical differences of sufficient degree and depth between Hamilton and Madison to settle the matter of authorship. Oddly enough, however, no one ever systematically set forth these differences in a manner that could authoritatively settle the controversy. And the question that still remains long after the smoke has cleared is why, if their theoretical differences were so pronounced, there should have been any dispute about the authorship in the first place. Or, to put this somewhat differently, if there were significant theoretical differences between them, why couldn't this controversy, involving no less than one-fifth of the essays, be resolved in short order, the more so as certain of the papers in dispute were, by any standards, among the most theoretical of the lot?

The fact is that it was only *after* the disputed papers controversy was resolved by Douglass Adair in the mid-1940s (see text below) that relatively coherent and plausible claims concerning philosophical differences between Hamilton and Madison writing as "Publius" were advanced. But, as I point out below, those who advanced this thesis—and that would include Adair—pretty much assumed what they wanted to prove. They began, that is, with the assumption that there must have been significant differences between them in their views of the Constitution, the nature of man, the need for government, and so forth. They then selectively combed the text, or, what is worse, manipulated the positions of Hamilton and Madison, to prove their point.

There is room for intelligent speculation about the whys and wherefores of this alleged "split personality" within the framework of my introductory remarks. For the better part of his political life Madison was an ally of Jefferson. No doubt for this reason alone,

18

revisionists feel the need to separate his thoughts from Hamilton's to make it appear that the two were very uneasy allies in the ratification struggle. But the thesis serves other purposes as well. By contrasting the republican Madison with the "authoritarian" Hamilton, it amends and clarifies the revisionists' position. For instance, in these terms Madison's contribution to our founding and institutions can explain why Jefferson was favorably disposed towards the Constitution—a fact that early revisionists avoided like the plague. At the same time, given the picture painted by Hamilton, the revisionists' interpretations gain credibility; that is, their charges can readily be accommodated to this view by maintaining that the system has in reality operated in accordance with Hamilton's presumed design to thwart democracy and protect vested interests.

The "split personality" thesis, taken as a whole and developed fully, can provide a sufficiently expansive framework to explain or account for virtually every twist and turn, theoretical or otherwise, in our constitutional development. If it were valid, however, it would for this very reason leave us at sea without a rudder. By denying that "Publius" expressed a consensus and by asserting that he gave us not one, but two or more constitutional moralities, it leaves us uncertain of our heritage. What is more, it simultaneously lays the groundwork for the revisionist interpretations of our constitutional heritage to claim legitimacy.

PUBLIUS—A SPLIT PERSONALITY?

In 1944, Douglass Adair published a seminal two-part article, "The Authorship of the Disputed Federalist Papers."[1] While this article is rightly celebrated for authoritatively settling the long-standing controversy surrounding the authorship of certain essays in *The Federalist* claimed by both Hamilton and Madison, it also advanced a thesis whose significance for scholars of the American political tradition far exceeds the resolution of this controversy.[2] Specifically, Adair wrote that though Hamilton and Madison "agreed that the proposed Constitution should be ratified and laid aside all differences to bring this about . . . the two statesmen's radical divergence on what constituted good government gave Publius truly a split personality" (DP, 55). Eight years later, in an article entitled "The Federalist—A Split Personality," Alpheus T. Mason echoed this thesis by maintaining that there are clearly discernible differences between Hamilton and Madison writing as Publius on basic issues and principles relative to the proposed Constitution.[3] And Gottfried Dietze, in writing the first book-length analysis of *The Federalist*, found

---

[1] This two-part article is reprinted in *Fame and the Founding Fathers: Essays by Douglass Adair*, ed. Trevor Colbourn (New York: W. W. Norton, 1974). All citations are to the reprint and will be designated DP.

[2] The disputed essays were 18, 19, 20, 62, 63, and 49 through 58, not an inconsiderable portion of the work. Adair's article sets forth the reasons for this dispute and thoroughly examines the scholarly controversies that ensued, matters well beyond my concern here.

[3] "The Federalist—A Split Personality," *American Historical Review* 57 (1952). Hereafter cited as SP.

Mason's "contributions" on this score to be "indispensable."[4] Accordingly, Dietze saw fit to deal with the contributions of John Jay, Madison, and Hamilton to *The Federalist* in separate sections and chapters on the grounds, we may presume, that their positions and theories are sufficiently different to warrant such treatment.

Clearly this split personality thesis has far-reaching implications for scholarly inquiry into our political tradition. Obviously, if the lines of argument in *The Federalist* are as divergent as Mason, Adair, and other scholars intimate,[5] then its status and role in our tradition must be reevaluated, particularly by those who have come to regard it as a relatively coherent and authoritative source for a fuller comprehension of the underlying principles of our constitutional system. Viewed from another perspective, however, the split personality thesis might lead us to a woefully inadequate understanding of the foundations of our political order. By emphasizing the differences between Hamilton and Madison, it could lead us to minimize or downplay the areas of substantial agreement surrounding the major underlying principles of the system. But, more significantly, the thesis would have us read *The Federalist* in a way not intended by its authors, that is, as the product of two pens, not one. And, because the authors regarded their work a coherent whole, it may well be that the "tensions" and seeming contradictions we find within its pages are not the result of differences between them on matters of principle or theory, but rather manifestations of basic, underlying difficulties— some of them perhaps insoluble—inherent in the proposed Constitution or republicanism.

In sum, the split personality thesis does pose difficulties for those who seek to come to grips with the teachings of *The Federalist* and, more generally, the nature of our political foundations. My purpose here is to critically examine this thesis with an eye to determining whether Publius does, as some scholars contend, speak with a forked tongue or whether, as equally serious students of the tradition hold,[6] the alleged theoretical divergences are either exaggerated or contrived.

---

[4]*The Federalist: A Classic on Federalism and Free Government* (Baltimore: Johns Hopkins Press, 1960). Hereafter cited in text as TF. Dietze writes at one point (TF, 19) that Adair's introduction of the notion of a "split personality" is "an old idea." Yet, he credits Alpheus T. Mason (TF, 21) with "having first elaborated the idea of the split personality." The fact is that the Mason article is but a pale version of Adair's.

It should be noted here that Dietze, in embracing Mason's thesis, eventually had to run up against a difficulty that Adair and Mason were able to avoid, namely, providing specific evidences of a split personality in the text of *The Federalist*. Hence (see TF, 267–75), Dietze had to be more circumspect in his claims regarding a split personality. For an extended treatment of this point see note 10 below.

[5]Those in this category would include Benjamin F. Wright, Roy P. Fairfield, and Max Beloff, whose introductions to their editions of *The Federalist* seem to be based on a tacit acceptance of this thesis. Beloff goes so far as to write: "The fact that the *Federalist* is not the work of a single mind is one of the reasons for which it must stand somewhat apart in any collection of the great texts in political science." "Introduction" to *The Federalist* (New York: Macmillan, 1948), vii.

[6]Among these students we find Clinton Rossiter, Martin Diamond, Willmoore Kendall, and Herbert J. Storing.

Split Personality Thesis: Development and Substance

At the outset we should note that, while Adair's use of the disputed papers controversy to advance the split personality thesis seems understandable enough at first glance, the two concerns are, upon examination, theoretically distinct. More specifically, theoretical analysis confined solely to *The Federalist* only establishes with a relatively high degree of certainty Madison's authorship of certain disputed essays (48, 49, 50, 51, 62, and 63).[7] This, in turn, is accomplished by linking the substance of essay 10, whose authorship is beyond dispute, with the concerns of the disputed essays, primarily 51. By no means, however, can we take the validation of Madison's claim to authorship of these disputed papers as validation of this thesis.

The resolution of the controversy over the disputed papers does touch base with the split personality thesis over the pivotal role of papers 10 and 51 for an understanding of the main pillars of Madison's thought. Both Adair and Mason use these essays as a nucleus for their arguments, which are strikingly similar in substance and mode. Both see the major differences between Hamilton and Madison as centering around the immediate issues of controlling factions and the proper and prudent scope of popular sovereignty. They even manage to widen the scope of these differences by relating to these key essays seemingly disparate concerns, such as the proper relationship between the state and national authorities and the responsibilities of the departments. All of this they are able to accomplish, as we might expect, by contrasting certain of Hamilton's arguments and positions set forth at various points in *The Federalist* with what they regard to be the logic of Madison's extended republic theory set forth in essays 10 and 51. With this overview in mind, let us take a closer look at their analysis.

Mason writes that ''John Quincy Adams did not take the trouble to spell it out, but he hit upon a most significant aspect of the 'diversity' in this great collaboration [*The Federalist*] when he described Hamilton's number 9 and Madison's number 10 as 'rival dissertations upon Faction and its remedy.' ''(SP, 636). But aside from arguing that Hamilton wanted to establish a ''consolidated system,'' ''Union under one government,'' ''perfect subordination of the states to the general authority of the union'' (all these goals presumably set forth by Hamilton in

---

[7]Two basic techniques of textual analysis—techniques employed to some extent by both Adair and Mason—that lead to this conclusion are (a) an examination of the essays' structure—e.g., the sequence of the essays according to subject, the internal organization of the various sections of the work; and (b) the apparent theoretical linkage between certain papers, no matter what their sequence or place in the overall organization. These techniques cannot, however, resolve the controversy over the authority of essays 18, 19, 20, and 52 through 58. In coming to his conclusions which essentially support Madison's claim to all of the disputed papers, Adair had to rely upon evidence external to *The Federalist* such as the whereabouts of the authors at various periods in the ratification contest. Adair's conclusions have been corroborated by statistical analyses of the prose styles and word usage of Hamilton, Madison, and Jay. See: Frederick Mantella and Daniel L. Wallace, *Inference and Disputed Authorship* (Reading, Mass.: Addison-Wesley, 1964).

Federalist 9) whereas Madison on the basis of essays 10 and 51 was a pluralist who felt the existence of viable states with residual sovereignty essential for the national government, Mason does not elaborate extensively on the nature of this "diversity."

Adair goes into this particular matter more extensively. He contends:

> Hamilton felt so strongly about the need for an overruling, irresponsible and unlimited government that it showed through even in his *Federalist* essays, in spite of his attempt to conceal his opinions in order to achieve ratification. Federalist 9 indicates clearly that he expected a continual use of military force would be required to keep the rebellious poor in their place. In this essay the union is advocated because it will permit the use of troops raised in one section of the country to stamp out revolts in other districts. . . . Essays 23 and 30 mirror his belief that no government would endure without unlimited fiscal and military power and foreshadow his doctrine of "liberal construction" (DP, 68).

And, after quoting from the latter part of essay 51 to the effect that the multiplicity and diversity of interests renders an "unjust combination of a majority of the whole very improbable, if not impracticable," he writes: "Madison, it is clear, had emancipated himself from the sterile dualistic view of society that was so common in the eighteenth century and that so obsessed Hamilton. Madison was one of the pioneers of 'pluralism' in political thought. Where Hamilton saw the corporate spirit of the several states poisonous to the union, Madison was aware that the preservation of the state governments could serve the cause of both liberty and union" (DP, 70).[8]

Likewise, both Adair and Mason detect authoritarian overtones in many of Hamilton's essays, overtones that, they maintain, are absent from Madison's contributions. Adair contends that in Federalist 51 Madison offers a republican remedy to Hamilton's "overruling, irresponsible, and unlimited government."[9] More specifically, in essay 51 Madison eschews the notion that a will, independent of society, is needed to prevent factious majority rule. And this, Adair argues,

---

[8]Federalist 35, written by Hamilton, would certainly tend to cast considerable doubt on Adair's contention concerning Hamilton's "dualistic" view of society. For instance, Hamilton argues that it would be "impracticable" for the House of Representatives to represent sympathetically "the interests and feelings of every part of the community." He goes on to say: "The idea of an actual representation of all classes of the people by persons of each class is altogether visionary."

[9]Adair sees Madison repudiating Hamilton's theory in arguing that the cure for factious majorities cannot be found "by creating a will of the community independent of the majority . . . because a power independent of the society may well espouse the unjust views of the major as the rightful interests of the minor party, and may possibly be turned against both parties" (51:268).

But this charge seems to overlook what Hamilton wrote elsewhere in *The Federalist* concerning republicanism. For instance, in essay 22 he rails against the Articles because equality of state representation leads to minority rule and violates "that fundamental maxim of republican government, which requires that the sense of the majority should prevail" (109).

sets him apart from Hamilton: "discussion of the executive in Federalist 71 reveals his dearest hope that the president would develop an 'independent will.' And his analysis of the powers of the Supreme Court in Number 78 was in time to provide an enduring sanction for the development of an independent and irresponsible judiciary" (DP, 68–69).

Mason develops Adair's contentions on this point more fully. Hamilton, he points out, favored a strong executive or at least one who would not bend "to every sudden breeze of passion or to every transient impulse which the people may receive from the arts of men, who flatter their prejudices to betray their interests" (71:369). Mason continues: "Hamilton placed perhaps even greater reliance on the federal judiciary—especially because of the provision for indefinite tenure of judges—as a safeguard against factions" (SP, 636–37).

For Mason there is also an "authoritarian" overtone in Hamilton's essays devoted to the executive and judiciary. "In essay 71," he writes, "one encounters Rousseau's sentiments, that though the 'people commonly *intend* the PUBLIC GOOD,' they do not 'always *reason right* about the means of promoting it.' The exalted role carved out for the executive and judiciary, especially the latter, is faintly suggestive of Rousseau's 'Legislator'—'a superior intelligence beholding all the passions of men without experiencing any of them.' " (SP, 637). But this, to Mason's way of thinking, raises the same kind of problem inherent in Hobbesian theory, namely, "does not such executive and judicial preeminence call for considerable qualification of those unseemly qualities Hamilton elsewhere attributed to the general run of mankind?" (SP, 637–38) Hamilton, Mason postulates, must have held to the proposition that possession of power would have a "purifying effect" on the officeholder (SP, 638). On the other hand, Mason maintains, Madison's solution to the problem of controlling government and factions rests upon the conflict and tensions between interests, sects, and classes—the operations of an unfettered pluralistic society.

THE EXPANDED SPLIT PERSONALITY THESIS CRITICALLY EXAMINED

While there are other points made by Adair and Mason, these are the key issues upon which the split personality thesis rests. These issues are, moreover, potentially far more crucial than either Adair or Mason seem willing to let on. It simply will not do to note these alleged differences and then proceed to point out that the areas of agreement between Hamilton and Madison were far greater and more significant than their differences, or that the differences between them come down merely to shades of grey.[10] The issues, as both Adair and Mason pose them,

---

[10]The distinctions that Mason notes begin to melt away in the last paragraphs of his article. He writes that one cannot "always be certain in identifying the stand of either Hamilton or Madison. Their interpretations become less categorical when either author enters the province of the other" (SP, 64).

Dietze has the most difficult time of all. Because his work is confined to *The Federalist*, unlike

involve the critical question. What kind of regime is it that *The Federalist* is recommending for the American people? If we are to accept the split personality thesis, half of Publius is advocating a republican form, the other half an oligarchy of sorts. And, if this be so, *The Federalist* can only be viewed as a jumble, at least with regard to the most important element of the proposed constitutional system.

Bearing this in mind, we can profitably examine these contentions starting first with those that seem to derive from the so-called diversity between essays 9 and 10.

First, it is certainly far from clear, as Adair contends, that Hamilton "expected a continual use of military force would be required to keep the rebellious poor in their place." Adair would appear to be referring to the very first sentence of Federalist 9 which reads, "A firm Union will be of the utmost moment to the peace and liberty of the States as a barrier against domestic faction and insurrection" (9:38). This statement as it stands is eminently sensible. In fact, Madison writing in Federalist 43 makes essentially the same point. For example, he quotes approvingly of a confederate republic: " 'should a popular insurrection happen in one of the States, the others are able to quell it. Should abuses creep into one part, they are reformed by those that remain sound' " (43:226). On this score, Madison is, in effect, repeating what Hamilton had stated in essay 9.

Perhaps more to the point of Hamilton's opening sentence is Madison's remark that the national government's "right to interpose" in cases of domestic violence and insurrection within these states "will generally prevent the necessity of exerting it" (43:226). Certainly from the examples and commentary in the very first paragraph of Federalist 9, this would seem to be the thrust of Hamilton's argument; that is, a "firm Union" will serve to prevent the "perpetual vibration between the extremes of tyranny and anarchy" (9:38).

In any event, Adair's contention that Hamilton envisioned "continual use of military force . . . to keep the rebellious poor in their place" cannot be sustained

---

Adair and Mason, he is restrained from quoting other writings and speeches. Thus Dietze's claims take on certain subtleties: "Madison sees in federalism a means for the creation of a system of federal power-balances . . . federalism is to him an institution devised to protect the states within federation" (TF, 269). Hamilton, however, "having practically precluded himself from pronouncing a theory of power-balances . . . puts the shock- or faction-absorbing function of the states in the background. Hamilton sees the remedy against factions in the states mainly in a strong national government. Federalism is a means for the creation of a system of power concentration." But this interpretation overlooks certain very direct observations by Hamilton on this score: "the State governments will, in all possible contingencies, afford complete security against invasions of the public liberty by the national authority" (28:141); or that "the State legislature" would be the "vigilant but suspicious and jealous guardians of the rights of the citizens against encroachments from the federal government" (26:134).

Likewise Dietze argues that Madison sought a "power-balance" among the branches through separation of powers, whereas Hamilton sought a "deconcentration of power from the legislature" (TF, 261). This distinction is very questionable for reasons set forth in the text below. In any event, the split between Hamilton and Madison certainly does narrow considerably when one is confined to the text of *The Federalist*.

from the text. What Adair has done is to extrapolate from Hamilton's other writings or speeches to reach this conclusion.

Second, to show that Hamilton believed in "unlimited" and "overruling" government Adair makes reference to essays 23 and 30 which deal, respectively, with the defense and taxation powers of the national government. Let us see what Hamilton says in these essays that could justify these charges.

With regard to the national powers to "raise armies," "build and equip fleets," and so forth, Hamilton writes: "These powers ought to exist without limitation, *because it is impossible to foresee or to define the extent and variety of national exigencies, and the correspondent extent and variety of the means which may be necessary to satisfy them*. The circumstances that endanger the safety of nations are infinite, and for this reason no constitutional shackles can wisely be imposed on the power to which the care of it is committed" (23:119). And in the very next paragraph he is to strike a theme that recurs in one fashion or another throughout *The Federalist*: the national government must possess the *means* necessary for the ends that are entrusted to its care. As he puts it: "the *means* ought to be proportioned to the *end*; the persons from whose agency the attainment of any *end* is expected ought to possess the *means* by which it is to be attained." This proposition rests upon "axioms as simple as they are universal" (119).

Hamilton is both instructive and logical about the matter of common defense and the powers that the national government must possess to fulfill its obligation; he never flinches from the conclusions that flow from these axioms. "Whether there ought to be a federal government entrusted with the care of the common defense," he writes, "is a question in the first instance open to discussion; but the moment it is decided in the affirmative, it will follow that the government ought to be clothed with all the powers requisite to complete execution of its trust" (23:119–20).

This same line of reasoning leads him to contend in Federalist 30 that the powers of the national government "to raise its own revenues by the ordinary methods of taxation" (that is, to possess the powers of sovereign states to requisition the necessary financial support to fulfill the ends entrusted to them) simply must replace reliance on the states to meet their requisitions (149).

The differences between Madison and Hamilton on these specific matters seem minuscule at best. Madison also subscribes to Hamilton's axioms regarding means and ends: "No axiom," according to Madison, "is more clearly established in law, or in reason, than that wherever the end is required, the means are authorized; wherever a general power to do a thing is given, every particular power necessary for doing it is included" (44:232). Again, when it comes to the matter of the national government's power to provide for the national defense, there seems to be no substantive difference between Hamilton and Madison. Madison writes: "The means of security can only be regulated by the means and danger of attack. They will, in fact, be ever determined by these rules and by no others. It is vain to oppose constitutional barriers to the impulse of self-preservation. It is worse than vain; because it plants in the Constitution itself necessary usurpations of power, every precedent of which is a germ of unnecessary and multiplied repetitions'' (41:210).

Finally, to the point of the differences between Hamilton and Madison concerning the powers of the national government, it is interesting to note how they describe the principal objectives of the proposed union. For Madison they are:

1. Security against foreign danger; 2. Regulation of the intercourse with foreign nations; 3. Maintenance of harmony and proper intercourse among the States; 4. Certain miscellaneous objects of general utility; 5. Restraint of the States from certain injurious acts; 6. Provisions for giving due efficacy to all these powers (41:210).

For Hamilton:

The principal purposes to be answered by Union are these—the common defense of the members; the preservation of the public peace, as well against internal convulsions as external attacks; the regulation of commerce with other nations and States; the superintendence of our intercourse, political and commercial, with foreign countries (23:119).

From this it would seem the two were remarkably close together on the substantive goals of the proposed system.

And, third, the charge that Hamilton in Federalist 9 advocates a ''consolidated system,'' ''a perfect subordination [of the states] to the general authority of the union,'' or, in other words, a unitary system, is also without textual foundation.

What Hamilton does do is enlist the authority of Montesquieu to answer critics of the proposed union who argue that an extensive republic must necessarily be short-lived. Using a lengthy quote from Montesquieu as a point of departure on the advantages of a ''CONFEDERATE REPUBLIC'' (9:40), Hamilton proceeds to argue that there is widespread misunderstanding concerning the essential elements or features of a confederacy. His purpose, it would appear, is to broaden the meaning or definition of confederacy so that the proposed system will fit within its confines. In any event, he concludes that ''a confederate republic seems simply to be 'an assemblage of societies,' or an association of two or more states into one state.'' The members of this association need not be considered as political equals, nor is the central government forbidden from acting directly upon individuals rather than through the governments of the member states. To argue otherwise, he contends, would be to adopt a position that is ''supported neither by principle nor precedent.'' He writes that ''the extent, modification, and objects of the federal authority [that is, the central government of a confederacy] are mere matters of discretion'' (41).[11]

---

[11]That Montesquieu might have misunderstood the relationship that existed between the central government and the components of the Lycian confederacy—a confederacy that both Montesquieu and Hamilton held up as a model—is explored by Christopher Wolfe, ''The Confederate Republic in Montesquieu,'' *Polity* 9 (Summer 1977).

It is in this context that the quote "perfect subordination to the general government" appears. The passage from which this phrase is taken reads as follows and comes immediately after the sentence quoted above relating to the "extent, modification, and objects of federal authority" being matters of "discretion":

> So long as the separate organizations of the members be not abolished; so long as it exists, by a constitutional necessity, for local purpose; though it should be in perfect subordination to the general authority of the union, it would still be, in fact and in theory, an association of states or a confederacy (9:41).

This is clearly presented by way of showing what *at a minimum* would constitute a confederacy and is consonant with his apparent end of broadening the definition of confederacy so as to include the proposed system. However, it is crucial to note that he feels the relationships stipulated in the Philadelphia Constitution are well "above" the stipulated minimum. The proposed system, he informs us in the sentence immediately following the above quote, "so far from implying an abolition of the State governments, makes them constituent parts of the national sovereignty, by allowing them a direct representation in the Senate, and leaves in their possession certain exclusive and very important portions of sovereign power." He goes on to write that this arrangement "fully corresponds, in every rational import of the terms, with the idea of federal government" (9:41).

His reference to "certain exclusive and very important portions of sovereign power" that are retained by the states certainly does not render him a champion of states' rights as they are contended for today. Yet such an admission certainly does cast grave doubts on the argument of the proponents of the split personality thesis who argue that Hamilton, unlike Madison, believed in a centralized and authoritarian system. And the fact is that, on these and other matters relating to federalism and state-national relations, there appears to be no principled difference between Hamilton and Madison. Both, for reasons set forth in Federalist 37, are necessarily vague and general about the relative powers of each government. Madison, for instance, is scarcely any more precise and informative than Hamilton when he writes that the powers of the national government are "few and defined," whereas those of "the State governments are numerous and general" (45: 238). Nor can Madison be viewed as a champion of states' rights in maintaining that the people, considered as a whole, should be free to repose their trust in whichever government, national or state, demonstrates "manifest and irresistible proofs of better administration." And in adding that "the State governments could have little to apprehend" from such a process "because it is only within a certain sphere that the federal power can, in the nature of things, be advantageously administered," he even undercuts the presumed *constitutional* status of the states' residual powers (46:241).

I should add, rather than relegating the matter to a footnote, that, instead of driving a wedge between Federalists 9 and 10, the students of the document would do well to read them as complementary.[12] Hamilton, to be sure, concentrates more on the traditional or formal arguments concerning the advantages to be derived from political union. However, in stressing the advantages of "ENLARGEMENT of the ORBIT" (chief among those principles of an improved science of politics), Hamilton consciously or unconsciously laid the groundwork for Madison to stress, as he had done at Philadelphia and in his writings, that the pluralistic nature of the proposed union would also operate to reduce the possibilities of factious rule or insurrection.[13] To put this otherwise: rather than being in opposition, both see the advantages of an extended republic from different perspectives.

The second major dimension of the split personality thesis, as I have said, involves the scope and degree of popular control. Hamilton, to be more exact, has been charged with backing off from the republican principle in those essays dealing with the executive and judicial powers and functions. Again, we can take up this matter point by point:

(a) Hamilton writes in Federalist 71, when discussing the veto power of the president:

> When occasions present themselves in which the interests of the people are at variance with their inclinations, it is the duty of the persons whom they have appointed to be the guardians of those interests to withstand the temporary delusion in order to give them time and opportunity for more cool and sedate reflection. Instances might be cited in which a conduct of this kind has saved the people from the very fatal consequences of their own mistakes, and has procured lasting monuments of their gratitude to the men who had the courage and magnanimity enough to serve them at the peril of their displeasure (71:370).

This, as far as I can tell, is the strongest statement that Hamilton makes on behalf of a president's using his powers to resist or thwart the will of a presumed majority. In essay 73 and elsewhere he urges the executive to use his veto power to protect the legitimate domain of executive authority and power against the encroachments of the legislature. With Madison, Hamilton believed that the legislative branch was most to be feared because of its inherent "propensity . . . to intrude upon the rights, and to absorb the powers, of the other departments" in order to advance the cause of one faction or another (379). Hamilton also believed that the veto should be exercised to protect the community "against the passing of bad laws, through haste, inadventure, or design" (380). But this stand is certainly not antirepublican, unless, of course, republicanism is equated with a sense-

---

[12]Ralph L. Ketcham even goes beyond Adair in driving a wedge between these two essays. See his "Notes on James Madison's Sources for the Tenth Federalist Paper," *Midwest Journal of Political Science* 1 (May 1957).

[13]See Martin Diamond, "The Federalist," in *A History of Political Philosophy*, ed. Leo Strauss and Joseph Cropsey (Chicago: Rand McNally, 1963).

less government. This use of the veto, moreover, is directed at the legislature, not the will of the people.

Hamilton goes on to write that the morality he is urging regarding the veto power is not based "upon the supposition of superior wisdom or virtue in the executive," but rather "upon the supposition that the legislature will not be infallible," and that there may be occasions when a factious spirit takes hold of the Congress that leads its members to pass legislation which upon due reflection they themselves "would condemn" (73:379–80).

Again, it is difficult to see how Hamilton's position on these matters differs from Madison's. Recall that Madison in discussing the utility of the Senate remarked that "such an institution may be sometimes necessary as a defense to the people against their own temporary errors and delusions." While the "cool and deliberate sense of the community ought . . . ultimately to prevail," he wrote, there are times when the people, actuated by passions or demagogues "may call for measures which they themselves will afterward be the most ready to lament and condemn" (63:325). At best, the advocates of the split personality thesis have a very shaky point on this particular issue. Yet, let us recall, the point is an extremely important one for their thesis.

(b) There are a number of things to note about Hamilton's argument for judicial review and the contentions of both Adair and Mason. First, the judicial review that Hamilton advocated was quite narrow in scope. He believed that the Courts should declare void only those legislative acts contrary to the "manifest tenor" of the Constitution (78:402). Before a statute could be declared unconstitutional, the Court would have to show an "irreconcilable variance" between the statute and the Constitution (78:403). The Court, according to the morality set forth by Hamilton, "should be bound down by strict rules and precedents" (78:406).

These rather rigid restrictions hardly support the notion that Hamilton provided a "sanction for the development of an . . . irresponsible judiciary."[14] Of course the Court has in recent years overstepped the boundaries set forth by Hamilton. Clearly, the blame for this lies not with Hamilton but with recent generations of legal scholars who have praised and justified judicial imperialism and supremacy.

Second, as we know, Hamilton invokes the "higher" or "fundamental law" theory to justify judicial review: "the prior act of a superior ought to be preferred to the subsequent act of an inferior and subordinate authority; and that accordingly, whenever a particular statute contravenes the Constitution, it will be the

---

[14]It can be maintained that Hamilton in Federalist 81 does not satisfactorily refute the charges of the Antifederalist "Brutus," who contended that the national judiciary "would be authorized to explain the constitution, not only according to its letter, but according to its spirit and intention." *The Antifederalist Papers*, ed. Morton Borden (East Lansing: Michigan State University Press, 1965), 230. In my view, the major shortcoming in his response is the failure to set forth clearly what he would consider an appropriate constitutional remedy for an habitual abuse of judicial power. But the charge that he provided a "sanction for the development of an . . . irresponsible judiciary" is unwarranted. See chapter 5.

duty of the judicial tribunals to adhere to the latter and disregard the former'' (78: 404). Quite obviously, he does not believe that legislative majorities, even those with strong popular support, have the authority to pass laws that contravene the Constitution. It is difficult to see how Madison could have held a different position. In Federalist 53, in trying to discover the grounds for the maxim ''that where annual elections end, tyranny begins,'' Madison remarks that it must have arisen in political systems where the body that possessed ''the supreme power of legislation'' also possessed the authority and power ''to change the form of government'' (277–78). ''Even in Great Britain,'' he notes, ''where the principles of political and civil liberty have been most discussed, and where we hear most of the rights of the Constitution, it is maintained that the authority of the Parliament is transcendent and uncontrollable as well with regard to the Constitution as the ordinary objects of legislative provision.'' In such systems, consequently, the legislative bodies can change ''the period of election'' through the very same processes by which they pass ordinary laws. But in America, he points out, it is ''well understood'' that there is a difference ''between a Constitution established by the people and unalterable by the government, and a law established by the government and alterable by the government'' (277).

Third, there can be no question that, if Hamilton had really wanted to establish the judiciary as the bulwark against majorities (the poor) bent upon exploiting minorities (the rich), he would have moderated his remarks about the addition of a bill of rights. Plainly, the addition of a bill of rights would only serve to enhance the authority of the Court.[15]

On this score, it can be argued that Hamilton (and certainly by all evidences Madison) wanted to skirt the bill-of-rights issue because it was a ''front'' under which the Antifederalists sought to drain the national government of vital powers (e.g., the authority for direct taxation). But another reason for Hamilton's animus towards a bill of rights is that the bill would be ineffective in curbing majority factions.[16] And still another, which confutes the charges that Hamilton was a monarchist, elitist, authoritarian, or the like, was his belief that a bill of rights, as traditionally understood, was inappropriate in a republican form of government such as that established by the Constitution. Rights, he points out, had traditionally been viewed as limitations on the power of the king towards his subjects, but, under the proposed system, the people rule. ''WE, THE PEOPLE of the United

---

[15]The more so, to use Hamilton's language, because the interpretation of the laws and Constitution ''is the proper and peculiar province of the courts'' (78:403).

[16]Hamilton goes beyond this to write that a ''bill of rights, in the sense and to the extent in which they are contended for, are not only unnecessary . . . but dangerous'' (84:443). We need not explore his argument on this point to see that, unlike the impression conveyed by the split personality advocates, Hamilton was not a mechanical politician who believed that formal constitutional restraints would serve to curb the abuses of majorities or the rulers. On this his heart beat at one with Madison. See, for example, 10:46 and 48:258.

States,'' he continues, constitutes ''a better recognition of popular rights than volumes of those aphorisms . . . which would sound much better in a treatise of ethics than in a constitution of government'' (84:443).

(c) To Mason's point that Madison did not share Hamilton's implicit belief in the purifying effects of power, the response must be that, in the first place, there is no basis, save pure speculation, for attributing any such belief to Hamilton writing as Publius. In the second place, there is a definite correspondence between Hamilton and Madison, not only with regard to the question of human nature, but also to the general character of those who would hold office in the proposed system.

Madison in Federalist 10 tells us that the extended republic holds out every prospect that the representatives of the people (certainly a healthy majority of them) will be those ''whose wisdom may best discern the true interest of their country and whose patriotism and love of justice will be least likely to sacrifice it to temporary or partial considerations.'' In fact, he even goes on to say, ''it may well happen that the public voice, pronounced by the representatives of the people, will be more consonant to the public good than if pronounced by the people themselves, convened for that purpose'' (47). He discusses this more fully in Federalist 57 where he spells out why he believes the system will normally operate to produce representatives of high caliber.[17]

Hamilton did not have occasion to speak to this point at length. It is clear, however, that he shared Madison's presumptions, namely, that the conditions associated with the extended republic, coupled with the ''Duty, gratitude, interest, and ambition'' of the representative himself, would operate to provide fit and responsible officeholders (57:297). For instance, Hamilton writes that ''the office of the President will seldom fall to the lot of any man who is not in an eminent degree endowed with the requisite qualifications.'' Why so? Largely because of the extensiveness of the republic:

> Talents for low intrigue, and the little arts of popularity, may alone suffice to elevate a man to the first honors in a single State; but it will require other talents, and a different kind of merit, to establish him in the esteem and confidence of the whole Union, or of so considerable a portion of it as would be necessary to make him a successful candidate for the distinguished office of President of the United States. It will not be too strong to say that there will be a constant probability of seeing the station filled by characters pre-eminent for ability and virtue (68:354).

---

[17]The end sought by Madison he sets forth at the beginning of Federalist 57: ''The aim of every political constitution is, or ought to be, first to obtain for rulers men who possess most wisdom to discern, and most virtue to pursue, the common good of society; and in the next place, to take most effectual precautions for keeping them virtuous whilst they continue to hold public trust'' (295). He spells out in the remainder of this essay why he believes the proposed system will approximate this goal. In this enterprise he does not conflict in the slightest with the presumptions of Hamilton.

The fact is, of course, that both Hamilton and Madison were fully aware of the dangers of faction. Both knew that men could be selfish and shortsighted—prone to place their short-term interests and gratifications above the long-term interests and well-being of either themselves or the nation. Consequently, one of the central concerns of the authors of *The Federalist* is, quite simply, this: given the nature of man, is it possible to institute a republican government that will not succumb to tyranny or majority oppression? A good deal of *The Federalist*—when the authors have the opportunity—centers on this and like questions.[18]

What is evident, to return to the split personality thesis, is that the charge that Hamilton believed in the "purifying effects" of power, or that he must have assumed this given his estimate of mankind, could equally apply to Madison. Put otherwise, whatever burden is placed upon Hamilton to show that the chief executive or members of the Supreme Court will be able to exercise their powers with the restraint necessary for a nontyrannical republican system falls as well upon Madison, perhaps even more so because it was his lot to defend Congress, that institution most likely to represent the very worst characteristics of the people.

SOME CONCLUSIONS

What I hope to have made abundantly clear is that a careful analysis of *The Federalist* does not lend support to the split personality thesis. Whatever plausibility this thesis does possess would appear to derive from the differences between Hamilton and Madison over matters political, economic, and otherwise that arose either before or after ratification. These differences are, of course, marked, and certainly would lead one to regard any collaboration by Hamilton and Madison as unlikely. But, as I have indicated, evidences of their differences, in the sense of antagonistic views on the nature of the Constitution, are not present in *The Federalist*.

This fact tends to confirm the commonly advanced proposition that each of Publius's component parts knew full well the dimensions of the task before them, that perhaps the opportunity for a stronger union might never again present itself, and that, in addition, a united and coherent defense of the proposed Constitution would require them to trim their theoretical sails, that is, to accommodate themselves and their thinking to the implicit values and assumptions of the document, as well as to the sensibilities of each other.

This analysis, it should be noted, does not bear upon serious questions that have been raised about *The Federalist*: To what extent does it reflect the concerns and thinking of the Framers? Does it represent the consensual views of those who favored ratification? Is it reflective of the predominant views of its time concern-

---

[18]For an analysis of the remarkable agreement that seemed to exist between Hamilton and Madison on the characteristics of human nature and how both argued effectively that the proposed system would "exploit" these characteristics to advantage, see James B. Scanlan, "The Federalist and Human Nature," *Review of Politics* 21 (October 1959).

ing the need for a stronger union? What the analysis does show is that two political thinkers and activists with divergent views, Hamilton and Madison, were in substantial agreement on the principal issues surrounding ratification and the nature of the proposed system. In this sense, at least, *The Federalist* is a "consensual" document, one well suited to serve as a benchmark in charting the course of our political development.

Finally, this analysis should not be read to imply that there are no tensions or contradictions in *The Federalist*. But the more important of these, it would appear, reflect problems implicit in the proposed Constitution or inherent in republicanism. As such, they reside in Publius as a whole, not as conflicting parts. Recall, for instance, that the proposed Constitution called for an entirely new relationship between the national government and the states: a relationship that did not fit any of the traditional categories known to Publius[19] or his contemporaries, and that defies precise delineation even today. Nor should we forget that the proposed system wedded republicanism to a new version of separation of powers, one calling for an independent and coordinate judiciary, a wedding that was bound to pose unforeseen problems, both theoretical and practical.[20] And it is, I would submit, the holistic perspective of *The Federalist* that holds out the best prospect for identifying, illuminating, and comprehending these and like concerns surrounding the foundations of our system.

---

[19]On this point, see: Martin Diamond, "What the Framers Meant by Federalism," in *Essays on Federalism*, ed. George C. S. Benson (Claremont, Calif.: Institute for Studies in Federalism, 1962).

[20]In Federalist 37, certainly one of the more reflective essays, Publius identifies and touches upon these and other "difficulties" that he regards as "inherent in the very nature of the undertaking referred to the convention" (182). What is more, he indicates why, in all likelihood, they will continue to persist so long as the system endures.

2

Majority Rule and the Extended Republic Theory of James Madison

INTRODUCTORY NOTE

Of all the Federalist essays, Federalist 10 is by far the most widely read and cited. Indeed, most students of the American political tradition have come to regard it as the document to which one must recur in order to understand the underlying theory of our constitutional system. Its assumptions, principles, and theorems form the foundations of what is commonly known as the ''Madisonian model'' which many close observers, scholars and practical politicians alike, believe best explains the nature and operations of the American political system. Thus, the essay enjoys a quasi-constitutional status.

That much may be said about Federalist 10 without too much fear of contradiction. However, principally because of its acknowledged and strategic role in fixing the character of the regime, it has been subjected to numerous readings and interpretations, and many of these can hardly be characterized as ''neutral.'' In this respect, I should remark, it would seem that many, if not most, analysts do not employ the essay as an ''eyepiece'' through which they might gain a clearer or more comprehensive picture of the American political system; rather, they seem to use it for purposes of finding theoretical support for conclusions they have already reached about the salient characteristics of the system and its operations. This often leads to a piecemeal and distorted interpretation of Madison's extended republic theory, a theory set forth not only in this essay but in his personal correspondence and at the Philadelphia Convention.

Charles Beard's *An Economic Interpretation of the Constitution of the United States*, a work that can be credited with sparking the enormous interest that has been shown in Federalist 10,* is perhaps the best example I can offer. Briefly put, Beard quotes extensively from a portion of the essay in an effort to show that Madison was a pre-Marxian Marxist who believed that the basic divisions in society would be economic, between the ''haves'' and the ''have nots.'' Yet, Beard was able to accomplish this only by deleting key sentences in the middle of the quoted portion—sentences that clearly indicate that Madison was very much aware of other and, as many analysts would argue, even more potentially devastating sources of division and conflict originating from dis-

---

*On this point see: Douglass Adair, ''The Tenth Federalist Revisited,'' in *Fame and the Founding Fathers: Essays by Douglass Adair*, ed. Trevor Colbourn (New York: W. W. Norton, 1974).

tinctly noneconomic sources involving passion and opinion. In his *Main Currents in American Thought*, Vernon Parrington is also guilty of the very same practice, though his elliptic surgery is more precise than Beard's. And both are also guilty of not pointing out another facet of his theory that does not so readily fit their preconceived notions: Madison also anticipated a "horizontal" conflict between different economic interests, not simply a "vertical" conflict between those with and those without property.

The modern critics of the "Madisonian model," though they subscribe to essentially the same revisionist thesis concerning Madison's underlying thoughts about the need to protect the "haves" from the "have nots" who constitute a majority, are less direct and more subtle in presenting their case. Thus, disentangling their arguments is sometimes a difficult matter. For instance, as we shall see in chapter 3, we find Madison's arguments for an extended republic mixed with and fused into his arguments concerning the necessity for the separation of powers. But other lines of argument seem designed to show that we cannot really take Madison's position very seriously, presumably because it will not withstand critical analysis. Madison presumes, for example, that the permanent and aggregate interests of the community and rights of citizens are not necessarily what the majority may hold them to be at any given moment; that, in other words, they have an existence quite apart from what majorities may will or think. This, however, makes no sense to many moderns who have come to regard man as the measure of all things. From their perspective Madison was offering up, much as our politicians of today are wont to do, sweet-sounding maxims designed to enlist popular support: rather than offering an "operational" theory, he was presenting an attractive and appealing rationale for minority rule.

These lines of analysis or argument are appealing primarily to those already convinced that our system is built on the foundations alleged by the revisionists. Put another way, they do not come to terms with Madison's argument on Madison's terms; they simply reject the presumptions that lie at the heart of his approach. For instance, those who do not believe in an objective moral order cannot "enter" Madison's system; they must summarily reject it or, as I have intimated, question his motives or sincerity. However, as I believe the following analysis will make clear, the central issue in the revisionists' critique is whether Madison makes his case that the rights of other citizens and the permanent and aggregate interests of the community can be protected in the proposed system without having to abandon the republican principle of majority rule. This, in my estimation, is both a legitimate and crucial question raised by the modern critics. Yet, it is also one they have not chosen to explore with any intellectual rigor.

A few words are in order about the last section of my analysis. It was written in 1975 shortly after New York City went bankrupt. I believed—and one has only to read William Buckley's *The Unmaking of a Mayor* to see why—that a major contributing cause of this bankruptcy was the practice of pandering to virtually every identifiable interest in the city.** I could also see that politics at the national level was alarmingly similar to that of New York, particularly after the enactment of the Great Society programs. While New York could turn to the national government for relief, the question arose in my mind, "Where can the national government turn once it runs out of money?"

My basic concern then and now, to put this in terms of my introductory remarks, is that the active, positive government along the lines suggested by Croly and initiated by the

---

**The Unmaking of a Mayor* (New Rochelle, N.Y.: Arlington House, 1977).

New Deal is in the long run incompatible with the conditions and processes necessary for the successful operation of the "Madisonian model." I see no reason to change my prognosis. Indeed, it has been borne out over the years, nor is there any indication that our leaders are about to change course. The principal reasons for my assessment—that groups will not willingly give up benefits or advantages once bestowed by the government whether they are needed any longer or not; that our present morality encourages groups to take full advantage of governmental largess; and, among others, that our elected officials seem incapable of resisting or tempering the demands of significant groups—are still operative. I would add only that the "new morality" that triggered this seemingly irreversible process has produced a state of affairs completely at odds with what it intended or promised. Rather than making the nation more of a nation in the manner Croly envisioned, it has served to make it less so.

MAJORITY RULE AND THE EXTENDED REPUBLIC THEORY OF JAMES MADISON

The American experience with self-government has long been the object of admiration by foreign observers. Principally for this reason students have pored over the records, debates, and pronouncements of our founding period with an eye to discovering the principles, theories, and beliefs that undergird the system and seem to have contributed to its success. Their interest has been more than academic. A belief, still widely held and for good reason, is that certain principles embodied in our constitutional framework are exportable, that underdeveloped nations, or nations embarking on the enterprise of deliberately creating governments, may benefit from our experience by incorporating certain of our principles into their political design.

But the results of these searches into our underlying principles have been less than encouraging. Rather than coming to substantial agreement, scholars seem hopelessly divided concerning even the most basic and important features of the American system. Were our institutions designed to allow for popular control of government or were they the product of men who actually feared republican government? Was the system really designed to provide for a unitary form wherein authority would be centralized in the national government, or was it intended to provide for an effective and meaningful division of powers between the states and national government? Was the President intended to be a prime mover among our branches of government or was this to be the function of Congress? These are only a few of the fundamental matters over which there has been lively dispute. The predictable result is great uncertainty concerning precisely what our basic principles are. Most certainly, it seems impossible to construct any coherent political theory that must have guided our Founding Fathers.

The situation is such that the contention advanced by John Roche seems warranted. He writes that the Framers are best understood "as extremely talented democratic politicians" and that the emergent Constitution was not "a triumph of architectonic genius," but rather "a patch-work sewn together under the pressure of both time and events.''[1] From this point of view, the search for coherent theory is necessarily doomed to failure; or, if not that, the underlying theoretical principles will at best be hazy, less than well developed, and often employed with an eye to their acceptability and workability given the political and social circumstances of the time. Moreover, we should not expect consistency in their application given the practical bent of the Framers.

Despite all this, there was one overriding question of enormous theoretical import that the Framers and presumably a majority of the American people answered affirmatively and unambiguously with the adoption of the Constitution; namely, they believed a republican and nontyrannical government over an extended territory possible. Certainly, in back of, or overarching their democratic caucusing, as Roche would have it, there must have been a prior and fairly wide consensus as to the feasibility of their undertaking. Admittedly not all shared this conviction—not, at any rate, to the degree and extent of the Constitution's more ardent proponents—and in many respects it can be viewed as one of the most, if not the most, basic issue(s) that divided the political leadership during the period of ratification. The issue, to be sure, may not have been put precisely in these terms on every occasion, but key debates over the role of the national government vis-à-vis the states, how secure the liberties of the people would be in the hands of the national government, the role and accountability of representatives in the national government, and popular recourse from abuses of power by the national government can be directly related to and subsumed under the more general question of the feasibility of a nontyrannical republic over an extended territory.

Our purpose here is a limited but important one. We will examine with some care Federalist 10, an essay in which Madison sets forth what is generally conceded to be the strongest argument for the workability of a stable, nontyrannical, and republican form of government over an extended territory. We will do so with certain critical questions in mind: What novel features or departures from traditional teachings does Madison advance? What presumptions must Madison have held in advancing his thesis? What changes in our social and political environment seem to bear upon critical elements of his argument? What conceivable developments might destroy or undermine the validity of his arguments? An examination of these and similar questions will hopefully provide some clues as to what the future holds for our republic.

The Extended Republic Theory

Federalist 10 presents us with a number of novel theses. In this respect, the main thrust of the essay, which stresses not only the workability but desirability of an extensive republic, is noteworthy. At the time Madison wrote, the traditional

---

[1]John Roche, ''The Founding Fathers: A Reform Caucus in Action,'' *American Political Science Review* 56 (March 1962), 814.

and widely accepted teaching held that a republican government—a government based upon the democratic principles of majority rule and political equality but one in which elected representatives would meet to conduct the business of the whole community—would be short-lived and marked by turbulence unless it operated upon a relatively small and homogeneous population within a relatively confined territorial expanse. Madison, however, advanced precisely the opposite proposition. In direct or ''pure'' democracies, where the entire people would meet to conduct the business of the community, and in small republics as well, the majority will more easily and readily feel ''a common passion or interest''; ''a communication and concert results from the form of government itself; and there is nothing to check the inducements to sacrifice the weaker party or an obnoxious individual'' (46). Thus, he reasoned, pure democracies and small republics were inherently ill-suited to control the effect of majority factions, that is, a majority ''united and actuated by some common impulse of passion, or of interest, adverse to the rights of other citizens, or to the permanent and aggregate interests of the community'' (43–44). But a large and extensive republic, he maintained, held out every prospect for controlling the effects of majority factions. Why so? Precisely because of the conditions necessitated by and associated with extensiveness. Extensiveness would require representation of some kind and that would serve, in his judgment, ''to refine and enlarge the public views, by passing them through the medium of a chosen body of citizens, whose wisdom may best discern the true interest of their country, and whose patriotism and love of justice will be least likely to sacrifice it to temporary or partial considerations'' (47). More: extensiveness would of necessity involve the inclusion of a greater number of parties and interests which would hamper the formation of factious majorities. In his words,

> Extend the sphere and you take in a greater variety of parties and interests; you make it less probable that a majority of the whole will have a common motive to invade the rights of other citizens; or if such a common motive exists, it will be more difficult for all who feel it to discover their own strength and to act in unison with each other. Besides other impediments, it may be remarked that, where there is a consciousness of unjust or dishonorable purposes, communication is always checked by distrust in proportion to the number whose concurrence is necessary (48).

Summing up this whole matter in the latter portion of Federalist 51, which is recognizably a reiteration of the argument presented in Federalist 10, Madison writes: ''among the great variety of interests, parties, and sects which it embraces, a coalition of a majority of the whole society could seldom take place on any other principles than those of justice and the general good'' (269).

Now, in setting forth his theory relative to the extended republic, Madison is ever mindful of the basic requirements of republicanism; namely, in the last analysis, a truly republican government ''derives all its power directly or indirectly from the great body of the people, and is administered by persons holding their offices during pleasure, for a limited period, or during good behavior.'' What is "essential to such a government," he takes pains to emphasize, is "that it be derived from the great body of society, not from an inconsiderable proportion, or a favored class of it" (39:194–95). His avowed strategic purpose in Federalist 10 is to convince the reader that in the extended republic the effects of majority faction can be controlled without violence to these republican principles. So much he makes clear at the outset of this essay and in the final paragraph he writes, with seeming confidence in his analysis, "we behold a republican remedy for the diseases most incident to republican government" (48).

His republican remedy for a republican disease, like his inversion of the traditional large versus small republic theories, is highly original but also enigmatic. As we shall see later, its enigmatic character derives from the obvious assumption that the attributes of extensiveness, representation, and multiplicity of interests will serve to thwart majority factions without doing violence to the republican principle. But, we are entitled to ask, since republicanism involves control by the "great body of the people," presumably at least a majority, how do the attributes of extensiveness serve to control this majority when it should be controlled, that is, when its ends are factious? Will such majorities somehow be "forced" to restrain themselves? If so, how can this be accomplished without recourse to some process or institution independent of the "great body of society" which would represent a significant departure from the republican principle?

One approach that leads to the heart of the enigma is to focus on solutions to the problem of majority factions that Madison expressly rejects. In doing this, we can best see what intellectual baggage Madison explicitly discarded or left by the wayside in the development of his theory. The results of such an undertaking are quite revealing in their own right largely because they stand in direct opposition to most of our contemporary interpretations of how the American system was "designed" to handle the problem of unjust and overpowering majorities.

One method that Madison rejects outright can be termed the traditionalist approach. It is the one that most readily comes to mind and finds its contemporary expression in the faith that some individuals place in certain of our institutions, most notably the Supreme Court. Quite simply this approach involves placing a veto power over actions of a majority in the hands of a select group. In Madison's time, for instance, theories of "mixed government" that would lodge such powers in the hands of the major social classes were prevalent and obviously could have been adapted to the American environment to provide a ready framework for such a solution. Yet, it must be emphasized that aside from the principle of representation that would require a legislative body, Madison at no point in Federalist 10 speaks of constitutional institutions as barriers to factious majorities. The means by which their effects will be controlled relate only to the noninstitutional factors associated with extensiveness that we have already noted. This fact, often overlooked by contemporary scholars, provides very strong, albeit indirect, evidence that Madison was aware that such institutions would rest upon nonrepublican foundations and would, moreover, at best be a precarious check on factious majorities. We need not, however, rely upon inferences. At other points he explicitly rejects any such approach. He writes that we cannot count on "enlightened statesmen" to control factions because they "will not always be at the helm," besides which, even if they were, they would be of little use since "indirect and remote considerations . . . rarely prevail over the immediate interest which one party may find in disregarding the rights of another or the good of the whole" (10:45). He flatly rejects creating a will in the community independent of the majority—that is, of the society itself. This he notes is the method that "prevails in all governments possessing an hereditary or self-appointed authority." "This, at best," he warns, "is but a precarious security because a power independent of the society may as well espouse the unjust views of the major, as the rightful interests, of the minor party, and may possibly be turned against both parties" (51:268).

Another approach to the problem of majority factions, one that at least seems to fascinate behaviorists concerned with the development and formation of the norms, attitudes, and values upon which political behavior is predicated, would be this: to produce and inculcate in the general population democratic values and norms with the end in mind of creating such a consensus that divisive issues (e.g., issues involving the truth or wisdom of basic values or ways of life of the society) would simply not arise in the political arena. Or, to put this into a more respectable framework, we know that every viable society rests upon some commonality of belief or, quite simply, it no longer remains a viable society. This commonality of belief—if, of course, it conforms with the known and tested standards of virtue—would serve to limit the boundaries of political discourse, particularly the introduction of factious proposals. In this connection, we cannot help but note that one of the critical functions of public education, at least as it was originally conceived, was to reinforce and bolster in each successive generation the fundamental ethics of this commonality.

With this we come to one of the most interesting and perplexing aspects of Madison's thought, to wit, his rejection of this approach for both normative and empirical reasons. For one thing, Madison seems adamant in rejecting methods that would serve to *eliminate* the causes of faction. "The latent causes of factions," he writes in Federalist 10, "are sown in the nature of man." And even if "no substantial occasion presents itself [such as attachment to different political leaders, or matters concerning "government" or "religion"] the most frivolous and fanciful distinctions have been sufficient to kindle their unfriendly passions and excite their most violent conflicts." It would be "impracticable" (at other points he suggests impossible) to give "to every citizen the same passions and the same interest" that, if it could be done, would surely serve to eliminate the causes of faction. Nor is he about to destroy liberty, the other means he perceives for eliminating the causes of faction. This would be analogous to "the annihilation of air, which is essential to animal life, because it imparts to fire its destructive agency" (44). From Madison's vantage point, there is little that can or should be done to eliminate factions. They will always be with us:

As long as the reason of man continues fallible, and he is at liberty to exercise it, different opinions will be formed. As long as the connection subsists between his reason and his self-love, his opinions and his passions will have a reciprocal influence on each other; and the former will be objects to which the latter will attach themselves (44).

And, as we might expect, he placed little reliance on appeals to a higher morality or religion in staying the hands of a majority faction. "They are not found to be such on the injustice and violence of individuals, and lose their efficacy in proportion to the number combined together, that is, in proportion as their efficacy becomes needful" (10:46). By the same token, he placed little faith in the sufficiency of written limitations to block factions. At other points in *The Federalist* (e.g., Federalist 48) and consonant with the general approach set forth in Federalist 10, he is somewhat disdainful of "parchment barricades" controlling the effects of factious groups. And even after his change of heart concerning the need for a bill of rights, it is apparent from his own language that he holds out limited and guarded prospects regarding their efficacy in curbing majority factions:

> It may be thought that all paper barriers against the power of the community are too weak to be worthy of attention. I am sensible they are not so strong as to satisfy gentlemen of every description who have seen and examined thoroughly the texture of such a defence; yet, as they have a tendency to impress some degree of respect for them, to establish the public opinion in their favor and rouse the attention of the whole community, it may be one means to control the majority from those acts to which they might be otherwise inclined.[2]

The perplexing aspect of Madison's theory in this respect can be put as follows: unlike many of his contemporary critics, Madison was an objectivist in the sense that he attached meaning to such terms as "justice," "permanent and aggregate interests of the community," and the "rights of other citizens." In his very definition of factions, for example, he uses this terminology to set such groups apart in a class by themselves on the rather obvious assumption that, by reference to such objective standards as "rights" and "permanent and aggregate interest," they could be operationally identified. For instance, justice, probably his highest end, is not to be equated with what any majority or "the great body of the people" may regard it to be at any given point in time; it embodies known and objective characteristics that are the measure of whether a group is factious. In sum, Madison was not a relativist.

In light of this and his depiction of majority factions, his assertion that a majority will "seldom" coalesce on any other principles than "those of justice and the general good" is startling. What kind of faith can we place in any such prediction?

---

[2]*The Annals of Congress*, 1st Congress, 1st Session, Philadelphia, April 8, 1789, 437.

Why are we to assume majorities will almost always act in a manner consistent with the public good? Factions, after all, are inevitable; they are the source of "the diseases most incident to republican government." Factious majorities, and this seems to be another of their inherent characteristics, will seldom, if ever, be dissuaded or show forbearance; they will press ahead with their demands no matter how unjust their cause, totally unaffected by appeals to a higher morality, justice, or the common good. Debate, deliberation, and reason, the characteristics of decent and orderly government, will be of no avail in modifying or thwarting their ambitions. They will introduce "instability, injustice and confusion" into our highest councils and when the opportunity presents itself—once, that is, they are the "superior force"—they will rule without regard for the "rules of justice and the rights of the minor party" (10:45).

Madison's answer centers on the extensiveness of the republic. And, as we have seen, he sees no need to depart from the republican principle that, of course, leaves majorities virtually unlimited. But, given the very formidable threat posed by majority factions to the existence of the republic, we are entitled to ask whether extensiveness alone is sufficient. To answer this, we must examine more thoroughly the arguments that he advances.

THE VIRTUES OF EXTENSIVENESS

The two attributes of extensiveness, already noted, that serve to control the effects of faction are representation and the multiplicity and diversity of interests. We shall discuss these in greater detail with an eye to determining how it is they might operate to accomplish this end consonant with republican principles.

At least one claim advanced by Madison on behalf of a system of representation in the context of a large republic seems self-evident. He observes that there must be an upward limit to the size of a representative assembly. The reasons for this are twofold: the assembly cannot be so large as to constitute a tumultuous mob incapable of conducting its assigned business in an orderly fashion; nor, by the canons implicit in republicanism, should it be so large that strict oligarchic internal rule is needed. Quite obviously, the larger the republic in terms of population, the more fit characters there will be to choose among for the limited number of positions in the legislature (10:47). To put this point in a familiar context, we can be reasonably certain, all things being equal, that a high school with 5,000 students will be able to field a better football team than one with but 500 students.

The greater number of fit characters means that the opportunities for selection of worthy representatives are increased. Extensiveness also provides other opportunities that are not so obvious. The larger the constituency, the less susceptible is the election to the "intrigues of the ambitious, or the bribes of the rich" (57:298). In other words, the possibilities of one man or a small group of men manipulating the electoral outcome are drastically diminished. The campaigns promise to be open contests wherein the voters will more likely be freed from the pernicious influences that all too frequently afflict small electoral districts.

And Madison seems to suggest something beyond this when in Federalist 10 he maintains that in large republics "it will be more difficult for unworthy candidates to practice with success the vicious arts, by which elections are too often carried" (47). Here, because he is contrasting the conditions of democracy with those of republicanism, we can without injustice take him to mean that extensiveness will diminish the opportunities for the election of demagogues. This rests on two assumptions that seem warranted in light of his general theory: first, the worthy candidates will be able to counteract the effects of the demagogue; and second, extensiveness will require a candidate to expose himself repeatedly to a variety of audiences, which means at a minimum that he cannot secure election by one passionate appeal in a setting where all the voters are present. Each candidate, in sum, will be forced to state his case repeatedly before different groups with sufficient opportunities for rebuttal by opposing candidates. This will serve to give the electorate sufficient opportunity to reason and deliberate.

These are forceful, though far less than compelling, arguments to the effect that the electorate would have a greater opportunity to select representatives "whose patriotism and love of justice will be least likely to sacrifice" the common good "to temporary or partial considerations." But Madison is less than convincing in telling us why the attention of the people will focus on men of the most attractive merit. The opportunity may be there but the motive may be lacking. To recur to our football team analogy, the coach of the high school with 5,000 students may by design, ignorance, or stupidity select the worst, not the best, available talent for the team. Conversely, the coach of the school with 500 students may be knowledgeable and conscientious and field a far better team.

Madison's clear assumption, stated in Federalist 57, is that the people will choose those "whose merit may best recommend" them "to the esteem and confidence of [their] country":

As they will have been distinguished by the preference of their fellow-citizens, we are to presume that in general they will be somewhat distinguished also by those qualities which entitle them to it, and which promise a sincere and scrupulous regard to the nature of their engagements (296).

Bearing this in mind, let us look at the end that Madison felt would be attained through representation to see how this relates to the majority faction problem. The representative assembly, for one thing, will constitute a "chosen body of citizens" that will "refine and enlarge the public view" and "whose wisdom may best discern the true interest of the country." Moreover, the representatives' "patriotism" and "love of justice," as we have mentioned, will presumably operate to prevent the sacrifice of the true interest to "temporary and partial considerations." And of this, Madison goes on to write, "it may well happen that the public voice, pronounced by the representatives of the people, will be more consonant to the public good than if pronounced by the people themselves, convened for the purpose" (10:47).

We can ask, apart from the fact that representatives are more capable and virtuous than the average constituent, why should the representative assembly possess this clearer conception of the common good? One obvious answer is that the representative assembly is so constituted that its members collectively, through their deliberations and debates, will provide a picture of the whole so that, unlike an ordinary constituent, the representative can weigh and measure with greater knowledge and certainty the impact of particular policies upon the whole country, not just one section or district. They are, in other words, strategically placed for this purpose. Contrasting the domains of the states and national government, for example, Madison writes:

> The great theatre of the United States presents a very different scene. The laws are so far from being uniform that they vary in every State; whilst the public affairs of the Union are spread throughout a very extensive region, and are extremely diversified by the local affairs connected with them, and can with difficulty be correctly learnt in any other place than in the central councils, to which a knowledge of them will be brought by the representative of every part of the empire (53:279).

Thus a policy that may have only a marginal benefit for a given geographical section of the country may have factious effects for another and eventually the whole nation. Or, it could be that a policy when viewed in the context of the whole may be seen as counterproductive. At least this much a representative will be in a better position to determine than constituents who, we must presume, will have more partial views.

Such a position regarding representation is easily reconciled with republicanism by assuming that, if the constituents possessed the same knowledge as their representatives, they, too, would see matters in the same light as their representatives and abandon their temporary or partial interests. For such a process to occur would require a fairly high degree of "communion" between the representatives and their constituents because the representatives would be obliged, in this variant of republicanism, to make as accurate a calculation as possible concerning what factors or values derived from a comprehension of the whole, if known to the constituents, would cause a shift in their thinking. Madison perceived this need for communion,[3] as we have termed it, but it presented him with serious problems. Critics of the proposed Constitution contended that the electoral districts under the new form of government would be so large that communion between constituents and the representatives would be virtually nonexistent. Madison was able to counter that the districts would be no larger than those found in certain of the existing states. Yet, on Madison's own showing this was hardly a satisfactory rejoinder. If, as he conceded, the population of the nation would grow and if, as he also conceded, there must be an upward limit to the size of the representative

---

[3]See especially Federalist essays 52 and 57 on this point.

assembly, the bonds of communion could not help but be severely weakened, if not entirely broken. Madison's general comment reflecting on this problem is noteworthy because it touches upon a theme that recurs throughout *The Federalist*:

> By enlarging too much the number of electors, you render the representative too little acquainted with all their local circumstances and lesser interests; as by reducing it too much, you render him unduly attached to these, and too little fit to comprehend and pursue great and national objects. The federal Constitution forms a happy combination in this respect; the great and aggregate interests being referred to the national, the local and particular to the State legislatures (10:47).

But, in suggesting the need for a division of authority between the states and national governments, Madison theoretically evades one problem only to introduce another that even to this day defies solution.

If representation itself provides at best only a very partial solution to controlling the effects of faction, what can be said of the other characteristics of an extended republic, namely, multiplicity and diversity of interest? The clearest statement of the desired effect of multiple interests is found in Federalist 51:

> Whilst all authority in it will be derived from and dependent on the society, the society itself will be broken into so many parts, interests and classes of citizens, that the rights of individuals, or of the minority, will be in a little danger from interested combinations of the majority. In a free government the security for civil rights must be the same as that for religious rights. It consists in the one case in the multiplicity of interests, and in the other in the multiplicity of sects. The degree of security in both cases will depend on the number of interests and sects; and this may be presumed to depend on the extent of country and number of people comprehended under the same government (268–69).

By recurring to Federalist 10, we find specific reasons that we have mentioned in another context as to why this state of affairs will prevail. Here, again, we find the conditions of the small and large republic contrasted. In the small republic, with fewer "distinct parties and interests," the likelihood increases that interests composing a majority will possess a common motive to oppress or otherwise abuse a minority. Beyond this, the opportunities for discovering and acting upon such a common motive are more abundant because of the "small compass" within which the interests operate. The opposite is true of the large republic that Madison envisions. The interests and parties will be so numerous that it will be difficult for them to discover a common motive for oppressive action. And even if such a motive does exist—and here Madison seems to feel geographical factors come into play—"it will be more difficult for all who feel it to discover their own strength, and to act in unison with each other." In this view of things, each interest is a small stone in a large mosaic.

In addition to all the difficulties attendant upon majority formation with such a diversity of interests, Madison cites another impediment: "where there is a consciousness of unjust or dishonorable purposes, communication is always checked by distrust in proportion to the number whose concurrence is necessary" (10:48). This, of course, presumes that there are recognized social norms regarding what constitutes an unjust or dishonorable purpose, even to the extent that factious leaders sense they are doing something wrong. To what extent this would really operate as an impediment, given Madison's characterization of factions, is somewhat questionable. However, and more important in light of his general theory, is the "distrust" that is bound to occur among the diverse interests. Given the picture painted by Madison, the degree of mutual suspicion might well be sufficient to preclude unified action. To this we might also add that organization for unified action would probably have to take on conspiratorial overtones because secrecy might well be required in plotting action contrary to the common morality. Thus, all the factors of extensiveness operate to render a successful conspiracy most unlikely.

Yet there are obvious problems with Madison's theory. Why will the extensiveness operate to thwart only factious majorities? Why, that is, won't the hurdles of interest diversity operate to prevent the formation of virtuous or nonfactious majorities? Still another and more crucial problem can be put as follows: Madison clearly didn't want an inert government, one incapable of making necessary decisions. And the fact is that the system he designed does make far-reaching decisions. Given this, how are we to tell whether factious majorities have been able in practice to overcome the hurdles of extensiveness? To answer these and like questions we must probe Madison's theory a bit further.

EXTENSIVENESS, INTERESTS, AND THE COMMON GOOD

A fruitful approach to the central problems posed by Madison's interest theory is to set forth and examine the currently fashionable interpretation of the American political process, which is presumably a logical outgrowth of the Madisonian system. In the course of this we will also have need to cast Madison's remarks on representation in a somewhat new light, one that links them more closely to his interest theory.

A standard but by no means universally accepted theory of American politics, derived from Madison's extensive republic theory, comes to this: there are, indeed, varied and numerous interests vying with each other; and, as Madison put it, the chief task of modern legislation is to regulate "these various and interfering interests."[4] Our political processes, both between and during elections, are best viewed as shifting alliances or coalitions of these various groups and interests.

---

[4]Most students readily acknowledge their indebtedness to Madison for an understanding of the general workings of the American system. See, for example, David Truman's classic, *The Governmental Process* (New York: Knopf, 1951).

The processes of decision making are slow, but through compromises, log rolling, and other give-and-take practices, a general consensus emerges on policy matters. Certain interest alliances, if strong enough, may block action, but, whether consensus is reached or not, the process is best understood as an interplay between the varied and numerous interests that comprise the republic.

This, in brief outline, is probably the most widely shared view of how the American political system operates at the national level with regard to those features with which we are concerned. It is also considered, as we have mentioned, to be the logical outgrowth of the Madisonian theory, which we have set forth in some detail. What we see at once, however, is that this account of the process does not deal with the key normative elements of Madison's theory. Put otherwise, our processes are viewed in terms of a collision of interests where it is assumed that the outcome of the collision accords with the common good largely because of the degree of consensus behind it. Absent from this depiction are such considerations as "the true interest" of the country, "the permanent and aggregate interests of the community," or the "general good." More to the point, while the foregoing account may be an accurate portrayal of the American system in its relevant dimensions, there is little reason to presume that we have a republican government free from the control of factions.

This matter can be put another way. Madison's theory, no matter how one chooses to read it, does not support the notion that the true interests of the country emerge through the resolution of interest conflict. For example, two or more factions may be the participants in any such conflict and one would be hard pressed to say that the ensuing result is likely to conform with the general or common good. Far from it: the presumption would have to be precisely the opposite. But Madison tells us this will seldom happen, and we are led to ask: what does the Madisonian theory require that is overlooked or ignored in our contemporary theory? If we were, in fact, following the Madisonian model, what would our political processes look like? How would they vary from what we have today as described by most observers?

The major difference, as we see it, is the emphasis that the Madisonian theory places on the cultivation and existence of a predominant independent force in our highest decision-making councils. What precisely do we mean by an independent force? In essence this: a group of decision-makers sufficiently detached from the immediate interests of a given controversy that they would serve more or less as a jury to judge the relative merits of the arguments and proposals advanced by the interested and contending parties. The members of the independent force would necessarily change from issue to issue as different interests become embroiled in controversy. Yet, the point is that on any given issue the force would be of sufficient size to hold the balance among contending interests.

The whole thrust of Madison's theoretical discourse leads us to this conclusion. To see this, we need only transpose Madison's thought a bit: suppose we do not, as Madison did, focus our attention on how the large republic will serve to control the effects of faction, but rather on how the large republic and the conditions associated with it will serve to produce an independent force of the kind described above. In other words, if we look to Madison's theory as an explanation of why it will come to pass that no interest group will become "a judge of its own cause," we are in a better position to understand how Madison's extended republic will control the effects of faction. Indeed, Madison as much as invites us to look at the matter this way when he laments the character of the decision-making process that has led to the undoing of republics:

> No man is allowed to be a judge of his own cause because his interest would certainly bias his judgment, and not improbably, corrupt his integrity. With equal, nay with greater reason, a body of men are unfit to be both judges and parties at the same time; yet what are many of the most important acts of legislation, but so many judicial determinations, not indeed concerning the rights of single persons, but concerning the rights of large bodies of citizens? And what are the different classes of the legislators but advocates and parties to the causes which they determine? (10:45)

If we transpose Madison's theory, we can readily see how the conditions that he identifies in the large republic will enhance the probabilities of an independent force. Let us detail some of these:

(a) Multiplicity and diversity of interests certainly reduce the possibilities of a widespread union of interest with common motives. Thus, on any given issue normally only a small proportion of the entire population is likely to be aroused or involved. As a result there will be a large independent force that can perform a "jury" function. In these terms the contrasts between the small and large republic are striking: in the small republic where the interests are fewer and the ties between individuals are such that most individuals are forced to take sides one way or the other, the possibilities of an independent and decisive force in the decision-making councils are considerably reduced.

(b) The independent force, freed from the interest bias that clouds and distorts judgment, is more likely to resort to the accepted norms of the community in making its decision. Certainly it will have no need to deviate markedly from the accepted norms; it has no axe to grind, nor does it seek favors that might impinge on the rights of others. In sum, there is every reason to suppose it would represent a stable and calm force during stress and conflict.

(c) Representation, aside from placing a third force at a critical juncture in the decision-making process, is bound to temper deliberations. Interest advocates possessed of a greater knowledge of the whole would be obliged to weigh the contentions of opposing interests. The outgrowth of this would be a debate in which passions are minimized in large part because the contending parties must come to grips with the issues, that is, with the long-term effects, the merits, and shortcomings of any given proposal with an eye to persuading the independent force.

(d) When issues arise where the prospects of an effective independent force seem unlikely—that is, issues that "mobilize" the entire community sentiment one way or another—Madison seems to presume one of two processes occurring. Where a common motive prevails there is less likelihood of factious behavior because all interests alike will perceive a common stake in the outcome. Such, for example, would normally be the case with respect to a foreign attack or intrigue. Where, as in the case of competing religious sects, a partial end is sought to the detriment of other sects, the fragmentation of interests will preclude any action.

With this before us we are able to perceive why nonfactious groups are in a far better position to achieve their ends through the system, and why it is that factions face almost insurmountable obstacles. To the extent that proposals do not impair the accepted rights of others, there is every presumption that the independent force will favor them if they are otherwise meritorious. In any event, members of the independent force will be able to do those things good and virtuous representatives should do: act in the true interest of the country. Stated otherwise, when there is no independent force, the possibilities of factious control are greatly increased.

If this view is substantially correct, it would seem to follow that the Madisonian theory presupposes what can be termed a low-key or relatively passive government. If it were otherwise, the problems of controlling the effects of faction would go well beyond those canvassed by Madison. A positive government would, more likely than not, serve to arouse the people; and, to the extent that it became the mechanism through which interests, factious or not, could achieve differential and favored treatment, it would increasingly become the object of capture or domination. Scarcely any interest could avoid being drawn into this political vortex. Soon "horse trading" and coalitional politics, all with the end of securing needed majorities, would become common practice. With this the prospects of an independent force would be greatly diminished. Moreover, as the government would be obliged to embark upon long-range programs that would necessarily favor one set of interests over another, the society would become increasingly polarized. To a lesser and lesser extent would issues be decided on the basis of the common good or the true interests of the nation. Rather, such decisions would be made with an eye on how to maintain and enlarge a winning coalition. In sum, an active government involves a form of bribery in which only a few can afford to remain neutral. And, on Madison's own showing, once this process begins, there is little, if any, hope that considerations of long-term national interest will arrest the tide.[5]

Active or positive government thus poses very critical problems for Madison's extended republic theory. Once a government has shifted gears from a more or less passive instrumentality that operates within a relatively narrow sphere to an instrumentality for the advancement of interests and purposes that are of enor-

---

[5]John C. Calhoun, one of the first major critics of the extensive republic theory, lays out a scenario very similar to this in his *A Disquisition on Government*, in *Union and Liberty: The Political Philosophy of John C. Calhoun*, ed. Ross M. Lence (Indianapolis: Liberty Fund, 1992). It would seem that because Calhoun was on the Southern side in the slavery controversy we have seen fit to ignore his warning.

mously broad scope, the best one can hope for consistent with the Madisonian theory is that the true interests of the country reside somewhere within the depths of the forces that propel the dominant interest coalitions, or that, at the very least, these forces do not contain strategically placed factions. But, in light of Madison's assumptions, these hopes are at best very dim.

The Modern Problem

With the foregoing in mind, we have at least some idea of where to look to determine whether Madison's solution to the problem of factions is any longer applicable to the American system as it presently operates. We shall briefly examine some of the characteristics of our present system with reference to Madison's basic assumptions and propositions.

In one respect—the continued growth of the United States—the conditions essential for a nontyrannical republic seem to have been immensely strengthened. Whether the effects of this growth have been offset by advanced systems of communication and travel is obviously a judgmental matter. However, because of our industrial and technological development, interest proliferation has been increasing at an enormous rate. Today there is virtually no sector of American life in which interest organizations do not abound, and many of these are highly organized for political action. Thus, one is safe in saying that one of the basic props of the Madisonian theory, multiplicity and diversity of interest, is quite sound.

Developments of another sort, however, present a very basic and serious threat to a republic free from the control of faction. We have already commented on the effects of positive government with reference to Madison's theory. In this regard, we have already witnessed a dramatic shift in our thinking about the legitimate role of government in our society. We can say that, since at least the advent of the New Deal, Madison's basic presumption regarding the role of government has been rendered inoperative. Since that time the dominant political forces have seen their main task as one of achieving "social democracy," which, when distilled, comes down to greater economic and social equality. The extent of the shift since the New Deal can hardly be exaggerated. What were formerly regarded as dispensations by government are now looked upon as vested rights. We now have entrenched interests in the bureaucracy whose very livelihood depends upon identifying social "wrongs" and developing long-range plans to ameliorate them. The quest for equality in all spheres of social life seemingly knows no bounds short of repealing the laws of nature. In this process, the government has massively intervened in precisely those areas of economic and social life where it is abundantly clear that the opportunities for factious influence abound. It has done so, moreover, where independent forces by the very nature of the situation are either weak or nonexistent.

Equally important in the disintegration of independent forces produced by positive government is the ideology that has justified and propelled positive government, namely, secular liberalism. The characteristics of this ideology hardly need recounting here. Yet we must not ignore two of its features that do bear upon our analysis. First, the push for social and economic equality moves us in a direction clearly fraught with danger. In an important sense, such movements, when carried to the extreme, embody the essence of what Madison seemed to regard as factionalism: namely, the attempt to reduce men as far as possible to the condition of sameness. A second and related feature worthy of note is a perverse form of relativism that exalts equality or, better said, transforms equality into the common good or the true interest of society, but simultaneously and dogmatically holds that it is meaningless to speak of national interest or the common good as something apart from and "above" the clash of particular interests. In this, the contemporary and prevalent ideology and Madison's theoretical presumptions, which were plainly not relativist, are poles apart.

Secular liberalism would pose no dangers in terms of Madison's extended republic theory save for its pervasiveness. Its simplicity and moral gloss make it the standard to which academics, the priests of the mass media, and, perhaps because of this, our political leaders, repair. It is the source of "respectable" opinion and those who operate most effectively within its confines are our "statesmen." Yet, its acceptance at the highest levels further diminishes the possibilities of an independent force in our decision-making assemblies. The ideology, being the measure of what is best for the country, serves to exclude from consideration measures, policies, and proposals at variance with its principles, no matter how prudential, worthy, or effective they may be. Even in the field of foreign policy, where we would expect to find a vast independent force at the national level, the effects of ideology on our policies are pronounced.[6] More than this, it threatens to incapacitate the national government in performing its requisite and primary functions, such as securing the common defense and providing for domestic tranquillity.

Finally, secular liberalism's attachment to pure democracy, as far as that is attainable in the United States, promises to reduce even further the possibilities of an independent force. The reforms of political parties and Congress, all designed in the name of greater democracy, have this effect. Not only would they create a decision-making structure that would *force* a division of the whole society along majority-minority lines, they would also assure that this cleavage was reflected in our decision-making bodies, thereby eliminating the possibilities of an independent force. Thus the benefits of diversity, one of the fundamental pillars of Madison's theory, would be lost in this rigid and constrictive framework.

A number of reasons can be adduced as to why we have not as yet evidenced the full effect of factions. The basic reason, as we see it, is to be found in the relative affluence of the American society. This is to say that interests caught up

---

[6]This Henry Regnery thoroughly documents in his "The Age of Liberalism," *Modern Age* 19 (Spring 1975).

in the politics of positive government have to date experienced little hardship. Quite the contrary. To this point in time, most of the interests have benefited. In addition, the potential independent forces have been, so to speak, bought off. Thus, positive government has generated an interest of its own that all but forecloses a significant number from showing forbearance. For any substantial group to try to arrest the process now in full operation would be considered an act of betrayal and bad faith that could only result in severe deprivations for the "guilty."

Yet the day of reckoning is inevitable. Hard and painful choices will have to be made as resources become scarcer. Circumstances not of human design or volition will force forbearance. The severity of withdrawal will depend in large measure on the sacrifices demanded of interests, and this, in turn, will depend on the extent to which government will be forced to curtail its activities. But as the tide of secular liberalism has not ebbed, we have every reason to believe the reactions will be severe. And the severity of the reaction will be compounded by the fact that the major interests, because of their strategic positions in society, can resort to forms of extortion to gain favored status or to hold at least whatever gains they have made. Those, for instance, performing essential services can always hold out the threat of a general strike. But whatever configuration politics does assume at this juncture, there is little prospect that the effects of faction can be controlled without resort to coercion. Whether coercive powers will be exercised moderately or in a relatively benevolent manner would seem to depend on whether the middle class will be able to act as a viable independent force.

One thing does emerge from this analysis. Madison's reliance on the extended republic to prevent the abuses of faction, like such devices formulated by the traditionalists, is far from foolproof. This can be seen in our increasing popular reliance on the feeblest of the traditional devices, a body presumably removed from the purely political arena (the Supreme Court) empowered to enforce written limitations (a Bill of Rights). This is indicative of the misdirection and sad state of our thinking about the problem of the nature of factions. It also constitutes a remarkable regression in our thinking about democratic government.

Certainly Madison cannot be faulted for not having seen the true dimensions of the problems associated with factions. Perhaps more clearly than other theorists who preceded him, he saw their root causes. Yet, he can be faulted for not having urged upon his audience the observance of that morality necessary for the perpetuation of the regime he envisioned.

3

Separation of Powers and the Madisonian Model: A Reply to the Critics

INTRODUCTORY NOTE

Separation of powers, in many respects the most important of our constitutional principles, is beyond any question the most misunderstood. And this misunderstanding is widespread; it is not simply confined to the ignorant and ill-informed. For instance, the revisionists and modern critics of our constitutional system who are found in abundance at our seats of higher learning point to separation of powers as proof positive that the Framers, while professing republicanism, were in fact building a system that would permanently entrench vested minorities. Somewhat astonishingly, many modern conservatives look upon separation of powers in essentially the same fashion: as a barrier to naked majorities that would trample on the rights of private property. Of course, quite unlike the liberal critics, the conservative looks with favor upon the Framers' handiwork. Nevertheless, the conservative who takes this position lends a good deal of credence to one of the main theses of revisionism that has remained constant over the years.

The revisionist position seems reasonable enough. A pure or pristine republican form—that is, one that conforms with certain modern definitions of republicanism—would by definition have to be structured or built in a manner consistent with the principles of political equality and majority rule. This alone means that there could be no place in such a system for separation of powers such as that built into that Philadelphia Constitution. But having granted this much, we are still left with the question of motives. Put otherwise, we can readily grant that the Constitution deviates from ''model'' republicanism as we would define it today, but we do not have to concede the revisionist points concerning the motives of the Framers. Indeed, what we see upon investigating the relationship between republicanism and separation of powers is that the revisionists' contentions simply lack any solid foundations.

That the Framers' conception of this relationship was worlds apart from that of the revisionists is readily apparent from even a cursory examination of the relevant documents. Madison, reflecting a widely shared view, conceived of republicanism in terms that would embrace the principle of separation of powers. For him the test of republicanism came down to whether those holding office, either by election or appointment, were accountable, either directly or indirectly, to the "great body of the people," not to any privileged or "favored class of it." On the face of it this would indicate that the Founders were not obsessed with "fine tuning" the constitutional machinery along lines suggested by the ideological pronouncements of the Warren Court. To their way of thinking, in other words, the issue at stake was whether sovereignty resided in the people, not whether the institutions would precisely mirror the opinions of the people or whether they possessed the authority to instantly enact the will of the majority, two factors that today seem to be uppermost in the minds of "reformers." They seemed to believe that as long as the system provided for popular sovereignty in the sense described by Madison, it would eventually move in the direction desired by or acceptable to the greater number. In this regard, their views toward the system can legitimately be compared to those we frequently encounter today with respect to the Supreme Court, namely, that over the long haul it will "follow the election returns" by which we mean it will not get too far "ahead" or too far "behind" the positions of persistent majorities. Beyond this, we may say, they were interested in institutions that would produce and reflect a consensus—a goal not incompatible with republicanism but one that, nevertheless, seems somewhat foreign to the mechanistic concerns of modern republican theory.

There are other perspectives from which we may view the relationship between republicanism and separation of powers, none of which supports the revisionists' claims. As I point out below, the most significant deviation from the republican principle—the equal representation in the Senate—is the result of a necessary compromise without which the Constitution would probably never have seen the light of day. But, in any event, it was a compromise agreed to with the greatest of reluctance on the part of the strong "nationalistic" contingent at the Convention, and for this reason alone could scarcely have been an integral part of any plan to entrench vested interests of the kind prominently mentioned by the revisionists. This example, however, poses a broader concern for which neither critics nor revisionists seem to have good answers: who, in fact, does benefit from the deviations from republicanism necessitated by the separation of powers? Again, it is one thing to say that there is a deviation, still another to say that the deviation was designed to benefit a specific, identifiable interest.

What I have said to this point takes on added force if we recall that the extended republic theory relies on "natural" or "given" factors to remedy the republican disease of majority faction; namely, on the multiplicity and diversity of interests that inhere in the extended republic. A point often overlooked is that this theory does not call for a separation of powers, judicial review, a bill of rights, or any constitutional barrier or mechanism to control the effects of faction. Consequently, the revisionists, conservatives, and others who view separation of powers as one of the principal devices designed to curb majorities are, in fact, superimposing their conceptions of the constitutional system on the Founders and then blaming or praising them, as the case may be, for something they did not do—not, at least, in the sense the revisionists, critics, and conservatives think.

While these and related matters will be explored more thoroughly below, what is apparent from what has been said is that separation of powers was primarily intended to perform a function other than controlling majorities. That function, as I make clear below, was to prevent tyranny and to prevent the governors—those who wield the powers of government—from ruling arbitrarily and capriciously to abuse and oppress the governed. And to accomplish this, they believed that the legislative, executive, and judicial functions had to be exercised by separate departments. This much at least must be understood to comprehend fully the role of separation of powers in the context of the difficulties confronting the Founders. To begin with, we see why the Founders had to scrap the Articles entirely rather than simply amend them. Once the decision had been made to establish a truly effective national government to provide for common goals such as defense, a concentration of powers in a unicameral legislature was, by their best lights, simply out of the question. Or, to put this the other way around, the structure of the Articles was perfectly satisfactory as long as the government could not effectively exercise the powers granted to it.

Certainly one of the chief problems facing the Framers was how to reconcile republicanism with separation of powers. But for them this problem was of a different order and character from what we might imagine on the basis of the revisionists' understanding. The Framers' chief concern was to prevent the Congress, in their view the predominant branch in our system, from usurping the executive and judicial functions. In retrospect, we can say that they followed a policy of weakening the strong (Congress) and strengthening the weak (the President and the Court), a policy that today we misleadingly label "checks and balances." Thus, for example, as part of the strengthening process, they gave the President a qualified veto and provided judges with life tenure during good behavior. To weaken Congress, they divided it. Yet, for all of this, they did not believe they had compromised republicanism, at least as they understood the term.

With this before us, I believe, we can appreciate one of the highly significant but subtle distortions of the Founders' thought that have contributed to our present constitutional crisis. It is a small step from the process I have described—weakening the strong and strengthening the weak—to the belief that the Framers designed a system wherein each of the departments should be *equal* and coordinate. Such a view, though widely accepted today, is at fundamental variance not only with the Framers' thought but with the plain language of the Constitution itself. However, leaving all of that to one side, once this step is taken it intrudes upon the traditional constitutional morality, and an opening is provided for what we have witnessed in recent decades: all branches being equal, one branch can lay claim to the powers of another, particularly when the advancement or achievement of our "rights" hangs in the balance. Of course, on the Framers' showing, this is very dangerous business because it can result in the concentration of powers they struggled, with good reason, to avoid. And it becomes even more dangerous when we mix in the further distortion concerning the Framers' views on judicial review because then, as we shall see in due course, the way is opened to make the weakest the strongest; in other words, to invert completely the Founders' design.

Finally, I should say a few words about my terminology in the analysis that follows. I use the expression "governmental tyranny" to describe what it is that the Framers sought to avoid through the separation of powers. Strictly speaking, and this is plain from the text of *The Federalist,* what the Framers sought to avoid was tyranny, pure and simple. I use the expression "governmental tyranny" because I think it important to distinguish between government oppression and "majority tyranny" in order to emphasize my basic point in answering modern critics of the Constitution. Now it is interesting to note that the term "majority tyranny" is never used by Publius because, we may surmise, the term tyranny had a very special meaning that rendered majority tyranny, as distinct from rule by majority factions, virtually impossible. The imprecision of terminology that abounds in our texts only reflects the fact, as I intimate in my conclusion, that few have taken the trouble to understand the system as the Founders understood it.

SEPARATION OF POWERS AND THE MADISONIAN MODEL:
A REPLY TO THE CRITICS

Central to most assessments of the democratic character of our constitutional order is the doctrine of separation of powers. Many, if not most, students of the American system have accepted the proposition that separation of powers was intentionally fused into our system to thwart majority rule in one way or another.[1] Indeed, the most persistently advanced democratic "reforms" of our institutions call for extensive modification or elimination of our system of separated powers because of the barriers that such a separation seems to pose to the implementation of the majority will.[2]

While populists around the turn of the century—James Allen Smith being the most notable—were among the first to give currency to the notion that the Constitution is a "reactionary" or "undemocratic" document,[3] modern students, going well beyond the populists' preoccupation with constitutional forms, have focused their attention on what is fashionably called the "Madisonian model"[4] and its underlying assumptions regarding the need, utility, and purpose of two of its most important elements, checks and balances and separation of powers. Their findings in one crucial respect are the same as those of the populists: through the constitutional mechanism of separation of powers, Madison sought to protect "certain minorities whose advantages of status, power, and wealth would, he thought, probably not be tolerated indefinitely by a constitutionally untrammeled majority."[5] In a similar vein, Eidelberg writes: "Madison wished to institute a system of checks and balances to preserve the Republic from the leveling spirit."[6] James MacGregor Burns puts this conclusion even more forcefully:

---

[1]In addition to those works cited below, a very partial listing of works that advance this thesis would be: David Spitz, *Democracy and the Challenge of Power* (New York: Columbia University Press, 1958); Robert A. Dahl and Charles E. Lindblom, *Politics, Economics and Welfare (*(New York: Harper, 1953); Richard Hofstadter, *The American Political Tradition* (New York: Knopf, 1948); Vernon L. Parrington, *Main Currents in American Thought,* 2 vols. (New York: Harcourt, Brace, and Company, 1927–30); and Henry Steele Commager, *Majority Rule and Minority Rights* (New York: Oxford University Press, 1943).

[2]The varied and numerous proposals for a more disciplined and responsible party system are the most notable. For an examination of these proposals see Austin Ranney, *The Doctrine of Responsible Party Government* (Urbana: University of Illinois Press, 1962) and Evron M. Kirkpatrick, "Toward a More Responsible Two-Party System: Political Science, Policy Science, or Pseudo-Science?" *American Political Science Review* 65 (December 1971).

[3]James Allen Smith, *The Spirit of American Government* (New York: Macmillan, 1907).

[4]The term "Madisonian model," very much in vogue today, was first used by James MacGregor Burns in *The Deadlock of Democracy* (Englewood Cliffs, N.J.: Prentice-Hall, 1963). Part I of the book, which deals with the obstacles to majority rule posed by the American political system, is entitled "The Madisonian Model."

[5]Robert A. Dahl, *A Preface to Democratic Theory* (Chicago: University of Chicago Press, 1956), 31. Hereafter cited as *Preface.*

[6]Paul Eidelberg, *The Philosophy of the American Constitution* (New York: Free Press, 1968), 153.

[Madison] was not content with a flimsy separation of power that lunging politicians could smash through like paper. He was calling for barricade after barricade against the thrust of a popular majority—and the ultimate and impassable barricade was a system of checks and balances that would use man's essential human nature—his interests, his passions, his ambitions, to control himself . . . . It was a stunning solution to the Framers' problem of checking the tyranny of the majority.[7]

Modern criticism, however, has gone beyond the populists, principally by pointing out that Madison, in his efforts to prevent tyrannical majorities from ruling, relied principally on institutional checks and balances while largely ignoring the critical role of social checks and balances in a pluralistic society. Dahl writes in his widely acclaimed *Preface to Democratic Theory:*

The Madisonian argument exaggerates the importance, in preventing tyranny, of specified checks to governmental officials by other specified governmental officials; it underestimates the importance of inherent social checks and balances existing in every pluralistic society. Without these social checks and balances, it is doubtful that the intragovernmental checks on officials would in fact operate to prevent tyranny; with them, it is doubtful that all of the intragovernmental checks of the Madisonian system as it operates in the United States are necessary to prevent tyranny.[8]

And along these same lines Burns critically asks certain very crucial questions with which we shall have occasion to deal later:

If, as Madison said, the first great protection against naked majority rule was the broader diversity of interests in a larger republic and hence the greater difficulty of concerting their "plans of oppression," why was not this enough? Why would not any popular majority representing such a variety of interests perforce become so broad and moderate in its goals as never to threaten any major or even minor or individual interest? Why was it necessary to have what Madison called "auxiliary precautions" of checks and balances built right into the frame of government?[9]

In sum, according to these critics, either Madison didn't or couldn't perceive the crucial role of social checks and balances, or he did perceive this role but

---

[7]Burns, 20–21.

[8]*Preface,* 22.

[9]Burns, 21. To the best of my knowledge this line of argument was first set forth by E. E. Schattschneider in his *Party Government* (New York: Farrar and Rinehart, 1942): "Madison's defense of federalism [his presentation in Federalist 10] annihilates his defense of the separation of powers. If the multiplicity of interests in a large republic makes tyrannical majorities impossible, the principal theoretical prop of the separation of powers has been demolished" (9). As we shall see, however, Madison does not introduce separation of powers as a device to check factious majorities.

persisted in his efforts to establish and justify even further unnecessary checks and balances to thwart majority rule.

My purpose here, quite simply, is to challenge these interpretations. This task is not an easy one, largely because the critics of the Madisonian model have been selective and partial in their elaboration of the model, especially with respect to the role and purpose of separation of powers. To put this otherwise, the Madisonian model is an intricate construct that attempts to realize and accommodate more than one crucial value or goal. Yet, more frequently than not, the present-day practice has been to judge the model on the basis of the degree to which it accords with a single value, namely, political equality, and its derivative majority rule. As we shall see, this practice not only distorts assessment of the model's democratic character, it also, and more importantly, excludes from our purview fundamental, normative considerations that better enable us to comprehend the model. At the very least a fuller examination of separation of powers and its place in the Madisonian model would seem prudent before advancing wholesale reform of our present institutions and practices.

With this end in mind, we shall examine the Madisonian model from three perspectives: (1) the purpose of separation of powers; (2) the compatibility between separation of powers and majority rule; and (3) the purposes of bicameralism (an integral component of Madison's separation of powers system) and their compatibility with majority rule. Throughout this analysis, I will deal with the contentions raised by Madison's critics, principally those of Dahl and Burns.[10]

SEPARATION OF POWERS

"The accumulation of all powers legislative, executive and judiciary, in the same hands, whether of one, a few or many, and whether hereditary, self-appointed, or elective," Madison wrote in Federalist 47, "may justly be pronounced the very definition of tyranny." Of this proposition he went so far as to say, "No political truth is certainly of greater intrinsic value, or is stamped with the authority of more enlightened patrons of liberty" (249).

Not only do the records of the Philadelphia Convention seem to bear out this assessment, the political writings of such figures as Adams and Jefferson, whose theories were otherwise markedly different, also reveal fundamental agreement on the proposition that accumulation of powers and tyranny were inseparable.[11]

---

[10]Most of what follows also critically bears upon salient aspects of the thesis advanced by Paul Eidelberg in *The Philosophy of the American Constitution*.

[11]Jefferson, for example, was most critical of the Virginia Constitution of 1776 precisely because the powers of government were concentrated. In his often-quoted words, "All the power of government, legislative, executive, and judiciary, result to the legislative body. The concentrating of these in the same hands is precisely the definition of despotic government. It will be no alleviation that these powers will be exercised by a plurality of hands and not by a single one. One hundred and

Moreover, as Madison correctly noted in Federalist 47, all but two of the states during the revolutionary era had attempted, albeit with very limited success, to provide in one fashion or another for separation of powers. In fact, in six of these state constitutions we even find specific declarations to this effect.[12] Beyond this, despite the in-built provisions in the Constitution designed to insure separation of powers, three of the last four of the original thirteen states to ratify the Constitution (Virginia, North Carolina, and Rhode Island) submitted recommendatory amendments designed, so it would seem, to reinforce this principle. The wording in each case was the same: "the legislative, executive, and judiciary powers of Government should be separate and distinct."[13]

While there did seem to be virtual unanimity on the need for separation of powers, the convention debates, as well as the state constitutions, reveal marked differences concerning the specifics of its implementation.[14] What is crucial to note, however, is that the Framers (and Madison as well) had consciously divorced the concept of separation of powers from that of the "mixed regime" with which it had been historically associated.[15] That is, the Framers retained essential elements of Montesquieu's teachings regarding the principle of separation of branches, but rejected the idea that the branches should represent the dominant social "classes" such as the democratic, aristocratic, and monarchical. In large part, this rejection was simply dictated by the realities of American society which

---

seventy-three despots would surely be as oppressive as one." [*Notes on the State of Virginia,* ed. William Peden (New York: W. W. Norton, 1954), 120.] It is also interesting to note that both of Jefferson's drafts of a constitution for the state of Virginia (1776 and 1783) contain specific provisions for separation of powers.

John Adams, unlike Jefferson, can be viewed as a proponent of a mixed or balanced government wherein distinct classes would be represented, each with a veto over proposed legislation. See his *A Defense of the Constitution of Government of the United States of America* in *The Works of John Adams,* ed. Charles Francis Adams (Boston: Little Brown, 1850–56), 4 and 5. It should be pointed out that Adams's views never gained currency because the social structure of the United States, very dissimilar to that of England, was not amenable to such a balanced government. On this point see M. J. C. Vile, *Constitutionalism and the Separation of Powers* (Oxford: Clarendon Press, 1967), 148–51. Also see our discussion below.

[12]These states were Georgia, Massachusetts, Virginia, Maryland, New Hampshire, and North Carolina. See *The Federal and State Constitutions,* ed. Francis N. Thorpe, 7 (Washington, D.C.: Government Printing Office, 1909).

[13]*Documents Illustrative of the Formation of the Union of the American States,* ed. Charles C. Tansill (Washington, D.C.: Government Printing Office, 1927) 1028–29, 1045, and 1053. Hereafter cited as *Documents Illustrative.*

[14]On the difficulties surrounding implementation of the doctrine, particularly with respect to the legislative and judicial branches, see Edward C. Corwin, "The Progress of Constitutional Theory Between the Declaration of Independence and the Meeting of the Philadelphia Convention," *The American Historical Review* 30 (April 1925).

[15]For two excellent works dealing with the development of the doctrine of separation of powers see M. J. C. Vile, *Constitutionalism and the Separation of Powers* (Oxford: Clarendon Press, 1967), and William B. Gwyn, *The Meaning of the Separation of Powers,* Tulane Studies in Political Science, 9 (New Orleans, La.: Tulane University Press, 1965).

did not possess the social divisions appropriate for a mixed regime as envisioned by Montesquieu. Charles Pinckney, among others, stressed this very point at the Philadelphia Convention:

> [the United] States contain but one order that can be assimilated to the British Nation, this is the order of Commons. They will not surely then attempt to form a Government consisting of three branches, two of which shall have nothing to represent. They will not have an Executive and Senate [hereditary] because the King and Lords of England are so. The same reasons do not exist and therefore the same provisions are not necessary.[16]

Likewise, it is clear that the goal sought through separation of powers was the avoidance of governmental tyranny—a goal long associated with the concept of a division of powers. Aristotle, for instance, provides us with an early example of a perceived relationship between a union of powers and tyranny. Tyranny, a perverted form of "perfect monarchy," he associated with capricious and arbitrary government wherein all powers, as we conceive of them today, were vested in the hands of one. "No freeman," he wrote, "if he can escape from it, will endure such a government."[17]

John Locke expanded upon Aristotle's formulation and provided us with the more modern conception of governmental tyranny:

> It is a mistake to think this fault is proper only to monarchies; other forms of government are liable to it as well as that. For wherever the power that is put in any hands for the government of the people and the preservation of their properties is applied to other ends, and made use of to impoverish, harass, or subdue them to the arbitrary and irregular commands of those that have it, there it presently becomes tyranny, whether those that thus use it are one or many.[18]

The link between Locke's thought, as well as Aristotle's, and American thought during the period preceding the adoption of the Constitution, is unmistakable. The *Essex Result* provides one of the most detailed elaborations on the necessity of a division of powers to avoid governmental tyranny:

> If the three powers are united, the government will be absolute, *whether these powers are in the hands of one or a large number.* The same party will be the legislator, accuser, judge and executioner; and what probability will

---

[16]*Documents Illustrative,* 273. Because we lacked such social "orders," Patrick Henry argued that any system of separation of powers would be ineffective. *The Debates in the Several State Conventions on the Adoption of the Federal Constitution,* ed. Jonathan Elliot, 5 vols. (Philadelphia: J. B. Lippincott Co., 1836), III, 165.

[17]*Politics,* trans. Benjamin Jowett (New York: Modern Library, 1943), Bk. 4, Ch. 11.

[18]*A Second Treatise of Civil Government* (Chicago: Gateway edition, 1955), Ch. 18, Sect. 201.

an accused person have of an acquittal, however innocent he may be, when his judge will also be a party.[19]

Moreover, any union of two powers was viewed as producing the same effect. If the legislative and judicial powers were joined, the laws would be "uncertain," and they would reflect on the "whims," "caprice," or "the prejudice of the judge." If the legislative and executive powers were united, "the security and protection of the subject would be a shadow—the executive power would make itself absolute, and the government end in a tyranny."[20]

That such a view of the matter was shared by Madison also seems beyond doubt. Quoting from Montesquieu's *Spirit of the Laws,* Madison in Federalist 47, the first essay devoted exclusively to separation of powers, endorses this very same line of reasoning:

> The reasons on which Montesquieu grounds his maxim are a further demonstration of his meaning. "When the legislative and executive powers are united in the same person or body," says he, "there can be no liberty, because apprehensions may arise lest *the same* monarch or senate should enact tyrannical laws, to *execute* them in a tyrannical manner." Again: "Were the power of judging joined with the legislative, the life and liberty of the subject would be exposed to arbitrary control, for *the judge* would then be *the legislator.* Were it joined to the executive power, *the judge* might behave with all the violence of *an oppressor.*" Some of these reasons are more fully explained in other passages; but briefly stated as they are here, they sufficiently establish the meaning which we have put on this celebrated maxim of this celebrated author (251).

We may say, then, that the chief end sought through separation of powers was avoidance of capricious and arbitrary government. The end, however, can be stated more precisely and positively. Article XXX of the Massachusetts Convention of 1780, in which we find the injunction that no branch shall exercise the functions of another, concludes "to the end it may be a government of laws and not of men."[21]

We have before us three facts that bear directly upon the modern interpretations of the Madisonian model to which we have referred. First, Madison's reference to tyranny in Federalist 47 is to governmental tyranny. This tyranny, quite simply, involves those in positions of authority using their powers arbitrarily and capriciously to abuse the nongovernmental portion of society. In this situation, the conflict comes down to the governors versus the governed as distinct from the

---

[19]*The Popular Sources of Political Authority: Documents on the Massachusetts Constitution of 1780,* eds. Oscar and Mary Handlin (Cambridge: Harvard University Press, 1966), 327.
[20]Ibid., 337–38.
[21]Ibid., 448.

problem of majority factions oppressing minorities discussed in Federalist 10. As obvious as this may seem, one of the chief weaknesses of modern criticism of the Madisonian model has been its failure to make this distinction regarding the source and kinds of tyranny.[22] Dahl, for instance, manages to lump Madison's concern with majority factions together with his treatment of the problem of governmental tyranny.[23] He does this by transforming Madison's explicit definition of tyranny in Federalist 47 (accumulation of all governmental powers) to conform with his own definition ("severe deprivation of a natural right")[24]—a definition best suited for an analysis of Federalist 10 and the problem of majority factions. Dahl then treats Madison's solutions to governmental tyranny as if they were solutions to majority tyranny as well.

The predictable result is that Dahl's analysis and presentation, not Madison's, is difficult to follow. For instance, the charge that Madison underestimated the importance of social checks and balances is manifestly false, particularly if one looks to Federalist 10 and his "solution" to the problem of *majority* tyranny. In this essay Madison cites such factors as the multiplicity of interests, the mutual suspicions that inevitably arise between interests, and the probability that representatives will be men "who possess the most attractive merit, and the most diffusive and established characters," as barriers to majority tyranny. At no point in the essay, save possibly with his brief mention of federalism, does Madison allude to institutional structures as barriers to majority rule, or conversely, as protectors of vested minorities. In sum, we do not find recourse to institutional barriers because Madison believed the social checks and balances inherent in the extended republic were an adequate protection against majority tyranny.[25] When we reach Federalist 47, however, Madison is obviously dealing with tyranny of a different order, namely, *governmental* tyranny. And because this tyranny is of a different order, his solution to the problem is markedly different and does concern

---

[22]The distinction between governmental tyranny and majority tyranny which seems to be blurred or ignored by many moderns was not lost upon John C. Calhoun. Throughout his *Disquisition* he treats these two sources of tyranny as distinct. *A Disquisition on Government* in *Union and Liberty: The Political Philosophy of John C. Calhoun,* ed. Ross M. Lence (Indianapolis: Liberty Fund, 1992).

[23]*Preface*, cf. Ch. 1.

[24]Ibid., 6–7.

[25]This particular confusion is reflected in the following passage from Dahl: "In retrospect, the logical and empirical deficiencies of Madison's own thought seem to have arisen in large part from his inability to reconcile two different goals. On the one hand, Madison substantially accepted the idea that all the adult citizens of a republic must be assigned equal rights, including the right to determine the general direction of government policy. . . . On the other hand, Madison wished to erect a political system that would guarantee the liberties of certain minorities whose advantages of status, power, and wealth would, he thought, probably not be tolerated indefinitely by a constitutionally untrammeled majority. Hence majorities had to be constitutionally inhibited" (31). Clearly Madison in Federalist 10 did not see the need to constitutionally inhibit majorities. Nor is his concern in Federalists 47 to 51, which deal with separation of powers, the constitutional inhibition of majority factions. In these papers his evident concern is with guaranteeing the liberties of the people from arbitrary and capricious government (see text below).

itself to a great degree with the constitutional checks and balances to which his critics refer. But, given the nature of his concern—control of a government or of those with governmental powers—it is impossible to see how he could have done otherwise.

This particular difficulty becomes more obvious when we turn to the major concern expressed by Burns, namely, if, as Madison indicates in Federalist 10, the diversity of interests is a sufficient guard against majority factions or majority tyranny, why then did Madison erect even further barricades against majority rule with a system of checks and balances?[26] Burns's question would be perfectly legitimate save for the fact that Madison was worried about two sources of tyranny, majority tyranny and, as I have shown, governmental tyranny. Burns has, along with Dahl, assumed that Madison's purpose in advocating a system of checks and balances was to thwart majority rule. But the assumption, as the text of *The Federalist* makes abundantly clear, is not warranted. Indeed, after the beginning two-thirds of Federalist 51, which deals with his solution to the problem of how to maintain the necessary partition of powers (in order to control, in Madison's words, "the abuses of government"), Madison changes focus and expressly identifies two distinct sources of tyranny (267). He writes: "*Second.* It is of great importance in a republic not only to guard the society against the oppression of its rulers [a matter that he has just finished treating in the preceding part of this essay], but to guard one part of the society against the injustice of the other part [the problem of minority and majority faction]" (268). What follows is unmistakably a reiteration of his "extended republic" theory more elaborately set forth in Federalist 10. Even the most cursory reading reveals this, as the following quote—the latter part of which is most interesting in light of the foregoing analysis—illustrates:

> In the extended republic of the United States, and among the great variety of interests, parties and sects which it embraces, a coalition of a majority of the whole society could seldom take place on any other principles than those of justice and the general good; and there being thus less danger to a minor from the will of the major party, there must be less pretext also, to provide for the security of the former, by introducing into the government a will not dependent on the latter; or in other words, a will independent of the society itself (269).[27]

A second point is this: through separation of powers, Madison sought to avoid governmental tyranny which, as we have seen, is closely related to arbitrary and capricious government. We can, of course, conceive of situations in which con-

---

[26]Cf. Burns, Ch. 1. Burns acknowledges that he is building upon Dahl's analysis.

[27]Notice that Madison, right after addressing himself to the issue of separation of powers, turns immediately to the problem of majority factions and declares this problem "solved" by social checks and balances which have nothing to do with constitutional checks and balances. At no point does separation of powers play a role in curbing majority factions.

centration of powers will not result in governmental tyranny—that is, those possessed of all governmental powers would not place themselves above the law or rule in their own private interests. So, it is fair to assume, could Madison. Yet Madison was concerned with fundamental principles on which to establish lasting constitutional procedures and forms. Therefore, we can readily imagine him responding that such instances would be exceptional, so exceptional as to prove the rule. Or, we can also imagine his answer to have taken this form: "Over an extended period of time a concentration of power will inevitably result in governmental tyranny. Benevolent dictators and philosopher kings are hard to come by."[28]

Madison's definition of tyranny presented in Federalist 47 is not ambiguous or meaningless, except, perhaps, to the extreme positivist. Dahl's difficulty in this respect is, again, of his own doing. Having supplied Madison with a definition of tyranny ("severe deprivation of a natural right"), he finds tyranny to have "no operational meaning" and "Madison's own definition . . . a trivial one."[29] Whatever merit Dahl's analysis of the meaning of tyranny may have in relation to majority factions is not applicable to governmental tyranny. Madison sought to avoid capricious and arbitrary government, which is characteristic of a government of men, not of laws.

Finally, and most importantly for our subsequent analysis, what is apparent, not only from those portions of *The Federalist* that deal with separation of powers but also from the work as a whole, is Madison's conviction that separation of powers is a *necessary* (thought not sufficient) condition for nontyrannical government. This, as we shall see, imposes a limitation on his theoretical development because other values and concerns have to be modified or reconciled with this basic requirement in mind.

SEPARATION OF POWERS AND MAJORITY RULE

As emphasized above, critics of the Madisonian model have been quick to point out the incompatibility between separation of powers and majority rule. In this context the critics view separation of powers as a device to protect minorities of wealth, status, and the like, and, as such, a gross departure from the republican principle of political equality.

In retrospect it is obvious that Madison did have to deal with two incompatible goals, though from his vantage point he had no qualms about which goal should

---

[28]In this connection, it is highly doubtful that Madison was concerned with majority tyranny as that term is normally used. He was concerned about majority factions that could perform a tyrannous act. Madison does acknowledge at least the possibility of this occurring ("seldom" is his word), but this is quite different from a permanent condition of tyranny associated with a concentration of governmental powers. On these grounds majority tyranny (i.e., the act of a factious majority) is not on the same theoretical plane as governmental tyranny.

[29]*Preface*, 24.

take precedence. But the incompatible goals were not, as some modern critics assert, majority rule and minority rights.[30] In Madison's mind, at least, these goals were not incompatible. The very first paragraph of Federalist 10, where he proposes a solution to the problem of majority factions, reveals this:

> Among the numerous advantages promised by a well-constructed Union, none deserves to be more accurately developed than its tendency to break and control the violence of faction. The friend of popular government never finds himself so much alarmed for their character and fate, as when he contemplates their propensity to this dangerous vice. He will not fail therefore to set a due value on any plan which, *without violating the principles to which he is attached,* provides a proper cure of it (43, emphasis added).

Madison proceeds then to set forth his famous theoretical ''solution'' to this problem by showing how the need for representation coupled with the multiplicity and diversity of interests in an extended republic by themselves provide ''a republican remedy for the diseases most incident to Republican Government'' (48). Moreover, we repeat, his solution does not involve institutional or constitutional mechanisms.

At various points in *The Federalist* and other writings, Madison seems fully aware of pure republicanism and what the structure of a model republican government would involve. Why, then, did he support checks and balances, which to all outward appearances would only serve to diffuse or dilute majority control and direction of government, essential elements of republicanism? In asking this question, perhaps the most important question relative to the criticisms directed at his model, we are focusing on one incompatibility of value goals that takes us a long way toward understanding the model and the form it takes. The answer, in light of what we have said in the previous section, is this: adequate provision for separation of powers, necessary for a nontyrannical government, imposes demands that in certain particulars are at variance with the principles of pure republicanism.

Let us tend carefully to the nature of this incompatibility, lest it be understood to mean that separation of powers imposes requirements that were intended to prohibit majority rule and protect specific minorities, as the critics contend. We can do this best by specifically considering the problems associated with the legislative branch which, on all sides, is considered the mainspring of the republican principle and whose very bicameralism is now viewed by contemporaries as prima facie evidence of the undemocratic character of the Madisonian model.

We cannot overestimate Madison's concern that the legislative body represented the greatest threat to separation of powers. On July 17 at the Philadelphia Convention, for instance, Madison set forth a theme that was to recur, principally

---

[30]Be they economic, property, social, or civil rights. The incompatibility cannot be couched in terms that would suggest that Madison believed in political equality but thought that some people were more equal than others. See *Preface*, 31.

in Federalists 48 to 50, where he discussed how to preserve the "necessary partition of powers":

> Experience had proved a tendency in our governments to throw all power
> into the Legislative vortex. The Executives of the States are in general little
> more than Cyphers; the legislatures omnipotent. If no effectual check be
> devised for restraining the instability of encroachments of the latter, a revo-
> lution of some kind or other would be inevitable. The preservation of Repub-
> lican Government therefore required some expedient for the purpose, but
> required evidently at the same time that in devising it, the genuine principles
> of that form should be kept in view.[31]

This passage also reveals Madison's desire to maximize simultaneously two
goals: republicanism and separation of powers.

Madison's concern on this score was, beyond any question, based on the fact
that the legislative body, consonant with republican principles, would possess the
vast bulk of the substantive powers of government. The problem, therefore, of
guarding against a concentration of powers in a republican government, he perceived, differed from that encountered in "mixed" monarchies. "The founders
of our republics," he writes in Federalist 48, have been so preoccupied with the
"danger to liberty from the overgrown and all-grasping prerogative of an hereditary magistrate" that they have overlooked "legislative usurpations" which, in a
republic, pose the greater threats to liberty (255–56).

Essays 48, 49, and 50 assume particular significance in understanding the answer that Madison eventually provides in essay 51. More importantly for our
purposes, they deal with the question of what role a majority is to play in maintaining separation of powers, which largely comes down to controlling the legislative branch vis-à-vis the other branches.

What, briefly, does Madison say in these essays? First, he contends in 48 that a
constitutional provision to the effect that each department should stay within its
boundary will definitely not suffice to preserve the necessary separation. Why?
For several reasons. "Experience assures us, that the necessary efficacy of [such
a] provision has been greatly over-rated; and that some more adequate defence is
indispensably necessary for the more feeble, against the more powerful members
of the government" (255). And because of the number, nature, and importance of
the powers vested in the legislature by the Constitution,

> it [the legislature] can with greater facility, mask under complicated and
> indirect measures, the encroachments which it makes on the co-ordinate
> departments. It is not unfrequently a question of real nicety in legislative
> bodies, whether the operation of a particular measure, will, or will not extend
> beyond the legislative sphere. On the other side, the executive power being
> restrained within a narrower compass, and being more simple in its nature;

---

[31]*Documents Illustrative,* 398–99.

and the judiciary being described by landmarks, still less uncertain, projects of usurpation by either of these departments, would immediately betray and defeat themselves (256).

Furthermore, because the legislature "alone has access to the pockets of the people, and . . . a prevailing influence over the pecuniary rewards of those who fill the other departments, a dependence is thus created in the latter, which gives still greater facility to encroachments of the former" (256).

Second, in Federalist 49 Madison addresses himself to the question of whether occasional appeals initiated by two-thirds of the members of two of the three branches calling for a constitutional convention would serve to maintain the necessary separation of powers.[32] Again, he is something more than skeptical. Such occasional appeals, he argues, could be thwarted by a one-third minority in any two branches; they would carry with them the implication that the government was defective, thereby seriously undermining that popular veneration of government which is necessary for "stability"; and, what is more, they would serve to arouse the "public passions" to a dangerous degree. "But the greatest objection of all," writes Madison, "is that the decisions which would probably result from such appeals, would not answer the purpose of maintaining the constitutional equilibrium of the government." Judges and members of the executive branch are relatively few "and can be personally known to a small part only of the people." In contrast, the legislators are "numerous," "are distributed and dwell among the people at large," and have "connections of blood, of friendship and of acquaintance [which] embrace a great proportion of the most influential part of the society." Given these conditions, "it could hardly be supposed" that the judicial and the executive branches "would have an equal chance for a favorable" resolution of any conflict with the legislature (261).

Finally, in Federalist 50, he considers whether periodic appeals to the people, at fixed intervals, would preserve the necessary partition. He also finds this proposal inadequate. If the interval between appeals is a short one, "the measures to be reviewed and rectified, will have been of recent date, and will be connected with all the circumstances which tend to vitiate and pervert the result of occasional revisions." On the other hand, if the interval is a relatively long one, the "distant prospect of public censure" probably would not serve as an adequate restraint on the more immediate motives of that department bent on encroachment (263). By way of illustrating his contentions regarding periodic appeals, he discusses the experience of Pennsylvania's "council of censors." This popularly elected council, which met in 1783–84, was, as Madison observes, charged with the responsibility of determining "whether the Constitution [of Pennsylvania] had been violated and whether the legislature and executive departments had encroached on each other." The results of this procedure, he notes, were predictable and far

---

[32]In this Madison is addressing himself to a scheme for preserving the independence of the branches set forth by Jefferson in his *Notes on Virginia.*

from satisfactory: the men who were elected to judge of the actions of the legislative and executive branches were, to a great extent, those who had served in
those very branches at the time the questionable actions were committed; party
animosities in the council were so severe that *"passion,* not *reason"* seemed to
dominate the proceedings; and the legislature felt no obligation to abide by the
decisions òf the council (264).

What can be said of Madison's analysis relative to republicanism and separation of powers? The most striking fact is that, for reasons specified, Madison is of
no mind to allow popular majorities to decide disputes between the branches of
government. This mode of resolution, he felt, was certain to result in legislative
tyranny because the experiences at the state level had shown that this branch
would most likely commit the transgressions and then would, for all intents and
purposes, act as the judge of its own actions. Thus, preservation of the partition
of powers necessitated this departure from the republican principle.

More revealing, in light of the contentions advanced by some contemporary
students, is the nature of this limitation. First, majority control is inhibited only
with respect to resolution of disputes between the branches on matters involving
their sphere of authority. This leaves popular majorities as free as the most ardent
populist could wish to initiate and enact any social policy to their liking. In this
regard, Madison's limitations scarcely touch upon curbing majority tyranny, and
then only by indirection.

Second, and equally important, Madison is not seeking to curb majority initia-
tive. There is no intimation that a popular majority itself would push for proposals
designed to obliterate the partition of powers.[33] On the contrary, it is the legislators themselves who, because they are operating as a small body in a context
relatively free from the restraints inherent to an extended republic,[34] would press
forward with such schemes and then, after the fact, seek popular endorsement.
Thus, the limitation is not directed at curbing majorities in the usual sense of that
term. And, in this connection, we cannot help but note Madison's total silence in
these essays about separation of powers being in any way related to prevention of
majority tyranny.

Finally, this very partial limitation on the sphere of majority decision making
is consonant with a broader theory of constitutionalism which Madison and most
of the Framers shared.[35] Within the confines of this theory, fundamental law or

---

[33]To this point he writes in Federalist 63, "The people can never wilfully betray their own
interests: But they may possibly be betrayed by the representatives of the people; and the danger will
be evidently greater where the whole legislative trust is lodged in the hands of one body of men, than
where the concurrence of separate and dissimilar bodies is required in every public act" (326–27).

[34]In this regard, Madison writes in Federalist 48 that it is against a legislature "which is sufficiently numerous to feel all the passions which actuate a multitude; yet not so numerous as to be
incapable of pursuing the objects of its passions, by means which reason prescribes . . . that the
people ought to indulge all their jealousy and exhaust all their precautions" (256).

[35]See Federalist 78, where this theory is articulated with respect to judicial review.

the Constitution could be changed only through an act as authoritative as the adoption of the Constitution itself (i.e., the amendment process). Separation of powers, inseparable as it is from the constitutional fabric, would certainly seem, on these grounds, to be immune to alteration or abolition by simple majorities. If, that is, popular majorities could legitimize basic alteration in the relative powers of the three branches, the way would be open to allowing basic constitutional alterations by simple legislative majorities.

The solution to the problem that Madison set out to resolve (how to maintain in practice the necessary partition of powers) is, as is well known, contained in Federalist 51. It "consists in giving to those who administer each department the necessary constitutional means and personal motives to resist encroachments of the others. The provision for defence must in this, as in all other cases, be made commensurate to the danger of attack." This would seemingly obviate the need for frequent or periodical appeals to the people. And Madison in elaborating on this solution continues: "Ambition must be made to counteract ambition. The interest of the man must be connected with the constitutional rights of the place. It may be a reflection on human nature, that such devices should be necessary to control the abuses of government. But what is government itself, but the greatest reflection on human nature?" (267)

While an evaluation of this solution is beyond our purposes here, two comments relative to it are in order:

1. Madison does rely upon constitutional or institutional mechanisms for maintenance of separation of powers. His reference to the "necessary constitutional means" in the context of the passage cited above is evidence of this. However, he is far from oblivious to the need for the proper type of internal motivation, a distinctly noninstitutional factor, to achieve this end. References to "personal motive," "ambition" counteracting "ambition," and the connection between the "interest of the man" and "the constitutional rights of the place" are abundant evidence to that effect. He may well have reasoned that proper constitutional provisions would unleash, protect, and even cultivate behavior patterns conducive to the end he sought.

Yet—and to the best of my knowledge this is a matter that has not been explored thoroughly—Madison must have presumed limits to the behavior he anticipated. His discussion, couched as it is in terms of conflict and competition, might well lead one to believe that such would be the normal state of affairs between the branches. But clearly, if this were the case, adoption of the model would be an open invitation to stalemate and catastrophe. For this reason, we can safely surmise that one unarticulated premise of the Madisonian system must have been that the members of the branches would hold substantially the same views regarding the legitimate domain of the three branches and that, moreover, these members would show a high degree of forbearance, high enough at any rate not to repeatedly push the system to the brink of collapse.

2. Madison's solution is, in his own words, directed to controlling the "abuses of government." He acknowledges at the end of this particular passage the more

general maxim of republican government—"dependence on the people is no doubt the primary control on government"—but he goes on to say, consistent with his teachings on this point, that "experience has taught mankind the necessity of auxiliary precautions" (267). Clearly the phrase "auxiliary precautions" refers to additional obstacles to governmental abuses and not to majority tyranny.[36]

BICAMERALISM AND MAJORITY RULE

For critics of the Madisonian system, as we have mentioned, the bicameral structure of Congress seems to provide incontrovertible evidence of Madison's hostility toward republicanism and his desire to protect vested minorities. At first glance, the case is a strong one which, without injustice, we may put as follows: separation of powers does not in theory, at least, require a bicameral legislature. Indeed, a bicameral legislature is a significant deviation from the republican principle, for it divides the purely democratic element of the Constitution, and this can only serve to diffuse, blunt, or obfuscate the will of popular majorities. In fact, while separation of legislative, executive, and judicial powers does not inherently represent a departure from pure principles of republicanism, bicameralism does. Moreover, a second or "upper" chamber cannot help but develop a "clubbishness" or sense of superiority that will set it apart from the "lower" house and transform it into a more "aristocratic" body with views markedly different from those of the "lower" chamber.[37]

At face value, these and like contentions are deceptively convincing, the more so as a second chamber is historically associated with institutions representative of the aristocratic class.[38] Yet, insofar as the Madisonian model is concerned, such views of the second chamber are far from the mark and serve only to conceal an important theoretical dimension of Madison's theory.

We must, in treating of bicameralism and its purpose, once again bear in mind Madison's overriding concern to maintain separation of powers in order to avoid governmental tyranny. This, we may say, was his principal reason for advocating

---

[36]Burns (22) mistakenly reads this as "auxiliary precautions" against majority tyranny. The error is understandable in light of his basic confusion concerning the purpose of separation of powers.

[37]This we submit as a composite argument drawn not only from the critical assessments of the Madisonian model in terms of its democratic character but from legislative behavioral studies as well. In any event, bicameralism certainly opens up the possibility of deadlock, and its very existence suggests that there can be two popular majorities on any given issue, a notion logically inconsistent with majoritarian theory.

[38]This, in one form or another, is what most of the critics of the Madisonian model contend bicameralism was intended to do. In this respect, they see the Framers (and Madison as well) attempting to create a "mixed government" along the lines advocated by John Adams. This interpretation was, no doubt, bolstered by Charles A. Beard's *An Economic Interpretation of the Constitution of the United States of America* (New York: The Macmillan Company, 1913) which related structural forms to economic interests. See also Malcolm P. Sharp, "The Classical Doctrine of the Separation of Powers," *University of Chicago Law Review* 2 (April 1935).

a divided legislature. So much we find in Federalist 51, where he writes of the impossibility of giving "each department an equal power of self-defence" because in republican governments "the legislative authority, necessarily, predominates." Therefore, he writes, the "weight of the legislative authority requires that it should be . . . divided" (267). In this assessment he was undoubtedly influenced by the fact that virtually all the major powers of government, consistent with the republican principle, were vested by the Constitution in Congress.

The need for two chambers to prevent governmental abuse was a recurrent theme in his thoughts and writings. In speaking to the Convention on June 26 he observed:

> A people deliberating in a temperate moment, and with the experience of other nations before them, on the plan of Government most likely to secure their happiness, would first be aware, that those charged with the public happiness, might betray their trust. An obvious precaution against this danger would be to divide the trust between different bodies of men, who might watch and check each other.[39]

A second chamber, he noted on this occasion, would serve "to protect the people against their rulers."

Again, in Federalist 62, when dealing specifically with the justifications for the Senate, he writes:

> First. It is a misfortune incident to republican government, though in a less degree than to other governments, that those who administer it, may forget their obligations to their constituents, and prove unfaithful to their important trust. In this point of view, a senate, as a second branch of the legislative assembly, distinct from, and dividing the power with, a first, must be in all cases a salutary check on the government. It doubles the security to the people, by requiring the concurrence of two distinct bodies in schemes of usurpation or perfidy, where the ambition or corruption of one, would otherwise be sufficient. This is a precaution founded on such clear principles, and now so well understood in the United States, that it would be more than superfluous to enlarge on it (321).

Clearly we see that in Madison's estimation the requirement of bicameralism necessitated a deviation from the pure republican structure. And we can also see clearly that this particular deviation is thoroughly consistent with and best understood in terms of his broader theory concerning the need to avoid governmental tyranny, as well as his fear of legislative usurpation. Moreover, his support of bicameralism is quite removed from any concern with majority tyranny or minority "rights" and, on the positive side, may even be viewed as an effort to preserve conditions necessary for popular majorities to form and operate free from governmental control.

---

[39]*Documents Illustrative*, 279.

While his concern with preventing governmental tyranny would alone justify his defense of bicameralism, Madison offers still another reason for it that does bear upon the problem of majority tyranny. It is at this point that bicameralism fits hand in glove with his concern to prevent majority tyranny. Since this coincidence clearly bears upon the republican character of the Madisonian model, I shall examine it with some care.

In his June 26 remarks at Philadelphia, Madison notes that a second end to be served by bicameralism is "to protect the people against the transient impressions into which they themselves might be led." And, in Federalist 63, after surveying six advantages of bicameralism "only as they relate to the representatives of the people," he continues:

> To a people as little blinded by prejudice or corrupted by flattery as those whom I address, I shall not scruple to add, that such an institution may be sometimes necessary as a defence to the people against their own temporary errors and delusion. As the cool and deliberate sense of the community ought, and actually will in all free governments, ultimately prevail over the views of its rulers; so there are particular moments in public affairs, when the people stimulated by some irregular passion, or some illicit advantage, or misled by the artful misrepresentations of interested men, may call for measures which they themselves will afterwards be the most ready to lament and condemn. In these critical moments, how salutary will be the interference of some temperate and respectable body of citizens, in order to check the misguided career, and to suspend the blow meditated by the people themselves, until reason, justice and truth, can regain their authority over the public mind (325–26)?

As if by way of answering those, such as Burns, who ask why the "solution" provided in Federalist 10 is not a sufficient barrier to majority tyranny, Madison writes:

> It may be suggested that a people spread over an extensive region, cannot like the crowded inhabitants of a small district, be subject to the infection of violent passions; or to the danger of combining in pursuit of unjust measures. I am far from denying that this is a distinction of peculiar importance. I have on the contrary endeavored in a former paper [Federalist 10], to show that it is one of the principal recommendations of a confederated republic. At the same time this advantage ought not to be considered as superseding the use of auxiliary precautions (326).

In the framework of Madison's thought, this "auxiliary precaution" is, so to speak, a "bonus" derived from his perceived need to protect the people from their government through bicameralism. Put otherwise, though needed to guard against governmental tyranny, the second chamber also provides a further "auxiliary precaution" against majorities. In these terms, which coincide with the manner in which Madison presents his theory, we must seriously question what seems to be a commonly held presumption to the effect that a second chamber was necessary quite apart from any role it might play with respect to the problem of majority tyranny and minority ''rights.''

We gain a further insight into this relationship between republicanism and bicameralism by examining the function the Senate is to perform in curbing majorities. Here the only deviation, if it can fairly be called that, from the republican principle relates to a matter of delay in responding to the wishes of a popular majority until such time as ''reason, justice and truth'' can ''regain their authority over the public mind.'' He seeks to insure that ''the cool and deliberate sense of the community'' will predominate—an end that, we may surmise, was primarily fostered by conditions associated with an extended republic, which likewise necessitated delay in the process of the formation of majorities.

Moreover, if we look to the factors that contribute to the Senate's effectiveness in performing this delay function, we see that they are fundamentally noninstitutional. In his speech of June 26 which bears directly upon majority factions and the role of a second chamber, Madison inquires, ''How is the danger in all cases of interested coalitions to oppress the minority to be guarded against?'' His answer: ''Among other means by the establishment of a body in the Government sufficiently respectable for its wisdom and virtue, to aid on such emergencies, the preponderance of justice by throwing its weight into that scale.''[40]

The Senate would serve as an institution composed of a ''temperate and respectable body of citizens'' who would, because of their ''wisdom and virtue,'' be capable of cultivating those ''internal restraints'' so necessary for the avoidance of majority tyranny. Failing this, the Senate would pose no difficulties for persistent majorities. In Madison's words, there is an ''irresistible force possessed by that branch of a free government, which has the people on its side.'' He continues:

> Against the force of the immediate representatives of the people, nothing will be able to maintain even the constitutional authority of the Senate, but such a display of enlightened policy, and attachment to the public good, as will divide with that branch of the legislature, the affections and support of the entire body of the people themselves (63:329–30).

Equally important, Madison does not urge a second house with in-built or entrenched minorities. Quite the contrary. Madison was most critical of the Connecticut compromise principally on grounds that it did deviate from the republican principle. His exchange with Paterson at the Convention on July 9 indicates this. Paterson in discussing ''the true principle of Representation'' calls it ''an expedient by which an assembly of certain individuals chosen by the people is substituted in place of the inconvenient meeting of the people themselves.'' Madison, in response to this, ''reminded Mr. Paterson that his doctrine of Representation

---

[40]Ibid., 281.

which was in its principle the genuine one, must for ever silence the pretensions of the small States to an equality of votes with the large ones. They ought to vote in the same proportion in which their citizens would do, if the people of all the States were collectively met.''[41]

By all evidence, Madison had to ''swallow hard'' in accepting the Connecticut compromise. In Federalist 62, he remarks that the compromise ''is allowed on all hands to be the result not of theory, but of a spirit of amity, and that mutual deference and concession which the peculiarity of our political situation rendered indispensable'' (320). But the proposed constitution, even with provision for equality of state representatives in the Senate, was, in his judgment, a ''lesser evil'' than the existing form of government under the Articles.

More to the point—save for southern sectional interests—Madison could not conceive of any interest in need of a structural protection in the Senate that might necessitate a deviation from the republican principle in either the mode of election or representation:

> He admitted that every peculiar interest whether in any class of citizens, or any description of States, ought to be secured as far as possible. Wherever there is danger of attack, there ought be given a constitutional power of defence. But he contended that the States were divided into different interests not by their difference of size, but by other circumstance; the most material of which resulted partly from climate, but principally from the effects of their having or not having slaves.[42]

Thus, he could write of the Connecticut compromise in Federalist 62:

> It must be acknowledged that this complicated check on legislation may in some instances be injurious as well as beneficial; and that the peculiar defence which it involves in favor of the smaller State, would be more rational, if any interests common to them, and distinct from those of the other States, would otherwise be exposed to a peculiar danger (320).

Yet, Madison's very line of reasoning on this point could be used to argue that the Connecticut compromise, though a deviation from republicanism, did not, in fact, entrench specific minorities. If, that is, no great dissimilarities of interests were to be found between the small and large states, there is no reason, a priori, to assume that this body would act to protect any specific minority or to thwart legitimate majorities. Perhaps for this reason, Madison could write in good conscience, ''it is not impossible that this part of the Constitution may be more convenient in practice than it appears in contemplation''[43] (320).

---

[41]Ibid., 345.
[42]Ibid., 310.

CONCLUSION

Though the foregoing analysis of separation of powers and its role in the Madisonian model opens upon new avenues for an exploration of the intended roles of the three branches in our constitutional system,[44] I shall make just two general observations that are directly related to this specific undertaking.

First, intelligent and meaningful evaluation of the Madisonian model makes sense only to the extent that we "enter" the model itself. This is true with respect to a full understanding of the values that Madison sought to maximize, the difficulties he encountered in this enterprise, and the evaluation of the model in terms of principles or norms such as those associated with liberal democracy. For instance, as this chapter illustrates, in Madison's framework of thought there was little to fear from Congress, acting in the capacity of a *translator* of a deliberate majority will. Nor did he feel that the Congress as constituted would be able to thwart persistent, and thus presumably mature and deliberate, majorities. What he did fear was Congress, with its enormous powers and prestige, acting as a force independent of society and imposing its will—much in the fashion of elected despots who presume to articulate the "general will"—on the whole society. Bearing this in mind, we can easily see that from Madison's point of view a more pristine form of republicanism, such as that advanced by his modern critics, would carry with it the probability of governmental tyranny.

We can state this another way: without effective separation of powers any system of government, even one in which republican values (i.e., political equality and majority rule) are fully realized, will degenerate into tyranny. The problem of governmental tyranny is, then, common to all forms of government. Madison most certainly must have subscribed to these or basically similar propositions. And, given this perception of the matter, we can scarcely fault him for his advocacy of separation of powers. But Madison's concerns went well beyond this: he had to "reconcile" the need for separation of powers with the principles of republicanism. He can, of course, be faulted for the form his reconciliation finally assumed, but one would have to deny the existence of governmental tyranny in order to ignore the problems it poses, particularly in the deliberate construction of a republican form of government.

This leads to a second general and related observation. One of the great hindrances to getting "inside" the Madisonian model, it would seem, has been a preoccupation with "one value" analysis.[45] Such analyses, because they do not

---

[43]Ibid. Madison's "wish" seems to have been realized. Writes Dahl, "The conclusion seems inevitable that the benefits and disadvantages flowing from equal state representation in the Senate are allocated in an entirely arbitrary fashion and cannot be shown to follow from any general principle." *Pluralistic Democracy in the United States: Conflict and Consent* (Chicago: Rand McNally, 1967), 125.

[44]For a pioneering effort in this direction see Martin Diamond, "Conservatives, Liberals, and the Constitution," in *Left, Right and Center,* ed. Robert A. Goldwin (Chicago: Rand McNally, 1969).

grasp the inner dimensions and tensions of the model, ultimately come down to a critique of the model without appreciation or consideration of the fundamental values upon which it rests, no matter how sensible or worthy they may be. Specifically, Madison's alleged theoretical shortcomings almost invariably relate to deviations from the principles of "liberal democracy" and political equality and its corollary of majority rule.[46] Principally on this score, Dahl concludes that Madison's theory will not bear up under examination and could with relative ease be placed "in the camp of the great antidemocratic theorists," such as Plato and Lenin. More: his theory centers "on the goal of avoiding majority control" and "goes about as far as . . . possible" in this direction "while still remaining within the rubric of democracy."[47]

Clearly, however, Madison's deviations from political equality, as we have seen, were trivial, the more so when compared with those attributed to him by his critics. More importantly, they were mandated by what Madison perceived to be a requisite for a republic without governmental tyranny. Indeed, the degree to which he was able simultaneously to maximize both the goals of republicanism and the necessary partition of powers is astonishing. Of course, one could say that Madison's concern with governmental tyranny was unfounded or exaggerated, or that the means he adopted to the end were inappropriate. Nevertheless, I submit, no sensible person immersed in the better part of the Western liberal tradition would ignore the potential danger of governmental tyranny. For this reason, if no other, Madison's concern still remains a challenge to the modern political theorist.

---

[45]I have borrowed this term from Professor Charles S. Hyneman.

[46]It is true that the model is also attacked on grounds that its structural forms prevent the realization of economic and social "democracy." But this is usually viewed as the very object of its presumed deviation from democratic principles.

[47]*Preface*, 32.

4

James Madison and the Principle of Federalism

INTRODUCTORY NOTE

Any penetrating treatment of state-national relations must, soon or late, deal with the teaching of James Madison because, far more than any other individual, he is responsible for our modern conception of federalism. From soon after the new government commenced operations under the Constitution until his death in 1836 he was the foremost spokesman for the proposition that our system occupied a "middle ground" between a consolidated or unitary form—one in which the general government possessed complete control over the component units—and the confederal form, wherein the constituent units retained their sovereignty. This middle-ground conception of our union is what American government textbooks commonly use in defining federalism when setting forth the fundamental principles upon which our system rests.

Madison recognized that this conception was not without its difficulties. In his final reflections on the nature of our union ("Notes on Nullification"), he acknowledges the argument that this middle-ground position, implying as it does a division of sovereignty between the national and state governments, may be theoretically untenable. Interestingly enough—by way, it would seem, of pointing up the disparity between theoretical speculation and practice—his response to this charge takes the form of pointing out that an understanding of the operations of our system depends on an awareness of this middle-ground principle or position. More significantly, at least from the viewpoint of the values and ends to be served by a division of powers between state and national authorities, he adds: it behooves "all . . . who are friends of a Government based on free principles to reflect, that by denying the possibility of a system partly federal [confederal] and partly consolidated [unitary], and who would convert ours into one either wholly federal or wholly consolidated, in neither of which forms have individual rights, public order, and external safety, been all duly maintained, they aim a deadly blow at the last hope of liberty on the face of the Earth."*

Many, particularly conservatives, have come to share Madison's views concerning federalism and its significance so that today it is widely regarded as one of the pillars of

---

*The Writings of James Madison, ed. Gaillard Hunt, 9 vols. (New York: G.P. Putnam's Sons, 1900–1910), IX, 606. Hereafter cited as Writings.

our constitutional order and freedoms. It is also widely regarded as one of our major contributions to the art of government. Yet, as the following section makes clear, when we look carefully at Madison's political career and his writings, it is difficult to see precisely what this contribution amounts to, or, for that matter, how it serves to bolster and protect our constitutional liberties. Indeed, if we look at the Supreme Court's record in this respect, a coherent articulation of the middle-ground position might well be impossible because, contrary to what Madison intimates, theory and practice do collide. Put otherwise—and this for reasons set forth below—there are not, and, it would seem, never can be rules, guides, injunctions or the like that can satisfactorily serve to perpetuate or maintain the division of powers called for by Madison's middle-ground (federal) position.

But if this is so, we may profitably ask, what is at stake between the revisionists and the traditionalists over the issue of federalism? The answer is somewhat involved and requires that we proceed a step at a time. First, we should note that from the outset of our constitutional experience controversy over state-national relations was inevitable. Even before the Constitutional Convention we can see a manifest "tension" in our official documents concerning the nature of the political relationship of the states to one another. This is evident, for example, in the Declaration of Independence. Its opening paragraph asserts that "one people" are dissolving the "political bands that have united them with another," a clause that suggests at least a feeling of unity or "oneness" among the colonies. That there were centripetal forces in operation at this time is clearly borne out by the convocation of the Continental Congresses and the subsequent ratification of the Articles of Confederation. But we also see evidences of centrifugal tendencies. The final paragraph of the Declaration is evidence of this, calling as it does for "Free and Independent States" with "full Power to levy War, conclude Peace, contract Alliances, establish Commerce, and to do all other Acts and Things which Independent States may of right do." And, although the Constitution was a decisive move toward greater unity, it certainly did not provide a definitive resolution of these tensions.

What seems clear is that the early revisionists, with the exception of Herbert Croly, associated the centralization of authority that resulted from the ratification of the Constitution with a departure from the democratic principles they had associated with the political decentralization under the Articles. The heroes for these revisionists were the early Republicans led by Jefferson who played upon and emphasized the centrifugal aspects of the tradition. While the record of these Republicans shows that the disputes over state-national authority were, for the most part, over issues far removed from any constitutional principle, they did serve to establish positions to which future politicians could repair to suit their purposes. With the coming of the Civil War, we do find, as I have noted, a constitutional crisis arising over the nature of the foundations of the union, with the South taking a position that would render the union little more than a confederacy—a position that, as the following essay shows, Madison strenuously opposed despite his general antipathy towards centralization of authority.

Modern revisionists, following the lead of Croly, have abandoned the Jeffersonian position. Though they pay due homage to what they understand to be Jeffersonian ideals, they find Hamilton's views on the necessity of a strong central government more suited to the achievement of these ideals. Yet, on this matter, the revisionists cannot rightly be called revisionists; that is, as the following selection shows, an extremely strong case can be made that Hamilton's view of the union was closer to what the Framers intended than Jefferson's or that advanced by Madison *after* the system was set in motion. In any event, it is generally conceded that Hamilton had much the better case concerning the scope of national powers. Moreover, his position corresponded far more closely to the teachings of *The Federalist* than that of Jefferson or of the later Madison.

For this reason, I find the position of many traditionalists in contemporary debates concerning federalism somewhat exasperating. Simply put, many traditionalists in their battle against the new constitutional morality simply assume, for instance, that Jefferson and eventually Madison articulated the Framers' views concerning the nature of the union and the proper scope of national authority relative to the states. And insofar as this puts the traditionalists on the side of "states' rights"—which it has had a pronounced tendency to do—the proponents of the new morality can claim to have the better case not only constitutionally but morally as well. More concretely, to take but one example, the civil rights issues of modern times have served to put the traditionalists on the defensive on both constitutional and moral grounds.

Yet, the basic issue between the traditionalists and the revisionists, as I see it, does not come down to the question of whether the national government has overextended its authority vis-à-vis the states according to some preconceived notions of how substantive powers ought to be divided between the two jurisdictions, but, rather, how or by what means the disputes over their relative domains are settled. Both logic and common sense tell us that controversies between the states and national government have to be settled by some agency of the national government. But—and this brings us back to reflect on the central element of the new constitutional morality—this agency need not be the Supreme Court, as the revisionists would have it. Rather, the constitutional morality set forth in *The Federalist* strongly suggests that the "common constituents" acting through Congress ought to have the last say concerning the proper division of authority between the national and state governments. In other words, consonant with the republican character of the system, Publius's teachings are that the people are the proper judge of the proper distribution of authority between the two layers of government. Such seems to have been the morality even at the time the Fourteenth Amendment was adopted: Section 5 of that amendment grants to Congress—significantly, not the courts—the authority to enforce the broad provisions of Section 1 (e.g., "due process of law," "equal protection of the laws") which can be used to severely limit state authority.

This should be taken to mean that, on the whole, I think Congress, particularly since the New Deal period, has acted responsibly. Its expansive use of the commerce power to intrude upon the states' police powers is, to say the least, imprudent. The entire system of federal grants-in-aid which give it leverage over the states leads to an inefficient and unresponsive government. Nevertheless, unlike many, if not most, *judicial* interventions into the realms traditionally reserved to the states, Congress's actions can be repealed or revised through the ordinary political processes.

The revisionists cannot abide by a political, as opposed to a judicial, resolution of issues surrounding state-national relations because of other aspects of federalism that are often overlooked today. Federalism, conceived not in terms of a division of sovereignty but as a principle that recognizes the states as equal constituent parts of the national government, has played and will continue to play an important role in our system. Part of the recognition—the "formal" part—is fused into our constitutional framework and processes (e.g., the equality of state representation in the Senate, the election of the President). But other and far more important aspects of this federalism so conceived are "informal," the product of an evolutionary growth. The most significant of these is the development of our party system with roots firmly planted at the state and local levels. Indeed, it is through the political parties that state and local interests find expression in the national councils, a fact that helps to insure that, in the resolution of state-national conflicts through the political processes, state and local interests will have to be reckoned with.

In this sense, federalism contributes to the "messiness" or "untidiness" of the constitutional system that the proponents of the new morality deplore. That is why they defend activist courts that operate through the Fourteenth Amendment to impose their will upon the states: the courts, that is, are perceived as rising above the parochialism that characterizes congressional deliberations and that often delays or forecloses needed "reforms." Beyond this, of course, the proponents of the new morality would sleep easier with disciplined, programmatic, and centrally controlled political parties that would be able to resist and overcome the centrifugal forces that arise from the mere existence of politically viable states.

JAMES MADISON AND THE PRINCIPLE OF FEDERALISM

Despite the prodigious efforts of biographers, analysts, and commentators over the decades, James Madison still remains an enigma. While he is widely hailed as the "father" of the Philadelphia Constitution, we find that he was, almost from the outset of its operations, schizophrenic about the nature of the political union it fashioned. To be more exact, his views or positions relating to the proper relationship between the state and national governments and their respective spheres of authority—that is, his posture towards issues that are subsumed today under the rubric "federalism"—shifted markedly during the course of his political career.[1] Clearly, this state of affairs casts doubts on the reliability of his views regarding the nature and character of the federal union. But, more importantly, it eventually leads us to inquire about the status of the federal principle itself. Could it be, in other words, that federalism, rather than being the product of a principled evolution from constitutional moorings, is really anchored only in political expediency wherein the relationship between the national and state governments at any given moment depends upon the mere will of the dominant political force?

---

[1]This view is generally accepted today even by Madison's most sympathetic biographers. For a dissenting view see Lance Banning, "The Hamiltonian Madison," *The Virginia Magazine* 92 (January 1984). Banning contends that "James Madison was never a 'nationalist,' not if that word is loaded with many of the connotations it has come to carry in recent histories of the 1780s. . . . Even as he led the nation through the framing and ratification of the Constitution, Madison expressed a lively fear of distant, energetic government, a fear he had displayed through the 1780s. . . . The great accomplishment of constitutional reformers had not been a radical redistribution of responsibilities from state to federal hands, but structural reforms allowing Congress to meet the needs that it had always been intended to secure. The innovations of 1787, from this point of view, were essentially conservative in their intent. So were the arguments of 1798, with which Madison's early understanding of the Constitution was not in conflict" (8–9).

As we will indicate in the text, Banning's position is perhaps tenable from the ratification period on, though it is not, in our judgment, the most plausible interpretation of Madison's contributions to *The Federalist*. However, Madison's remarks in the Philadelphia Convention and prior to it clearly indicate that Banning is off the mark in arguing that Madison was never a "nationalist."

Madison's views and positions on federalism are intriguing largely because they do invite us to ask this and related questions. And the reasons are not hard to discover. In the first place, as we shall see, Madison's conception of federalism changed significantly soon after the new Constitution began to operate. Moreover, even after this initial change, he was not entirely consistent in his outlook or in his answers to very important questions inherent in his conception of federalism. And, beyond this, we find that at various stages of his career he had to contend with tensions between theory and practice. These circumstances naturally give rise to serious questions concerning his teachings: after making accommodation to political reality, what principles or elements of federalism remain intact? Or, to phrase this concern somewhat differently, are there rules, tests, standards, or guidelines derivable from his theory of federalism that remained relatively "pure" or constant over time? What aspects of his theory or teachings might serve us today in resolving conflicts between state and national jurisdictions or defining the proper spheres of each?[2] What, in short, do Madison's thoughts, trials, and tribulations teach us about the federal principle?

Surveying Madison's thoughts on federalism with an eye toward answering these and like questions is not an easy matter, and it is best that we set forth our procedure at the outset. First, we must deal with Madison the "nationalist," that is, with Madison during what we will call his "first" or "nationalist" stage, which runs from almost the beginning of his political career to his famous break with Hamilton over the incorporation of a national bank in the very first session of Congress. After this break, we confront the so-called "strict constructionist" Madison who held to a narrow view of national authority. This represents his "second" or, as we put it at times, "shifting" phase, for, as we shall see, he wavered in his rules concerning constitutional construction.[3] We will initially be concerned with Madison's nationalism and the reasons for his abandonment of this position.

While we can divide Madison's views of state-national relations into two relatively distinct phases without much difficulty, his theoretical positions and views are not so readily amenable to such delineation. Writing as "Publius" in *The Federalist,* Madison can be read to stake out two positions: the nationalist, and one which, as we see in retrospect, is thoroughly compatible with his later and more restrictive views concerning national authority vis-à-vis the states. As

---

[2]An excellent work that raises broader concerns not unlike those implicit in Madison's "theory" and, at the same time, delves into the critical question whether, indeed, there is any such "animal" as "federalism" is S. Rufus Davis, *The Federal Principle: A Journey Through Time in Quest of a Meaning* (Berkeley: University of California Press, 1978).

[3]Of course, Madison's life can be divided into any number of logical segments. Our division seems reasonable because our concern is with Madison's views on federalism or the relationship between the state and national authority. Moreover, as we note, within his second period his positions are not easily categorized, although his abiding concern is to preserve a system of "divided sovereignty" in order to avoid the dangers he associates with either confederate or unitary systems.

we will indicate, his *Federalist* position is probably best understood as national-istic because it does conform on virtually all salient points with Hamilton's view of the proposed Union. Nevertheless, as we will also make clear, there is no gainsaying the "other" position that forms the theoretical framework for under-standing the perplexing problems that he confronted throughout his second phase. Showing this, as well as why it is so difficult to abstract from his writing and actions much by way of systematic or coherent views of federalism, is the focus of our concern after the initial sections.

MADISON: THE NATIONALIST

What seems clear is that experiences under the Articles had convinced Madison of the need for a stronger and more energetic national government. While this view was, no doubt, commonly held, it is safe to say that Madison's opinions on what form the new government should take were not so widely shared. In his famous letter to Washington on the eve of the Philadelphia Convention, he set forth his candid views concerning the nature of state-national relations he would like to see obtain under a new constitution. Conceding that the "consolidation of the whole into one simple republic would be" both "inexpedient" and "unattain-able," he adopted a "middle ground" position that would "support the due supremacy of the national authority" while not excluding "the local authorities wherever they can be subordinately useful."[4] His vision called for a national government "armed with positive and complete authority in all cases that require uniformity" and, beyond this, "a negative *in all cases whatsoever* on the acts of the States." This negative he deemed "absolutely necessary" not only with re-gard to state actions that might contravene or impinge upon national authority, but also as a "control on the internal vicissitudes of State policy, and the aggres-sions of interested majorities on the rights of minorities and of individuals."[5] In sum, Madison envisioned a negative national power that could reach down into the distinctly internal affairs of the states.

These views flowed logically from what he perceived to be the major weakness of the Articles. Aside from noting the mutability and multiplicity of laws at the state level, he found that their "injustice betrays a defect still more alarming"[6]— a defect that he believed could be supplied only by a stronger and more extensive government. Anticipating the argument he was to develop in Federalist 10, he maintained that the difficulties and injustices prevalent within the states, "con-trary to prevailing Theory," were not to be found "in proportion" to the "extent, but to the narrowness of their limits."[7] At the same time, Madison also faulted

---

[4]Letter to George Washington, April 16, 1787. *Writings,* II, 344–45.
[5]Ibid., 346.
[6]Ibid., 366.
[7]Ibid., 368.

the government under the Articles for its inability to act to advance the common interests of the states. To this point he wrote: "How much has the national dignity, interest, and revenue suffered from this cause? Instances of inferior moment are the want of uniformity in the laws concerning naturalization and literary property; of provision for national seminaries, for grants of incorporation for national purposes, for canals and other works of general utility, which may at present be defeated by the perverseness of particular States whose concurrence is necessary"[8]—ends that are particularly noteworthy in light of the views he was subsequently to express in his second phase.

Madison's strong nationalism manifested itself in the Philadelphia Convention. For instance, he was chief architect of the Virginia Plan, which, as one student has correctly remarked, "envisioned a unitary national government effectively freed from and dominant over the states."[9] By providing for the popular election of the lower house, which in turn would select the membership of the upper chamber, and by placing the responsibility for electing an executive and choosing judges with both these bodies, the plan established the foundations of a national government virtually independent of the states. Beyond this, the negative over state legislation for which Madison longed was granted to the national legislature, which was empowered "to negative all laws passed by the several States, contravening in the opinion of the National Legislature the articles of Union." To be sure, the plan called for a "Council of revision" composed of "the Executive and a convenient number of the National Judiciary" which could overturn this legislative veto unless extra-majorities in both chambers were to reaffirm the original negative.[10] Nevertheless, final jurisdiction over the proper scope of state authority was, in effect, lodged in the hands of the national government. And, what is more, consonant with its unitary character, the plan vested the national legislature with the authority "to legislate in all cases to which the separate States are incompetent, or in which the harmony of the United States may be interrupted by the exercise of individual legislation."[11]

Perhaps more telling than these structural arrangements and formal procedures were Madison's arguments against the states' rights position. At one point, to give, as he put it, "full force" to the arguments against a national government such as that envisioned in the Virginia Plan, he asks his fellow delegates to speculate on the consequences of giving an "indefinite power . . . to the General

---

[8]Ibid., 363.

[9]John Roche, "The Founding Fathers: A Reform Caucus in Action," *American Political Science Review* 56 (March 1962), 804.

[10]*The Debates in the Several State Conventions on the Adoption of the Federal Constitution,* ed. Jonathan Elliot, 5 vols. (Philadelphia: J. B. Lippincott Co., 1836), V, 128. Hereafter cited as Elliot.

[11]Ibid., 127. Vested with this power the scope of national authority would seem to be virtually unlimited. At any rate, provisions such as this hardly support Banning's thesis. (See note 1, this chapter.)

Legislature'' thereby reducing the "States . . . to corporations dependent on the General Legislature." Reasoning in a manner consonant with the views he had expressed earlier to Washington, he saw no reason why under this arrangement the legislature would deprive the states of any power so long as its continued exercise by the states was either desired by the people or "beneficial." He points to the examples of the states, particularly Connecticut, where "all the Townships are incorporated, and have a certain limited jurisdiction" and asks rhetorically: "have the Representatives or the people of the Townships in the Legislature ever endeavored to despoil the Townships of any part of their local authority?" He concludes that this has not been the case insofar as "this local authority is convenient to the people." And he sees no reason why this same relationship or condition should not obtain between the states and a national government vested with indefinite powers: "As far as its [national government] operation would be practicable it could not in this view be improper; as far as it would be impracticable, the conveniency of the General Government itself would concur with that of the people in the maintenance of subordinate Governments." Beyond this, he did not believe that "the people would . . . be less free, as members of one great Republic, than as members of thirteen small ones." Thus, even "supposing a tendency in the General Government to absorb the State Governments no fatal consequences could result." However, state encroachments on national authority, he felt, would have fatal consequences; a judgment he believed was borne out by "the experiment we are now making to prevent the calamity."[12]

As we know, of course, Madison did not get all he wanted at the Philadelphia Convention. Writing to Jefferson shortly after the Convention, he expresses his concerns about the final product, concerns that again reflect his nationalist point of view. He considers the lack of an effective negative over the states, such as that provided for in the Virginia Plan, to be one of the principal defects of the proposed Constitution. "Without such a check in the whole over the parts," he maintains, "our system involves the evil of imperia in imperio."[13] He is particularly concerned that the states might encroach upon the national government principally because of their critically important constitutive functions: "The Senate will represent the States in their political capacity; the other House will represent the people of the States in their individual capacities . . . . The President also derives his appointment from the States, and is periodically accountable to them." "This dependence of the General on the local authorities," he writes, "seems effectually to guard the latter against any dangerous encroachment of the former; whilst the latter, within their respective limits, will be continually sensible of the abridgement of their power, and be stimulated by ambition to resume the surrendered portion of it."[14] For all of this, however, he does not rule out the possibility that an "esprit de corps will . . . exist in the National Government" that might serve to

---

[12]Ibid., 222.

[13]Letter to Thomas Jefferson, October 24, 1787. *Writings,* V, 23.

[14]Ibid., 25.

resist such dangerous encroachments by the states.[15] This, at least, seems to be his hope.

The lack of an effective negative also bothered him, as we might expect, because of his concern "to secure individuals against encroachments on their rights." In this connection, he observes, a "serious evil" arises from the "mutability" of the state laws while their "injustices" have become "so frequent and so flagrant as to alarm the most steadfast friends of Republicanism." Such laws, he argues, have done more to prepare the "Public mind for a general reform, than those which accrued to our national character and interest from the inadequacy of the Confederation to its immediate objects." "The restraints against paper emissions, and violations of contract" he describes as "short of the mark": "Injustice may be effected by such an infinitude of legislative expedients that where the disposition exists it can only be controlled by some provision which reaches all cases whatsoever. The partial provision made, supposes the disposition which will evade it." Having noted this, he then proceeds to a lengthy discussion of why it is that "private rights will be more secure under the Guardianship of the General Government than under the State Government,"[16] a discussion that anticipates the arguments of his famous tenth Federalist.

Madison as Publius

For obvious reasons Madison had to abandon certain of his arguments and positions in his contributions to *The Federalist* simply because the movement toward a stronger union had entered a new phase; outwardly, at least, arguments over the form of this union had been settled at Philadelphia and now the task—at least as Madison seemed to perceive it—was to present a united front to marshal support for its adoption.[17] While, as we have remarked, Madison's contributions to *The Federalist* can be looked upon as providing the grounds for his restrictive views on national authority (a matter we will turn to later),[18] his nationalism clearly shows through in at least three significant ways. First, he sets forth in Federalist 10 and in the latter part of Federalist 51 the virtues of the proposed extended or large republic: "In the extended republic of the United States, and among the great variety of interests, parties, and sects which it embraces, a coalition of the majority of the whole society could seldom take place on any other

---

[15]Ibid., 26.

[16]Ibid., 27–28.

[17]*The Federalist* was intended to be read and comprehended as the work of one pen, not three. In fact, contrary to the views of Douglass Adair, Alpheus T. Mason, and others, the text of *The Federalist* does not reveal any fundamental or significant differences between its principal authors on the major principles of the Constitution. On this point see chapter 1.

[18]William W. Crosskey did look upon *The Federalist* in such a fashion. In his view, Jeffersonians and states' rights partisans managed to use *The Federalist* to completely distort the intentions of the Founders who, in fact, wanted a unitary or consolidated government. *Politics and the Constitution in the United States,* 2 vols. (Chicago: University of Chicago Press, 1953), I, 8–11.

principles than those of justice and the general good" (269). Extensiveness, he notes, also requires "the delegation of the government . . . to a small number of citizens elected by the rest" (10:46). And, from his perspective, the chances of obtaining virtuous and knowledgeable representatives were greater in the large than the small republic. Thus, the multiplicity and diversity of interests combined with representation by "fit characters" provided what he believed to be a "republican remedy for the diseases most incident to republican government," namely, a cure for the ravages of "majority factions" (10:48). In this regard, he summarily dismisses the possibility that minority factions would ever gain control of the constitutional apparatus. Such a faction, he writes, "may clog the administration, it may convulse the society; but it will be unable to execute and mask its violence under the forms of the Constitution" (10:45).

On this score, Madison seemed to believe that there was an inverse relationship between extent of territory and susceptibility to the evils of faction. He held out no prospect that "pure" democracies, wherein the citizens "assemble and administer the government in person," could avoid the evils of faction. The nature of such democracies would "admit of no cure for the mischiefs of faction" since "impulse" and "opportunity" could so easily coincide among majorities: "A common passion or interest will, in almost every case, be felt by a majority of the whole; a communication and concert result from the form of government itself; and there is nothing to check the inducements to sacrifice the weaker party or an obnoxious individual" (10:46). But small republics were, in his view, susceptible to the very same dangers. For example, Madison held out little prospect for just, stable, and republican government in Rhode Island outside the confines of union: "the insecurity of rights under the popular form of government within such narrow limits," he writes, "would be displayed by such reiterated oppressions of factious majorities that some power altogether independent of the people would soon be called for by the voice of the very factions whose misrule had proved the necessity of it" (51:269).

Second, he reiterates and expands upon his concern that the states will encroach upon the national government. He observes, once again, that the experiences of confederacies both "ancient and modern" conclusively show the proclivity of their members "to despoil the general government of its authorities, with a very ineffectual capacity in the latter to defend itself against the encroachments" (45: 236). And, though he concedes that the proposed constitutional system is quite dissimilar to these confederacies, he does not believe their experiences should be "wholly disregarded." He firmly held to the proposition that the states could more than fend for themselves in any conflict with the national government. On this point, he writes: "The State governments will have the advantage of the Federal government, whether we compare them in respect to the immediate dependence of the one on the other; to the weight of personal influence which each side will possess; to the powers respectively vested in them; to the predilection and probable support of the people; to the disposition and faculty of resisting and frustrating the measures of each other" (45:237).

And third, there can be no question that Madison viewed the Constitution as providing for a national government with full and sufficient powers to discharge the responsibilities placed upon it. While we will deal with this aspect of Madison's thought in another context, a good indication of the extent of his nationalism is the absence of any substantial differences between him and Hamilton—his principal collaborator and acknowledged nationalist—concerning the scope of national power. Indeed, what is somewhat astonishing is the similarity of their positions on key issues. In the first place, they both agree that the national government must possess the means necessary for the ends that are entrusted to its care. Hamilton writes as follows to this effect: "the means ought to be proportioned to the end; the persons from whose agency the attainment of any end is expected ought to possess the means by which it is to be attained." This proposition, he contends, rests upon "axioms as simple as they are universal" (31:15). Madison similarly maintains: "No axiom is more clearly established in law, or in reason, than that wherever the end is required, the means are authorized; wherever a general power to do a thing is given, every particular power necessary for doing it is included"[19] (44:232).

Moreover, principally because the national government was charged with the responsibility of providing for the national defense, both men were opposed to placing any a priori limitations on the powers of the national government. Writing with regard to the national powers to provide for the national defense (e.g., "raise armies," "build and equip fleets") Hamilton puts the matter this way: "These powers ought to exist without limitation, *because it is impossible to foresee or to define the extent and variety of national exigencies, and the correspondent extent and variety of the means which may be necessary to satisfy them.* The circumstances that endanger the safety of nations are infinite, and for this reason no constitutional shackles can wisely be imposed on the power to which the care of it is committed" (23:11). On this same issue, Madison contends: "The means of security can only be regulated by the means and danger of attack. They will, in fact, be ever determined by these rules and by no others. It is vain to oppose constitutional barriers to the impulse of self-preservation. It is worse than vain; because it plants in the Constitution itself necessary usurpations of power, every precedent of which is a germ of unnecessary and multiplied repetitions" (41:210).[20]

---

[19]On Madison's interpretation of the "necessary and proper" clause set forth in Federalist 44, David Epstein notes: "He [Madison] treats 'necessary and proper' as if it meant necessary *or* proper, i.e., as if Congress may make all laws which shall be necessary *and* all laws which shall be proper— rather than only those laws which are both. . . . That is, the permitted category includes all necessary and all proper laws, and excludes only those which are neither." *The Political Theory of "The Federalist"* (Chicago: University of Chicago Press, 1984), 44. This, of course, constitutes further evidence of Madison's nationalist vision at this point in time.

[20]Often overlooked is the degree to which Madison's position (and Hamilton's as well) provides a reasonable basis for a completely consolidated system. Harry Jaffa argued at the height of the Cold War that a credible and comprehensive civil defense policy was needed to deter a Soviet first strike;

And, among other points of similarity, we find that both hold to the proposition that the extent of national powers vis-à-vis the states will depend on their "common constituents," who, in Madison's words, "ought not surely to be precluded from giving most of the confidence where they may discover it to be most due" (46:241). In a similar vein, Hamilton concludes: "If the federal government should overpass the just bounds of its authority and make a tyrannical use of its powers, the people, whose creature it is, must appeal to the standard they have formed, and take such measure to redress the injury done to the Constitution as the exigency may suggest and prudence justify" (33:160).

Despite the ambiguities and difficulties associated with Madison's position in *The Federalist*—as well as with Hamilton's, for that matter—a convincing case can be made that, from the early 1780s until shortly after the commencement of the system he helped to fashion, Madison was an energetic proponent of a strong national government. True enough, his nationalism assumed, as he put it in his letter to Washington, a "middle ground" that did not call for the abolition of the state governments. Nor did he envision a consolidated government wherein the national government would assume control over all functions. On the contrary, he could see the states performing numerous and vital functions. Yet, for all of this, the relative authority of the two governments with respect to one another did not, in his view, depend upon known and fixed constitutional rules, stipulations, or principles. Rather, in his judgment, the lines would (and should) depend upon two highly related factors: the wishes of the "common constituents" and the administrative capacities and competence of the two governments. In this scheme of things, there was no body of functions or powers that could be marked out as irrevocably within the domain of state authority. Instead, echoing the position he set forth in the Convention, Madison felt that over time it would be abundantly clear that "it is only within a certain sphere that the federal power can, in the nature of things, be advantageously administered" (46:241).

The "federalism" of Madison's nationalist phase can appropriately be characterized as "pragmatic." The boundary lines between the national and state authorities would be worked out over time; however, at any given point these lines could be altered. Moreover, Madison's approach made allowances for the fact that the national government might have to intrude upon even recognized and established areas of state authority in order to fulfill its responsibilities, particu-

---

a policy that would be concerned with the structural design of buildings so that they would protect their occupants better in case of attack, as well as the "redesigning of our great urban centers, and indeed the entire country, into 'nuclear' neighborhoods that are self-sufficient for survival purposes." "The Case for a Stronger National Government," *A Nation of States,* ed. Robert A. Goldwin (1st ed.; Chicago: Rand McNally & Co., 1964).

By the same token one might argue that our economic survival in the highly competitive world economy now requires, more than ever before, that we produce students with a relatively high degree of sophistication in mathematics and the sciences. From this it is but a short step to the proposition that to secure a sufficient number of such students there is need for the national government to set down curriculum requirements for the primary and secondary schools across the nation.

larly national defense. Hence, the lines between the two jurisdictions could never be considered as unalterably fixed.

MADISON: THE STRICT CONSTRUCTIONIST

What we have said to this point indicates that Madison's views toward state-national relations were straightforward and consistent. Certainly they pose no insoluble theoretical dilemmas. However, with his position on the incorporation of a national bank on constitutional grounds in 1791, we come to the second phase of his career. Put otherwise, at this point we witness an abrupt change in his approach to federalism, an approach, as we have already mentioned, that leads to practical and theoretical difficulties that he never resolves satisfactorily.[21] Nevertheless, by exploring them we do gain an insight into precisely why state-national relations have been a perennial source of controversy. Indeed, largely because our modern conception of federalism parallels that which we find in Madison's second stage, the problems that Madison wrestled with also stand at the heart of our contemporary controversies.

Now Madison's previous record as a proponent of a strong national government would seem to leave no doubts about what stance he would adopt towards the constitutionality of incorporating a national bank.[22] Yet, astonishingly enough, when the issue did come before the House he actually led the opposition to this measure, basing his arguments on strict constitutional construction. ''The power of incorporation itself, as called for in this measure,'' he argued, ''could never be deemed an accessory or subaltern power, to be deduced by implication, as a means of executing another power; it was in its nature a distinct, an independent and substantive prerogative, which not being enumerated in the Constitution, could never have been meant to be included in it, and not being included, could never be rightfully exercised.''[23] Moreover, at another level, he contended that no meaning of the necessary and proper clause ''can be admitted that would give an unlimited discretion to Congress.'' Therefore, he reasoned, ''its meaning must,''

---

[21]Madison's famed ''break'' with Hamilton did not come over the bank issue. In retrospect, it occurred in 1790 with Madison's opposition to Hamilton's plan for the funding and assumption of state war debts. We begin Madison's second phase with the bank matter because this controversy involved what amounted to an official repudiation of his ''nationalist'' position.

[22]Here we refer not only to his prior positions but his behavior in the first Congress as well. He had expertly maneuvered a bill of rights through the House without having to make concessions to the states' rights partisans—concessions that would have severely weakened the national government. For instance, he resisted efforts to include the word ''expressly'' in what is now the Tenth Amendment so that it would have read: ''The powers not *expressly* delegated to the United States by the Constitution, nor prohibited to it by the States, are reserved to the States respectively, or the people.'' Likewise, his backing of a bill to provide funding for a purely scientific expedition to discover the causes of compass needle variations just prior to the debate over the national bank belied his own position with respect to the status of the ''general welfare'' clause. In other words, his position on the national bank could hardly have been anticipated.

[23]*The Annals of Congress,* 1st Congress, 2d Session, February 2, 1791, 1900.

given "the natural and obvious force of the terms and the context, be limited to means necessary to the end incident to the nature of the specified powers." "The essential characteristic of the Government as composed of limited and enumerated powers would be destroyed," he warned, "if instead of direct and incidental means, any means could be used which, in the language of the preamble of the bill, might be conceived to be conducive to the successful conducting of the finances, or might be conceived to tend to give facility to the obtaining of loans."[24]

This shift, of course, prompts serious questions: What reasons can be adduced for Madison's rather sudden switch? Is it that he perceived a new way of looking at the political system devised at Philadelphia? If so, what caused this change of perception? And, in any event, what are we to make of the federal principle? These questions lead to others with still broader concerns: can the mere fact of such a reversal be taken as evidence that there was a lack of consensus at the Convention concerning the scope of national authority vis-à-vis the states?[25]

---

[24]Ibid., 1898.

[25]In this regard, it should be noted that Madison, in the debate over the national bank and at various points in his second stage, brings the understanding of those who participated in the state ratification debates to bear as a standard for proper constitutional interpretation. For instance, in attacking the liberality of breadth of Marshall's interpretation of "necessary and proper," he writes: "those who shared in what passed in the State Conventions, thro' which the people ratified the Constitution, with respect to the extent of the powers vested in Congress, cannot easily be persuaded that the avowal of such a rule would not have prevented its ratification." Letter to Spencer Roane, September 2, 1819, in *Writings*, VIII, 450–51.

Likewise, contrary to the thrust of his overall stance, he justified a liberal or broad interpretation of Congress's powers "to lay and collect taxes, duties, imposts, and excises" and "to regulate commerce with foreign nations"—broad enough, at any rate, to embrace the use of tariffs to encourage domestic manufactures—by references to ratifying convention debates. In this, however, we see one of the difficulties in employing this method. Among the New England states Madison acknowledges that only the debates of Massachusetts "have been preserved." He can only infer that such a liberal interpretation was shared by Connecticut and Rhode Island since they were "the most thickly peopled of all the States, and having of course their thoughts most turned to the subject of manufactures." As for Virginia and North Carolina, whose "debates have been preserved," he does not believe any "adverse inferences can be drawn"; nor does he perceive the "slightest indication," though there were no records of the debates available, that either of the two Southernmost states "viewed the encouragement of manufactures as not within the general power over trade to be transferred to the government of the U.S." *Writings*, IX, 329–30. In other words, the evidence is scanty, to say the least.

Nevertheless, we may look upon this approach as an excellent tactic on Madison's part because, while his views might be disputed, they could never be controverted. Put otherwise, Madison certainly could not pretend that his views on "necessary and proper" represented the clear consensus of the Philadelphia Convention, if for no other reason than that, at the time of the national bank controversy, too many of the Framers were still alive. By shifting, so to speak, to the ratifying conventions to determine intent, his grounds, though highly questionable, were still more defensible. To see this, we need only imagine how publication of his own Convention notes would have undermined not only his initial position with respect to the bank, but all of those predicated on a "strict" construction.

Could it be that the Framers, to put this differently, simply took care to carve out the powers they felt it essential for the national government to possess, leaving the question of how far the exercise of these powers could intrude upon the residual powers an "open" matter to be worked out over time through the political processes much in the manner *The Federalist* suggests? And, if this be the case, is it not "legitimate" for one's views of state-national powers to vary according to the issues at stake in any particular controversy? This, of course, leads us back to the question of the constitutional status of federalism.

We will probably never know what caused Madison's change of heart. But the most frequently advanced explanations would lead us to believe that, contrary to Madison's professions, his change is attributable to factors far removed from the constitutional arguments he advances. One such explanation is that Madison, along with his fellow Virginians, viewed the incorporation of a national bank as serving Northern interests at the expense of the South. In this vein, Gaillard Hunt, certainly not an unfriendly biographer, perceives him as reacting against Hamilton's "inflexible devotion to a government of strongly centralized power" because Madison "knew . . . that Hamilton's system was repugnant to a great majority of the people of America, whose attachments were local or sectional." And, in taking this stance, Hunt continues, "Madison secured the favor of the people of Virginia as he had never secured it before, and he now stood for the first time upon the firm ground of a public man who has behind him a constituency practically undivided in its support of him." If this means, Hunt argues, "base motives of expediency must be attributed" to Madison, so, too, must they be attributed "to the former Federalists in Virginia who now acted with him."[26] In this regard, Hunt does not overlook the possibility that Madison and others may have fallen under Jefferson's spell: "The truth is that Madison now had a party chief. This chief neither directed nor suggested Madison's opposition to Hamilton's consolidation policy, but his political conduct was now influenced by Jefferson's stronger personality and extraordinary power of attracting men to him."[27]

Irving Brant offers a more principled explanation of Madison's behavior. In his account, Madison "saw the need to impose general checks against a mounting federal imperialism." But, because he faced "hostile majorities" in Congress, he was forced to turn "to the Constitution" even though its "ends and means presented a panorama of uncertainties." With the bank incorporation, Madison pre-

---

[26]Gaillard Hunt, *The Life of James Madison* (New York: Doubleday, Page & Co., 1902), 211.

[27]Ibid., 212. Irving Brant, Madison's premier biographer, seems keen on proving that Madison was his own man, not simply Jefferson's chief lieutenant. To this end Brant writes: "It is part of the long-prevalent myth that Jefferson broke with Hamilton over funding and assumption and carried Madison along with him, thus rupturing the Madison-Hamilton friendship. Actually the break between Madison and Hamilton became complete before Jefferson reached home from six years in France. Jefferson was a last-state observer of the crucial events by which Madison brought 'Jeffersonian Democracy' into existence two years before Jefferson's political genius gave it that name." *The Fourth President: The Life of James Madison* (Indianapolis: The Bobbs-Merrill Co., 1970), 247.

sumably found an issue that he could use to push for a doctrine of strict construction that might serve to stem dangerous centralization.[28] Beyond this, according to Brant, Madison's actions are understandable in another light: during his tenure in the House, he became not only an opponent of "the new money power grasping for control of the nation" but also the defender of "farmers, mechanics, storekeepers, small manufacturers—the American wayside of life— against organized commercial and financial interests with the government as their instrument."[29]

Still another, more conceptual, explanation is offered by Marvin Meyers. In his view, Madison must be regarded as "a working statesman" who sought to achieve an "effective balance among the actual and shifting forces of American politics." Consequently, when he perceived that "the concentration of power in the national government appeared to threaten freedom, corrupt government, or drive substantial parties or sections to despair, he would organize countervailing powers and emphasize anticentralist, libertarian principles." Conversely, when the centrifugal force of local interests or presumed minority rights threatened needed and effective national authority, "Madison would throw his weight to the center and emphasize the principle of majority rule." According to Meyers, Madison's chief objective in this rather flexible policy "was the perfection of a lasting American republic."[30]

---

[28]Irving Brant, *James Madison: Father of the Constitution, 1787–1800,* 6 vols. (Indianapolis: The Bobbs-Merrill Co., 1950), III, 332.

[29]Ibid., 333. However, Forrest McDonald, among others, casts a different light on Madison's behavior particularly with respect to Hamilton's debt assumption plan. "The tactic Madison and his allies employed, as it gradually emerged, was to seek out the most vulnerable part of Hamilton's proposals, block the passage of that part, and hold the line there until they could negotiate a bargain favorable to their region and to themselves." *Alexander Hamilton: A Biography* (New York: W.W. Norton & Co., 1979), 175. Madison, it would appear, wanted the capital located on the Potomac to insure the success of his land speculations.

[30]Marvin Myers, *The Mind of the Founder: James Madison* (Hanover and London: University Press of New England, 1982), xiii. Peter Schotten shares much the same view as Meyers concerning Madison's behavior. In his view, Madison stood between the strong nationalists and the states' rights partisans by "constantly seeking moderation and often opposing what he took to be the dangerous, dominant teaching of the time." Peter Schotten, "Joseph Story," *American Political Thought,* ed. Morton J. Frisch and Richard G. Stevens (2d ed.; Itasca, Illinois: F.E. Peacock, 1983), 140.

There are enormous difficulties associated with the Meyers-Schotten position. For instance, leaving aside the fact that a good deal of Madison's behavior in this area can apparently be explained in terms of normal interest-oriented politics, we cannot help but note that this "balance" theory, unless refined considerably, really tells us only that he shifted his positions in a seemingly contradictory manner. To argue that he sought balance would require that we have a pretty good notion of the balance he sought. Only with a developed notion of balance or equilibrium is it possible to explain the whys and wherefores of his actions and, thus, to defend him against the charges of acting on the basis of expediency, not principle. For instance, as we point out in the text, it is difficult to see why within such a short period Madison signs the national bank bill and vetoes an internal improvements measure. The answer "balance" is no answer at all in the absence of a notion of what constitutes

But there are serious problems with those explanations that move us away from simple political expediency to more altruistic motives in accounting for Madison's turnabout concerning the scope of national powers. Not the least of these is that these explanations bring into question broader aspects of his theory, particularly his arguments relating to the workability and desirability of the extended republic. In this connection, we need only recall that Madison, writing as Publius, had maintained that the national government under the proposed Constitution would secure the rights and liberties of the people to a far greater degree than the state governments; that the multiplicity and diversity of interests in the extended republic rendered it unlikely that majority factions would rule; that the republican foundations of the system were sufficient to thwart minority factions; and, *inter alia,* that the states would enjoy a pronounced advantage over the national government in any disputes relative to their respective jurisdictions. In writing to this effect, he was only reiterating somewhat more systematically what he had said or written on other occasions over the years. Yet, the charitable explanations would have us abandon one or more of these contentions which stand at the very heart of his argument for the proposed Constitution. For instance, we are asked to believe that, within a period of two years—i.e., in the very first Congress— contrary to his previous position based on both history and firsthand experience, he had come to conclude that the states desperately needed protection from the national government;[31] or that minority factions had actually gained control of the national government. Thus, to the degree these explanations are correct, something would seem to be drastically amiss with his extended republic theory, something that could not be remedied by repeated expostulations on the modes of proper constitutional interpretation.

---

balance for him. And, judging from the timing of his initial opposition to the national bank (see text) and the responses from other states to his Virginia Resolution, we are left to wonder what factors he took into account in formulating his conception of "balance."

Then, too, whatever his conception of balance, there is the question of his ability to assess the relevant political and social forces that could lead to this balance. According to Edward Burns: "He [Madison] seemed to have only a vague perception of the forces making for national dominance and the destruction of States' rights. He recognized that a substantial increase in the number of States and the presence of an external danger would be likely to strengthen the general government at the expense of the States, but he overlooked other factors making for the same result, among them the rapid growth of the North in comparison with the South, the weakening of the old local attachments with the expansion of population into the Western country, the improvement of transportation facilities, and, most of all, the development of a more complex economic life. By a curious irony of fate he himself contributed about as much as anyone to the centralizing tendency." *James Madison: Philosopher of the Constitution* (New York: Octagon Books, 1973), 125.

[31] Of Madison's position on the national bank, for instance, Brant writes: "the spectacle of chronic abuse of federal power propelled him into a lifelong argument against some of the most important principles he had helped to plant in the Constitution." III, 332. Yet, by almost any standard, Brant's assessment seems distorted. What, for example, are these "chronic abuses" to which he refers? And, after all, how "chronic" could they have been?

In addition to this, as we might gather from these explanations, we can expect to encounter difficulties in formulating easily transmissible rules or principles from Madison's approach in determining the proper state-national boundaries. Put otherwise, they suggest that ends or goals—whether for reasons of expediency or basic conviction—play a decisive role in his thinking about the constitutional boundaries between state and national power. And, even if it is true, as Meyers contends, that Madison was playing the role of "working statesman"—a role that would warrant his picking and choosing sides as the circumstances dictated—we still must face the question whether he did so by applying consistent rules and principles that can be communicated to future leaders who might like to play this same role.

These explanations certainly point to the conclusion that the major and endur- ing principles to be derived from Madison's thoughts on federalism will have to be found in the context of a wider, extra-constitutional framework. In other words, Madison's federalism does not reduce itself to a simple set of rules or principles presumably derived from the constitutional language. Rather, it involves a com- plex of considerations not the least of which would appear to be transcendent and distinctly nonconstitutional considerations and goals. This is a matter to which we shall return by way of discussing his legacy.

The Compound Republic

We do not mean to imply in the foregoing that there was no theoretical justifi- cation based on constitutional grounds for Madison's reversal. On the contrary, as we have taken care to point out, there did exist a theoretical framework to accommodate his position, elements of which he himself had set forth in *The Federalist* during his nationalist days. With the bank issue what we witness, in effect, is Madison jumping from one approach to state-national relations to an- other. And having chosen, in Brant's words, "the narrow path," Madison could find justification for it in *The Federalist*. However, this "narrow" approach, though at first glance theoretically more attractive than that of the nationalists, on further examination gives rise to problems and concerns that were never satisfac- torily resolved in *The Federalist* and still remain very much with us today.

A convenient point of departure for surveying the key components of this framework, as well as how it differs from the old, is Federalist 39. This essay represents his most comprehensive overview of the proposed system from the vantage point of its federal character, and it also points to the theoretical problems and difficulties to which we have referred.

In Federalist 39, Madison sets out to answer "the adversaries of the proposed Constitution" who argue that its Framers did not preserve the "federal form, which regards the Union as a *Confederacy* of sovereign states"; that, instead, they established a "*national* government, which regards the Union as a *consolidation* of the States" (196). The first thing we note about this passage is Madison's use of the term "federal."[32] For him, as for the Founding Fathers, the words "federal" and "confederal" or "confederacy" were used interchangeably. Likewise, for Madison and others of the time, the terms "national" or "consolidated" were used to describe governments that we today would call unitary—systems wherein sovereignty resides in the central government. Today, of course, we use the term "federal," at least with regard to our constitutional system, to denote a division of sovereignty between the state and national governments. This terminological difficulty manifests the novelty of our constitutional arrangement in this respect; that is, at the time of founding there was no generally accepted term to describe the distribution of authority between the central government and the component units (i.e., the states) such as that contemplated in the Constitution.[33]

Madison was quite aware of the "novelty of the undertaking." The Framers were, so to speak, trying to navigate in uncharted waters. While, he writes, "the existing Confederation is founded on principles which are fallacious"—so much so that it must be abandoned—"other confederacies which could be consulted as precedents, have been vitiated by the same erroneous principles." As a result, he observes, the history of confederacies "furnish[es] no other light than that of beacons, which give warning of the course to be shunned, without pointing out that which ought to be pursued" (37:182). In his last reflections on the nature of the system, written toward the very end of his life, he is to argue that for an understanding of the American political system it is necessary "to abandon the abstract and technical modes of expounding and designating its character; and to view it as laid down in the charter which constitutes it, as a system, hitherto without a model; neither a simple or a consolidated Government nor a Government altogether confederate." "The division and distribution of powers," he remarks, are "nowhere else to be found; a nondescript, to be tested and explained by itself alone."[34]

To answer critics of the proposed Constitution who had evidenced concern about its departure from the federal (confederal) principle and to determine its "real character," Madison proposes five tests: (a) "the foundation on which it is to be established"; (b) "the sources from which its ordinary powers are to be drawn"; (c) "the operation of those powers"; (d) "the extent of them"; and (e) "the authority by which future changes in the government are to be introduced" (39:196). Two of these tests—(a) and (d)—which relate to the foundations of the system and the extent of the powers of the national government, are to concern

---

[32]On this matter of usage see Martin Diamond, "What the Framers Meant by Federalism," *Essays on Federalism,* ed. George C. S. Benson (Claremont, California: The Institute for Studies in Federalism, 1962).

[33]Madison in Federalist 51 calls our republic "compound" (268). It could also be described as a "composite" of the confederal and national principles. But the fact is that no word existed to describe it.

[34]"Notes on Nullification," 1835–36. *Writings,* IX, 600–601.

Madison throughout his life. The other tests scarcely involve any problems or controversy at all. As for (b), since "the House of Representatives will derive its powers from the people; and the people will be represented in the same proportion, and on the same principle, as they are in the legislature of a particular state," the proposed system partakes of a national character. But the Senate, wherein there is provision for equality of state representation—a recognition of the states "as political and coequal societies"—embodies the federal principle. Thus, with regard to test (b), the system is "mixed" since it embodies both the federal or confederal and national principles (39:197). Test (c) relating to the "operations" of the national powers is easily answered: because the national government will operate directly upon the individual citizens composing it, and not through the states as intermediaries, it is national in this regard. Test (e), though a bit more involved, poses no real difficulties. This method for change is not national because "the supreme and ultimate authority" does not "reside in the *majority* of the people of the Union." Nor is it federal, since the concurrence of each state is not necessary for alteration. As Publius puts this: "The mode provided by the plan of the convention is not founded on either" national or federal principles. Yet it does bear a cousinly resemblance to them. To the extent that the procedure requires the concurrence of an extra-majority of the states, "it departs from the *national* and advances towards the *federal* character." However, to the degree the process does not require unanimity among the states, "it loses again the *federal* and partakes of the *national* character" (39:198).

However, difficulties do arise with regard to tests (a) and (d). While there is an interrelationship between these two tests that accounts for a good deal of Madison's observations about federalism, we do best to begin by examining them separately. Turning first to (a), Madison writes that the foundation of the Union is "federal." In this respect, he notes, the "assent and ratification" to the Constitution is not to be given by the people as "comprising one entire nation, but as composing the distinct and independent States to which they respectively belong" (39:196). At first blush this would suggest that the Constitution is a compact between sovereign and equal states very much along the lines of the Articles. A closer examination of why Madison labels the foundation "federal," however, does not support this view. In context he is applying the term "federal" to the mechanics of ratification; that is, it is through state conventions specially elected and convened that the Constitution is to be ratified. This mode of procedure is consonant with the federal principle. But the parties to the Constitution are not the states operating in their political capacities, the arrangement under the Articles. On the contrary, Madison is clear throughout his discussion on the crucial point: "the Constitution is to be founded on the assent and ratification of the people of America," not the states as political entities. "It is to be," he affirms, "the assent and ratification of the several States, derived from the supreme authority in each State—the authority of the people themselves" (39:196).[35]

---

[35]John Marshall in *McCulloch v. Maryland* puts this matter quite lucidly in rejecting the Maryland

Though at times unduly vague, Madison is consistent throughout his career in maintaining that the Constitution is founded on the "assent and ratification" of the people. True enough, the Virginia Resolutions, which Madison authored to denounce the Alien and Sedition Acts, assert the "right" of the states "to interpose" their authority "for arresting the progress of the evil, for maintaining, within the respective limits, the authorities, rights, and liberties pertaining to them"—a "right" that devolves from the position that "the powers of the federal government" result "from the compact to which the states are parties."[36] But in the Virginia Report, which he wrote by way of justifying these Resolutions against the criticisms of other states, he clarifies this matter. He notes here that the word "state" is used in different senses in different contexts: "it sometimes means the separate sections of territory occupied by the political societies within each; sometimes the particular governments established by those societies; sometimes those societies as organized into those particular governments; and lastly, it means the people composing those political societies, in their highest sovereign capacity." And, he continues, "whatever different construction of the term 'states,' in the resolution, may have been entertained, all will at least concur in the last mentioned; because in that sense the Constitution was submitted to the 'states;' they are consequently parties to the compact from which the powers of the federal government result."[37] Nevertheless, we hasten to add, while this clarification does render him consistent concerning the foundations of the union, we should not conclude that his arguments concerning interposition are constitutionally sound. Quite the contrary. As we shall see, this clarification undercuts the theoretical ground upon which the Resolutions are based. (See, for instance, note 69.)

This conception of the foundations of the Constitution and the national government played a critical role in his repudiation of the doctrine of nullification as it was advanced by South Carolina. During his final reflections on the nature of the union, he argues: "The main pillar of nullification is the assumption that sovereignty is a unit, at once indivisible and unalienable; that the states therefore indi-

---

contention that the Constitution is a compact between the states. "It would be difficult to sustain [Maryland's] proposition. The convention which framed the Constitution was, indeed, elected by the state legislatures. But the instrument, when it came from their hands, was a mere proposal, without obligation, or pretensions to it. It was reported to the then existing Congress of the United States, with a request that it might 'be submitted to a convention of delegates, chosen in each state, by the people thereof, under the recommendation of its legislature, for their assent and ratification.' This mode of proceeding was adopted; and by the convention, by Congress, and by the state legislatures, the instrument was submitted to the people. They acted upon it, in the only manner in which they can act safely, effectively, and wisely, on such a subject, by assembling in convention. It is true, they assembled in their several states; and where else should they have assembled? No political dreamer was ever wild enough to think of breaking down the lines which separate the states, and of compounding the American people into one common mass. Of consequence, when they act, they act in their states. But the measures they adopt do not, on that account, cease to be the measures of the people themselves, or become the measures of the state governments." 4 Wheaton 403 (1819).

[36]Elliot, IV, 528.
[37]Ibid., 547.

vidually retain it entirely as they originally held it, and, consequently that no portion of it can belong to the U.S." "But," he asks rhetorically, "is not the Constitution itself necessarily the offspring of a sovereign authority? What but the highest political authority, could make such a Constitution?" He answers that the "sovereignty" that created such a Constitution "resides not in a single state but in the people of each of the several states, uniting with those of the others in the express and solemn compact which forms the Constitution."[38] Nor, in this connection, could Madison entertain the proposition implicit in nullification, namely, "that . . . every party to a compact, has a right to take for granted, that its construction is the infallible one, and to act upon it against the construction of all others, having an equal right to expound the instrument, nay against the regular exposition of the constituted authorities, with the tacit sanction of the community." This "doctrine" he termed "subversive of all constitutions, all laws, and all compacts."[39] What is more, from his vantage point, the proponents of nullification were forced to deny reality to support their position; that is, they had to look upon the Constitution as "a treaty, a league, or at most a confederacy among nations, as independent and sovereign, in relation to each other, as before the charter which calls itself a Constitution was formed."[40]

Despite this, we must note, Madison did not deny the right of a state to rebel against national authority. In answering the question what remedies are available "against the usurpation of power" by the national government other than the "right of the States individually to annul or resist them," he responds that, if recourse to constitutional processes should fail (e.g., "Ballotboxes & Hustings"), "and the power usurped be sustained in its oppressive exercise on a minority by a majority, the final recourse to be pursued by the minority, must be a subject of calculation, in which the degree of oppression, the means of resistance, the consequences of its failure, and consequences of its success must be the elements." In this case, the minority would have no choice "but to rally to its reserved rights . . . and to decide between acquiescence and resistance, according to the calculations above stated."[41] But the right in question is not, perforce, a constitutional right; it is found in a higher authority, according to Madison, "the law of nature and of nature's God."[42]

As Marvin Meyers notes, the Virginia Resolutions did serve to drive the national debate at a critical juncture in our history to "the roots of political order and the nature of the Union."[43] Moreover, they opened up a line of argument that

[38]"Notes on Nullification." *Writings*, IX, 600–601.

[39]Ibid., 599.

[40]Ibid., 588.

[41]Ibid., 597–98.

[42]Ibid., 598–99.

[43]Meyers, op. cit., xxxviii. What is more, in suggesting that state legislatures can speak for the constituent majorities within the states, Madison helped lay the groundwork for nullification. See text below on this point.

was highly susceptible to exploitation by the later proponents of nullification. Nevertheless, Madison's view of the founding, consistent throughout his career, provided no theoretical support for these proponents. On the contrary, his conception of founding can be considered the major centripetal "force" in his theory of federalism.

THE PROBLEM OF DIVIDED SOVEREIGNTY

Where real difficulties do arise, as our discussion of founding intimates, is over test (d), the "extent" of the powers of the national government. It is with respect to this concern that we see the full dimensions of Madison's change of views concerning the nature of the Union. Significant portions of his analysis in Federalist 39 seem to be fully compatible with the positions and thoughts expressed in his second phase. For instance, he does tell us with respect to this test that the government is not "national"—i.e., unitary— in character. "The idea of a national government," he writes, "involves in it, not only an authority over the individual citizens, but an indefinite supremacy over all persons and things, so far as they are objects of lawful government." In such systems, he points out, "all local authorities are subordinate to the supreme; and may be controlled, directed, or abolished by it at pleasure." But, because the jurisdiction of the "proposed government extends to certain enumerated objects only, and leaves the several States a residuary and inviolable sovereignty over all other objects," it "cannot be deemed a national one" (39:19). Only in the final paragraph of the essay does he come around to labeling the new government "federal" with respect to extent of powers.[44]

At various points in his writings, Madison has occasion to recur to a notion of "divided sovereignty" that derives from his conception of the extent of national powers. In his "Notes on Nullification," for instance, he writes that "the constitutions of the States, made by the people as separated into States, were made by a sovereign authority residing in each of the States, to the extent of the objects embraced by their respective constitutions. And if the states be thus sovereign, though short of so many of the essential attributes of sovereignty, the United States by virtue of the sovereign attributes with which they are endowed, may, to that extent, be sovereign, tho' destitute of the attributes of which the States are not shorn."[45] On this point, he maintains that "those who deny the possibility of a political system, with a divided sovereignty like that of the U.S. must choose between a government purely consolidated, and an association of Governments

---

[44]What students of *The Federalist* have not, to our knowledge, noted is that Madison is clearly in error in labeling the extent of powers "federal." Obviously, by his own standards, it is neither "federal" nor "national." If it were truly "federal," then the extent of powers would be determined by the states. Madison's error is understandable in light of the fact that, as we have noted, no word existed to describe the power relationship he sets forth.

[45]"Notes on Nullification." *Writings,* IX, 600.

purely federal,'' two forms that have in his view proved fatally defective over the course of history. Our ''compound system,'' ''partly federal and partly consolidated,'' he goes on to say, ''has been successful beyond any of the forms of Government, ancient or modern, with which it may be compared.''[46]

Madison, writing in *The Federalist*, tells us something about the character or nature of the residual powers of the states. As we might expect, he is not too specific. In Federalist 10, for example, he envisions the ''great and aggregate interests being referred to the national government, the local and particular to the State legislatures'' (47). In most cases he indicates the scope and nature of the states' residual powers by spelling out in some detail the powers of the national government. His most definitive statement concerning this division is to be found in Federalist 45:

> The powers delegated by the proposed Constitution to the federal government are few and defined. Those which are to remain in the States are numerous and indefinite. The former will be exercised principally on external objects, as war, peace, negotiation, and foreign commerce; with which last the power of taxation will, for the most part, be connected. The powers reserved to the several States will extend to all objects which, in the ordinary course of affairs, concern the lives, liberties, and properties of the people, and the internal order, improvement, and property of the States (238).[47]

While there are obvious problems associated with this concept of ''divided sovereignty,'' some of which we will discuss later, we may provisionally note one aspect of this matter that is not so obvious: the divided sovereignty, as pictured by Madison, may be accepted as a fact; yet, there are different ways of looking at this fact in formulating a conception of the relative constitutional powers of the state and national governments. Proof of this is that Hamilton, writing in Federalist 9, seemed to share the conception of divided sovereignty that Madison advanced in Federalist 39. ''The proposed Constitution,'' in his words, ''so far from implying an abolition of the State governments, makes them a constituent part of the national sovereignty . . . and leaves in their possession certain exclusive and very important portions of sovereign powers'' (41).[48] But Hamilton surely did not come to look upon this division in the same way as Madison, namely, as a limi-

---

[46]Ibid., 605–6.

[47]Of this particular passage Irving Brant writes: ''Quoted out of context, as it has been many times, this appears to carry Madison's strict construction back to the *Federalist* papers. In reality he was minimizing the sacrifice of state sovereignty in order to bulwark [*sic*] a doctrine of implied powers as broad as Marshall's'' (III, 182). Brant, in our view, is correct in his assessment. Nevertheless, we are still left to deal with the matter of the states' ''inviolable sovereignty.'' It seems evident that Madison wanted to avoid spelling out the contents of that sovereignty.

[48]Hamilton may have been referring here to the states' role in constituting the national government. For example, he might have viewed the state legislatures as exercising a portion of sovereignty in electing senators. However, in context, Madison's ''inviolable sovereignty'' seems to be of another order.

tation on the extent of the exercise of the delegated powers of the national government.

Beyond this, as our previous remarks would suggest, it is doubtful—despite Madison's assertion to the contrary—that the states' residual powers could be considered "inviolable." At the very least, Madison's theory as set forth in *The Federalist* points to a "tension" on this score, for, as we have seen, it cannot entertain the notion of any limits on the exercise of powers necessary for the national defense. And we can readily imagine the national government intruding upon the states' domain, and legitimately so, to defend the Union against foreign attack. However, and very much to the point, Madison did not conceive of the national government's having a blank check; that is, he recognized that the first clause of Article I, Section 8, which authorizes Congress "To lay and collect Taxes, Duties, Imposts, and Excises, to pay the Debts, and provide for the common Defense and general Welfare of the United States," could be (and, indeed, was by certain Antifederalists) interpreted to provide the national government with "an unlimited commission to exercise every power which may be alleged to be necessary for the common defense or general welfare" (41:214). In other words, such an interpretation, he believed, would render the system virtually unitary with respect to extent of powers. Consequently, he seems keen on refuting any such reading: "For what purpose," he asks, "could the enumeration of particular powers be inserted, if these and all others were meant to be included in the preceding general power?" By way of answering, he remarks, "Nothing is more natural or common than first to use a general phrase, and then to explain and qualify it by a recital of particulars." Thus, he contends, the particulars or enumerated powers can be exercised in accordance with the goals or intent expressed in the "general phrase" (41:215).

Madison also employs the "inadmissible latitude of construction" principle in his criticism of Marshall's decision in *McCulloch v. Maryland*. His argument is not that Marshall reached the wrong conclusion concerning the constitutionality of the national bank—a position that he could hardly take since he had, as President, switched sides on this measure. Rather, he argues that the test developed by Marshall in determining the legitimate extent of national powers was far too "broad" and "pliant." Specifically, he objected to the "high sanction given to a latitude in expounding the Constitution which seems to break down the landmarks intended by a specification of the Powers of Congress, and to substitute for a definite connection between means and ends, a Legislative discretion as to the former to which no practical limit can be assigned." "Ends and means," he observes, "may shift their character at the will and according to the ingenuity of the Legislative Body. What is an end in one case may be a means in another; nay in the same case, may be either an end or a means at the Legislative option."[49] In this regard, he felt that a major source of "the error in expounding the Constitu-

---

[49]Letter to Spencer Roane, September 2, 1819. *Writings,* XIII, 448.

tion'' is to be found ''in the use made of the species of sovereignty implied in the nature of government''; namely, that ''the specified powers vested in Congress . . . are sovereign powers, and that as such they carry with them an unlimited discretion as to the means of executing them.'' But, Madison is quick to point out, ''limited government may be limited in its sovereignty as well with respect to the means as to the objects of its powers; and that to give an extent to the former superseding the limits to the latter, is in effect to convert a limited into an unlimited Government.'' In this respect, he held that there is a ''reasonable medium between expounding the Constitution with the strictness of a penal law, or other ordinary statute, and expounding it with a laxity which may vary its essential character, and encroach on the local sovereignties with which it was meant to be reconcilable.''[50]

Madison, in his post-nationalist phase, makes good use of the proposition that no phrase or clause of the Constitution should be interpreted in such a way as to give the national government an ''unlimited commission.'' The most notable of these is probably his veto in 1817 of an internal improvements bill, one of his last acts as President. In his veto message, which also constituted his farewell message, he warned that an improper interpretation of the ''common Defense and general Welfare'' clause would give Congress ''a general power of legislation instead of the defined and limited one'' intended. Citing the ''supreme Law of the Land'' clause, he contended that such an interpretation ''would have the effect of subjecting both the Constitution and the laws of the several States in all cases not specifically exempted to be superseded by laws of Congress.''[51] Towards the end of his message, he applies the same principle in more general terms: he cannot see how the power for internal improvements can ''be deduced from any part'' of the express powers ''without an inadmissible latitude of construction.'' And without ''adequate landmarks'' he feared that ''the permanent success of the Constitution'' which ''depended on a definite partition of powers between the General and the State Governments'' would be endangered.[52]

THE FINAL SAY: NATION OR STATES?

From what we have said to this point, we can readily see that Madison's task in preserving the divided sovereignty would have been easier if he could have substantively identified those portions of ''inviolable sovereignty'' retained by the states.[53] This is to say, if he could somehow draw a line between the two jurisdictions, then the task of maintaining the proper division would be immensely

---

[50]Ibid., 451–52.

[51]Veto Message, March 3, 1817. *Writings,* XIII, 387.

[52]Ibid., 388.

[53]We may construe one line of argument employed by Madison as an effort to delineate the national and state powers; namely, if the means derived from the ''necessary and proper'' clause to

facilitated. More concretely, in his criticisms of Marshall, he seems to advance the proposition that the states' residual powers or authority do place limitations on the means that the national government may use in executing its delegated powers. Yet, he does not specify what these residual powers are. But, it seems clear that coming to the "reasonable medium" he calls for would be far easier with at least some specification of areas within the sovereign domain of the states. What seems equally clear, moreover, is that Madison was fully aware of the impossibility of spelling out a substantive division or allocation of powers between the state and national governments, just as he could perceive the futility of attempting "a positive enumeration of the powers necessary and proper" for the exercise of delegated powers (44:232). This, it would seem, accounts for the fact that, when he writes of the division of powers, he does so in general, not specific, terms. Indeed, he speaks not so much of powers but of the different objectives, goals, and purposes of the two jurisdictions.

But if the powers cannot be substantively divided so that the parties have a pretty clear idea of where they stand relative to one another, then the answer to maintaining a division must be sought by providing procedures to settle differences as they arise. And, returning to Federalist 39, we see that Madison, immediately after writing of the states' "residual and inviolable sovereignty," turns to the crucial matter of how controversies should be settled. Here he declares that "the tribunal which is ultimately to decide, is to be established under the general government." This, he is quick to add, "does not change the principle of the

---

carry out the end seems "greater," more significant or sweeping, than the end to be achieved, then the presumption must be that the national government does not possess the constitutional authority to employ the means. Otherwise, so the argument goes, the Framers would have expressly granted the national government the authority to utilize the means.

This line of argument, however, was not without pitfalls for Madison. For instance (see note 57), Madison believed the tariff and commerce powers authorized the Congress to pursue policies that would encourage domestic manufactures. To the objection that "the Constitution might easily have been made more explicit and precise" regarding this authority, he responds: "the same remark might be made on so many other parts of the instrument, and, indeed, on so many parts of every instrument of a complex character, that, if completely obviated, it would swell every paragraph into a page and every page into a volume; and, in so doing, have the effect of multiplying the topics for criticism and controversy." Letter to Joseph C. Cabell, October 30, 1828. *Writings,* IX, 325.

While an examination of Madison's views on such matters as inherent powers is only at second remove related to our purpose here, we should also note that he was not entirely consistent in adhering to the "strict" constructionism commonly attributed to him. According to Burns: "The records of the State Department proved that West Florida had not been ceded by Spain to France along with Louisiana in 1800, and consequently could not have been sold to the United States by the French three years later. Even Napoleon himself finally advised the American government that it did not have the shadow of a claim to support its contentions. But these considerations did not deter Madison. He was convinced that West Florida 'was essential to our interest.' In the summer of 1810 a revolution, engineered by Americans, broke out in the province. A declaration of independence was issued, followed by a request for annexation to the United States. Soon afterward Madison issued a proclamation taking formal possession of the disputed territory, thereby completing what has been called 'the most disgraceful diplomatic transaction of our history'" (Burns, 19–20).

case''; this tribunal is to decide controversies "impartially . . . according to the rules of the Constitution." To secure this impartiality, he writes, "all the usual and most effective precautions have been taken." Such a "tribunal," he concludes, "is clearly essential to prevent an appeal to the sword and a dissolution of the compact; and that it ought to be established under the general rather than under the local governments . . . is a position not likely to be combated" (198).[54]

It is with regard to the issues raised in this passage that the major difficulties associated with Madison's "second phase" federalism seem to arise. In the first place, it seems a bit disingenuous for him to maintain that the controversies are to be settled "according to the rules of the Constitution." This suggests that the Constitution does contain known rules for the resolution of such conflicts that the tribunal can and should apply. But, save for very obvious and flagrant cases—and these, in the nature of the case, would usually involve state encroachment on national authority—it is difficult to discern any such rules. To see this we need only take important areas where conflict could easily have been foreseen. For instance, what rules does the Constitution set forth for the impartial resolution of state-national conflicts that arise over the meaning of the "necessary and proper" clause? Or what rules do we find for impartially determining the scope and nature of the commerce power relative to the residual powers of the states? In any event, as we have already seen, integral to any dispute over the proper boundaries between state and national jurisdictions is the issue of what "tests" or rules ought to be employed. This is to say, if agreement could be reached over the rules for the settlement of disputes, controversies between the jurisdictions would substantially subside. Indeed, to the extent any such rules could be refined, such conflict might conceivably disappear altogether. In short, Madison, in referring to such rules, seems to beg the question.

We can look at the passage in another light that would, at first glance, seem to make more sense; namely, by "rules of the Constitution" Madison was referring simply to procedures called for by the Constitution; that is, for example, disputes are to be settled by a national authority, not by the states. But looking at the phrase from this perspective is not without enormous drawbacks. The fact is that Madison, even writing as Publius, is not at all unambiguous about how disputes should be settled. Quite the contrary. We need only recall here his position in Federalist 46, namely that the jurisdictional lines "will not depend merely on the comparative ambition or address of the different governments." Rather, he holds, "the

---

[54]It is not at all clear from this passage that Madison is referring to the Supreme Court in his reference to "some such tribunal." It would appear that he wants to avoid a forthright statement to the effect that the Supreme Court will be the final arbiter. And the phrase "ought to be established" is also somewhat puzzling since the Court *is* established by the Constitution. Indeed, one could read this passage to mean that an impartial tribunal will be established by the national government once the system is set in operation. However, in his later writings, Madison does maintain that the "tribunal" to which he refers in this passage is the Supreme Court. See text below.

ultimate authority, wherever the derivative may be found, resides in the people alone. Truth, no less than decency requires that the event in every case should be supposed to depend on the sentiments and sanction of the common constituents.'' And, beyond this, he writes: ''If . . . the people should in future become more partial to the federal than to the State governments, the change can only result from such manifest and irresistible proofs of better administration, as will overcome all their antecedent propensities'' toward the state governments. If this does turn out to be the case, he does not believe the people should ''be precluded from giving most of their confidence where they may discover it to be most due'' (241).

We have, then, on the face of it, two answers to the procedural question of who should decide: a tribunal, presumably the Supreme Court, or the common constituents. It might be argued, of course, that Madison really provides only one answer: he believed that the Supreme Court should make an initial ruling that the ''common constituents'' could overturn through the amendment process, if they so desired. But this interpretation seems most unlikely, because it is an open invitation to frequent debate about fundamental constituent principles, a debate that could only undermine public confidence in the Constitution. On this matter, the words of Federalist 49 are quite relevant: ''The danger of disturbing the public tranquility by interesting too strongly the public passions, is a still more serious objection against a frequent reference of constitutional questions to the decision of the whole society'' (260).

But if, as seems likely, the ''common constituent'' solution does not mean the people acting in their constituent capacity (i.e., amending the Constitution), then we must ask: How or by what means are the common constituents to settle these jurisdictional disputes? How are they to adjust the boundary line between the national and state authorities? The most obvious answer would seem to be through Congress, since it is the only institution that can be said to represent the common constituents. This, of course, would be to lend a presumptive legitimacy to whatever decision Congress—the institution most likely to encroach upon the states' domain—may make concerning the extent of national powers vis-à-vis the states. This would oblige those who might contend that the national government has overstepped its bounds to make their case in the political arena in hopes of persuading Congress to reverse itself. What this means, in turn, is that Madison looked upon the disputes surrounding state-national relations as primarily political issues to be settled through distinctly political, not judicial or constituent, processes. Such a solution is certainly consonant with Madison's nationalistic views and, in slightly different form, it comes to play a significant role in his second phase thinking.

While this solution is tantamount to making Congress, the chief repository of national powers, the judge of the extent, Madison, writing as Publius, did not see any real dangers to the states' residual sovereignty resulting from this. Indeed, as we have already noted, he believed the common constituents would have a distinct propensity to favor the states over the national government should there be any conflict. Certain of his points in this respect are noteworthy in light of his later thoughts concerning state-national relations. On one side, Madison believed that "the prepossessions, which the members of Congress will carry into the federal government, will generally be favorable to the States." Congress under the Articles, he observes, paid "an undue attention to the local prejudices, interests, and views of the particular States" (46:242). And, while he sees every prospect that the new national government "will . . . embrace a more enlarged plan of policy," its members surely will "be disinclined to invade the rights of the individual States, or the prerogatives of their governments." However, he does not believe such a "reciprocal" disinclination would be found in state governments bent upon augmenting "their prerogative by defalcation from the federal government" (46:242).

But what if the national government were to "feel an equal disposition with the State government to extend its power beyond the due limits"? (46:242) Madison answers this question at some length and provides still another, though distinctly nonconstitutional, solution to state-national controversies. He notes that, "should an unwarrantable measure of the federal government be unpopular in particular States, which would seldom fail to be the case, or even a warrantable measure be so, which may sometimes be the case, the means of opposition to it are powerful and at hand" (46:242). "The disquietude of the people; their repugnance, and, perhaps, refusal to cooperate" coupled with "the frowns of the executive magistracy of the State" and "embarrassments created by legislative devices" would pose difficulties "in any State" and "very serious impediments" "in a large State." And if, he continues, "several adjoining States" were to act "in unison," they would "present obstructions which the federal government would hardly be willing to encounter" (46:243).

The situation, from Madison's perspective, could only worsen if the federal government were to undertake "ambitious encroachments . . . on the authority of the State government." Such encroachments, he writes, "would be signals of general alarm. Every government would espouse the common case. A correspondence would be opened. Plans of resistance would be concerted. One spirit would animate and conduct the whole. The same combinations, in short, would result from an apprehension of the federal, as was produced by the dread of a foreign, yoke; and unless the projected innovations should be voluntarily renounced, the same appeal to a trial of force would be made in the one case as was made in the other." Yet, Madison can scarcely envision this occurring: "Who," he asks, "would be the parties" in such a showdown? He answers: "A few representatives of the people would be opposed to the people themselves; or rather one set of representatives would be contending against thirteen sets of representatives, with the whole body of their common constituents on the side of the latter" (46:243).

Madison, not content to rest his case on these grounds alone, turns to the "visionary supposition that the federal government might over time set out to accumulate a military force for the projects of ambition." Aside from arguing that the national government could not conceivably raise an army large enough for this purpose, he ridicules the notion that ''the people and the States should, for a sufficient period of time, elect an uninterrupted succession of men ready to betray both; that the traitors should, throughout this period, uniformly and systematically pursue some fixed plan for the extension of the military establishment; that the governments and the people of the States should silently and patiently behold the gathering storm, and continue to supply the materials, until it should be prepared to burst on their own heads'' (46:244). In sum, he holds that ''the federal government'' under the forms of the proposed Constitution ''is sufficiently dependent on the people'' and that ''it will be restrained'' by this ''dependence from forming schemes obnoxious to their constituents'' (46:245).

THE FINAL SAY: COURTS OR CONGRESS?

As we have indicated, all of the theoretical difficulties that flow from *The Federalist* manifest themselves in Madison's second phase. To be sure, they take on an added complexity, but in the last analysis they come down to a search for a suitable procedure or process for settling controversies within his system of divided sovereignty. As we might expect, it is a search in which we find Madison again shifting ground, so much so that he appears to provide no definitive answer to this critical concern. This can best be illustrated by examining some of his salient positions.

We can fruitfully begin with his 1831 response to the charge of inconsistency leveled against him for assenting as President (1817) to the creation of a national bank. In this response he argues that an authoritative status attaches to constitutional interpretations that are grounded on a seemingly enduring consensus that finds expression in the political branches of the national government. In maintaining this, he of course has to face up to a theoretical question that arises from his conception of the Constitution as binding and fundamental law; namely, having sworn to uphold the Constitution, was he not bound, as President, to adhere to ''his own construction of it,'' however different that construction might be from the ''consensual'' construction?[55] This he answers by contending that even the ''most ardent theorist'' would ''find it impossible to adhere, and act officially upon, his solitary opinions as to the meaning of the law or Constitution, in opposition to a construction reduced to practice during a reasonable period of time; more especially when no prospect existed of a change of construction by the public or its agents.'' In effect, he argues, ''the true and safe construction of a constitution'' is to be found in ''the uniform sanction of successive legislative bodies, through a period of years . . . under . . . varied parties,'' rather than in ''the opinions of every new Legislature'' which may fall under the spell of ''the

---

[55]Letter to Charles Jared Ingersoll, June 25, 1831. *Letters and Other Writings of James Madison,* ed. William C. Rives and Philip R. Fendall, (New York: R. Worthington, 1884), IV, 185.

spirit of party'' or the ''eloquence and address of popular statesmen, themselves, perhaps, under the influence of the same misleading causes.''[56]

More specifically with regard to the national bank, he notes that its original foundation had been the subject of ''ample discussion in its passage through the several branches.'' Moreover, during its twenty years of existence it had received ''annual legislative recognition'' and ''the entire acquiesence of all local authority, as well as of the nation at large.'' He concludes: ''a veto from the Executive under these circumstances, with an admission of the expediency and almost necessity of the measure, would have been a defiance of all obligations derived from a course of precedents amounting to the requisite evidence of the national judgment and intention.''[57]

Yet, in the very same year that Madison signed the bank bill, he saw fit—as we have remarked previously—to veto the internal improvements bill on virtually the same grounds he took in his original opposition to the bank. In his veto message, however, he is evidently concerned with the matter of precedents and consent. Aside from remarking that the ''power to construct roads and canals'' cannot be derived from the Constitution without ''an inadmissible latitude of construction,'' he also notes that the ''assent of the States,'' as provided for in the bill, cannot extend the powers of Congress into areas beyond those ''specified and provided for in the Constitution.''[58] Nor could Madison find sufficient ''precedent'' for the assumption of such a power despite the fact that during the Jefferson administration he had personally overseen extensive internal improvement projects. In this instance Madison holds that the national government can secure this power only through the amendment process.[59]

---

[56]Ibid., 185–86.

[57]Ibid., 186. Madison uses the same argument to support the position that the Congressional power ''to lay and collect taxes, duties, and excises'' along with the power ''to regulate commerce with foreign nations'' conveys the authority to encourage domestic manufactures. After noting that this was the understanding of the members of the ''first session of the first Congress'' many of whom ''had been members of the federal Convention,'' he writes: ''A further evidence in support of the Congress's power to protect and foster manufactures by regulation of trade, an evidence that ought of itself to settle the question, is the uniform and practical sanction given to the power, by the General Government for nearly 40 years with a concurrence or acquiesence of every State Government throughout the same period; and it may be added through all the vicissitude of Party, which marked the period.'' To this he adds, ''And may it not be fairly left to the unbiased judgment of all men of experience and of intelligence, to decide which is most to be relied on for a sound and safe test of the meaning of a Constitution, a uniform interpretation by all the successive authorities under it, commencing with its birth, and continued for a long period, thro' the varied state of political contests, or the opinion of every new legislature heated as it may be by the strife of parties, or warped as often happens by the eager pursuit of some favorite object; or carried away possibly by the power of eloquence, or captivating address of a few popular Statesmen, themselves influenced, perhaps, by the same misleading causes.'' Letter to Joseph C. Cabell, September 18, 1828. *Writings*, IX, 333–34.

[58]Veto Message, March 3, 1817. *Writings*, XIII, 388.

[59]This instance shows the futility of trying to impose one's views of federalism on the system.

While his reversal on the bank issue does help us to determine what constitutes a lasting consensus among the common constituents regarding state-national boundaries, it also raises a number of questions and concerns, some of which are intensified by his veto of the internal improvements bill. To begin with, what is sufficient precedent for a given constitutional construction? After all, what seems clear is that Madison could easily have found ample precedent to sign the internal improvements bill had he been so inclined for the very reasons he advances in justification for reversing his position on the bank. Assuming precedent to be a legitimate consideration in judging of the constitutionality of a measure, unless we can specify what constitutes *sufficient* precedent with some degree of precision, it cannot very well serve the ends that Madison had in mind; namely, a high degree of certainty, stability, and continuity concerning the meaning of the Constitution which is necessary for a decent and orderly government characterized by liberty. We might find, as the very examples before us suggest, that what is sufficient precedent for one might not be so for another. Consequently, over a period of years marked by abrupt changes in partisan sentiment, grounds would exist for both claiming and denying the existence of sufficient precedents.

Similar concerns arise with determining what we have called the ''consensus'' among the common constituents. It would seem that, on the basis of what Madison writes in this regard, we have good reason to presume such a consensus if the political parties have held the same constitutional construction for a ''reasonable'' period of time. Yet, what if a sizeable minority of one of the parties—perhaps say, the representatives of a particular geographical region—has, over the years, consistently opposed the construction given by legislative majorities? Are we to say, then, that a consensus exists? Or do we make this determination, as Madison seems to suggest, on an estimate of the possibilities of ''a change in the public opinion''?

In addition to reliance on precedent and consensus as a means for fixing the proper state-national boundaries, Madison also perceived a role that the states might play. Because he was particularly anxious in the later part of his life to dissociate the Virginia Resolutions and Report which he authored from the doctrine of nullification advanced by South Carolina, he was compelled to differentiate, at least to some degree, the proper and improper constitutional modes of state protest against what the states considered to be intrusions on their authority. This endeavor can be viewed as a modification and refinement of his views presented in Federalist 46, where, as we have seen, he discusses the states' role in containing the national government.

In his ''Notes on Nullification,'' written during the last two years of his life, Madison contends that the Virginia Resolutions, far from justifying nullification,

---

Future Presidents and Congresses would come along with different views and, after they had worked their will, recourse could eventually be had to Madison's argument from ''precedent.''

were primarily intended to "produce a conviction everywhere . . . that the Constitution had been violated by the obnoxious [Alien and Sedition] acts and to procure a concurrence and cooperation of the other States in effectuating a repeal of the acts."[60] However, the text of the Resolutions suggests that its purpose went well beyond this rather modest political goal. Its third, and most controversial resolution, read: "that, in case of a deliberate, palpable, and dangerous exercise of other powers, not granted by the said compact [the Constitution], the states who are parties thereto have the right, and are in duty bound, to interpose, for arresting the progress of the evil, and for maintaining, within their limits, the authorities, rights, and liberties appertaining to them."[61] The seventh resolution appeals "to the like disposition in other states, in confidence that they will concur with this commonwealth in declaring, as it does hereby declare, that the acts aforesaid are unconstitutional; and that the necessary and proper measures will be taken, by each, for cooperating with this state, in maintaining, unimpaired, the authorities, rights, and liberties, reserved to the states respectively, or to the people."[62]

Madison in his "Notes on Nullification" dwells upon these resolutions to distinguish their meaning and intent from that of the nullification doctrine advanced by South Carolina. But his basic concern is a narrow one; namely, that his resolutions do not assert the right of a single state "to arrest or annul an act of the General Government which it may deem unconstitutional." Rather, he points out, throughout the Resolutions the right of the interposition is said to reside in the "States"—the plural, rather than singular, reference. To this effect, he writes: "by the rightful authority to interpose . . . was meant, not the authority of the States *singly* and *separately,* but their authority as the *parties* to the Constitution; the authority which, in fact, made the Constitution; the authority which being paramount to the Constitution was paramount to the authorities constituted by it, to the Judiciary as well as the other institutions." In this vein, he goes on, "There cannot be different laws in different states on subjects within the compact without subverting its fundamental principles, and rendering it as abortive in practice as it would be in theory." Indeed, he notes, "the persevering differences among the States on the constitutionality of Federal acts" would be sufficient to cause turmoil in the system.[63]

Madison's rejection of nullification and defense of the Virginia Resolutions does make sense on at least two grounds. The most obvious, of course, is that to acknowledge the right of nullification by a single state would undoubtedly lead to chaos ultimately destructive of the Union. Indeed, why he chose to direct his argument only against nullification by a *single* state is baffling since the same

---

[60]*Writings,* IX, 574–75.

[61]Elliot, IV, 528.

[62]Ibid., 529.

[63]"Notes on Nullification." *Writings,* IX, 576–77.

consequences would flow in rough proportion as the states are less than unanimous in nullifying a particular national law. Of greater significance in light of his other views on this matter is his defense of interposition on purely political grounds; that is, as a formal, structured, and organized protest. At this level he believes the effort resulted in ''a triumph over the obnoxious acts, and an apparent abandonment of them forever.'' And, while he concedes that some contend the Resolutions did not have this effect, he maintains that their impact ''may be safely left to the recollection of those who were co-temporary with the crisis, and to the researches of those who were not, taking for their guides the reception given to the proceedings by the Republican party everywhere, and the pains taken by it, in multiplying republications of them [the Virginia Resolutions] in newspapers and in other forms.''[64]

Beyond this there are very serious problems with interposition, so serious that it is highly doubtful that it could ever represent a workable means or method for the settlement of state-national tensions. On the practical side, it should be noted, interposition, however it might be exercised by a state, presumably could be resorted to only when all the states had come to agreement concerning its appropriateness or necessity. We say ''presumably'' because Madison is not exactly straightforward on this question. However, he does write of the states' interposing in ''their collective character as parties to and creators of the Constitution.''[65] His evident concern would seem to be providing for uniformity of law among the states in the interposition process in order to avoid the potential chaos inherent in the doctrine of nullification by a single state. To this point he writes that the purpose ''to be attained by the invited cooperation with Virginia'' was ''to maintain within the several States their respective authorities, rights, and liberties, which could not be constitutionally different in different States, not inconsistent with a sameness in the authority and laws of the U.S. in all and in each.''[66] In any event, Madison does not indicate that he believes anything short of unanimity— e.g., two-thirds or three-fourths of the states—is sufficient to ''trigger'' interposition.

Bearing this in mind, there is every reason to believe that interposition would never prove an effective barrier to national encroachments. It is hardly possible, for reasons that Madison spells out in *The Federalist*, that Congress would pass a law so blatantly intrusive that all of the states—or even three-fourths or two-

---

[64]Ibid., 595. One beneficial effect of interposition from Madison's point of view might be its bearing upon the establishment of ''precedent'' for the exercise of national power such as that he refers to in explaining his shift on the bank issues. Certainly, if a number of states were to interpose to protest a given policy or action, it would be difficult to argue at a future date that the policy enjoyed the kind of consensual support to which Madison refers.

[65]Ibid., 581.

[66]Ibid., 593–94.

thirds—would act to interpose. The negative reception accorded the Virginia Resolutions should have made this much abundantly clear to Madison, the more so
as he regarded his case against the national government as conclusive.[67] Moreover, reliance on interposition could well prove counterproductive from the states'
point of view; that is, if, perchance, the national government were intent on encroaching on the states, the unanimity (or extra-majority) requirement would
make it extremely difficult for the states to resist. What is more, the states' failure
to interpose effectively could be taken to bestow constitutionality on the questionable national laws. Thus, at this level, interposition would seem to be totally
inadequate for the very purposes Madison had in mind. In fact, to rely upon it
would serve to give the national government a relatively free hand in setting state-
national boundaries.

On the theoretical side, Madison contends that the import of the Virginia Resolution was "to show that the authority to interpose existed, and was a resort
beyond that of the Supreme Court . . . or any authority derived from the Constitution."[68] However, in his depiction of the process there is a serious flaw that
stems from the fact that, if interposition proceeds from the state legislatures in the
manner he suggests, then it is the state governments, not the constituent majorities
in the states, that are determining the division of authority. Clearly, given Madison's own conception of our constitutional foundations, the state governments
have no more authority to do this than the national government. What this means
is that, even if all the states were to agree to interpose, their subsequent actions
would lack constitutional sanction.[69]

Why Madison involved himself so deeply in such an exercise and why, afterwards, he sought to justify it on the grounds that he does is puzzling, particularly
in light of Article V which provides an easier and constitutional means of redress.
What is apparent is that his efforts to "fuse" the states into the process of resolving state-national controversies cannot be taken seriously from a constitutional
point of view. Save for the amendment process—and even here there are difficulties—the states, for all practical purposes, are constitutionally "locked" into the

---

[67]In his words, these acts were a "deliberate, palpable, and dangerous" exercise of powers by the
national government "not granted" by the Constitution. Elliot, IV, 547.

[68]"Notes on Nullification." *Writings,* IX, 592.

[69]As Edward Burns notes: "Madison was guilty of at least a minor inconsistency in his defense of
the ultimate right of the States collectively to interpret the division of sovereignty. The Virginia
Resolutions were adopted by the State legislature, and they had invited similar action by the legislatures of other States. The people in the States, however, not the State governments, were the parties
to the constitutional compact, according to his own contention" (150). Madison, as Burns remarks,
did admit as much to Jefferson in December 1798. Yet, in his "Notes on Nullification," he does not
bother to mention this "inconsistency."

From our vantage point this is hardly a "minor" inconsistency. Rather, it is further evidence that
this protest was motivated by distinctly political, not constitutional, concerns. What is more, it is not
at all insignificant because it does provide some ground for the doctrine of nullification; namely, that
a state legislature can pretend to speak for the constituent majorities within its state.

system at a decided disadvantage compared to the national government.[70] Nevertheless, much as he had in *The Federalist*, Madison looks upon the states as a political force that must somehow be factored into the final resolution. Viewed from this perspective, his doctrine of interposition makes sense: it provides an outlet for the expression of views from the states that prudent politicians at the national level would do well to heed. In the last analysis, to judge from what he does say about it in relation to the Alien and Sedition Acts, he did look upon interposition in this fashion.

Finally, Madison's views on the Court as an arbiter of state-national boundaries in his second stage retain the ambiguities we encountered in *The Federalist*. More than once he reaffirms and amplifies his position as set forth in Federalist 39. At one point, he maintains that "the provision immediately and ordinarily relied on" for the settlement of "controversies . . . concerning the partition line between the powers belonging to the Federal and State government . . . is manifestly the Supreme Court of the United States, clothed as it is with a jurisdiction 'in controversies to which the United States shall be a party' . . . and being so constituted as to render it independent and impartial in its decisions." He adds that "other and ulterior resorts" for the settlement of controversies "would remain, in the elective process, in the hands of the people themselves, the joining constituents of the parties, and in the provision made by the Constitution for amending itself."[71]

On another occasion he puts the Court's role in a wider context. To secure "the rights and powers of the States in their individual capacities, against an undue preponderance of the powers granted to the government over them in their united capacity, the Constitution has relied on, (1) the responsibility of the Senators and Representatives in the Legislature of the U.S. to the Legislatures and people of the states; (2) the responsibility of the President to the people of the U.S.; and (3) the liability of the Executive and Judicial functionaries of the U.S. to impeachment by the Representatives of the people of the States, in one branch of the Legislature . . . and trial by the Representatives of the States, in the other branch." While conceding that "time alone" will determine whether "this structure of Government" will operate to preserve the legitimate rights and powers of the states, he feels that thus far (1830) "sufficient control, in the popular will," has been exercised over the "Executive and Legislative Departments." Such, he notes, was the case with the Alien and Sedition Laws when "the first election that

---

[70]Toward the end of the Virginia Report he does acknowledge the amendment alternative. "It is no less certain that other means might have been employed which are strictly within the limits of the Constitution." Two-thirds of the state legislatures, he writes, "by an application to Congress" could "have obtained a convention" for the purpose of "an explanatory amendment to the Constitution." However, he glosses over the matter: "If the General Assembly, after declaring the two acts to be unconstitutional, (the first and most obvious proceeding on the subject,) did not undertake to point out to the other states a choice among the further measures that might become necessary and proper, the reserve will not be misconstrued by liberal minds into any culpable imputation." Elliot, IV, 579.

[71]Letter to N.P. Trist, February 15, 1830. *Writings*, IX, 358.

ensued after their passage put an end to them." Moreover, in his opinion, "whatever may have been the character of the other acts, in the judgment of many of us, it is but true, that they have generally accorded with the view of a majority of the States and of the people."[72]

Turning specifically to the Supreme Court in this context, he maintains that the "thirty-ninth number of *The Federalist*" embodies both the "prevailing view" at the time of founding and the "view that has continued to prevail" concerning the settlement of controversies between the national and state governments: namely, the Supreme Court is "the tribunal which is ultimately to decide." He is quick to add this "concession of . . . power to the Supreme Court, in cases falling within the course of its functions . . . has not always been rightly exercised." But, though the courts have on occasion rendered decisions "which have incurred serious and extensive disapprobation," Madison still gives the judiciary and, presumably, the Supreme Court, high marks: "with but few exceptions, the course of the Judiciary has been hitherto sustained by the predominant sense of the nation."[73]

In this context Madison was not so much concerned with the Court setting forth general principles or standards for determining state-national boundaries or restraining the national government, as with the capacity of the national government to enforce its laws uniformly among the states. He emphasizes "the utter inefficiency of a supremacy in a law of the land, without a supremacy in the exposition and execution of the law." What is more, he argues, without national judicial supremacy "all equipoise between the Federal Government and the State Governments" would be destroyed: "whilst the functions of the Federal Government are directly or indirectly elected by and responsible to the states, and the functionaries of the states are in their appointment and responsibility wholly independent of the U.S., no constitutional control of any sort belonged to the United States over the States." What is "evident" from this, according to Madison, is that without national judicial supremacy "it would be in the power of the States, individually, to pass unauthorized laws, and carry them into complete effect, anything in the Constitution and law of the U.S. to the contrary notwithstanding."[74]

What we see from the foregoing is that there are two aspects or dimensions of Madison's position regarding the role of the Court: one that deals with its role relative to the states; the other that concerns its authority relative to the other branches of the national government, principally Congress. The first of these, the one that Madison emphasizes here, is relatively free from difficulties. The Court, this is to say, is indispensable for the reasons that Madison sets forth. Yet, in Madison's view, the Court is obliged to nullify national laws that encroach upon the states' residual powers. But, in this respect, he does not advance our under-

---

[72]Letter to Edward Everett, August 1830. *Writings,* IX, 396–97.
[73]Ibid., 397.
[74]Ibid., 398.

standing of the principles, standards, norms, or doctrines the Court is to use in making its determinations much beyond what he writes in *The Federalist*.

Theoretical and practical problems beyond those raised in *The Federalist* do emerge, however, in his second phase. One very practical concern, and one that he notes in his Virginia Report, is "that there may be instances of usurped power, which the forms of the Constitution would never draw within the control of the judicial department." And still another, potentially more serious problem that he mentions in the same context is that "the judicial department," like the legislative and executive, "may exercise or sanction dangerous powers beyond the grant of the Constitution."[75] These difficulties, as we might expect, he brings to the fore by way of justifying his doctrine of interposition, a doctrine that, as we have seen, offers no effective remedy.

But the chief difficulty with Madison's position concerns, once again, the relationship between the Court and the people operating in their political capacities through the elective departments of the national government. Madison informs us, consistent with his *Federalist* views, that the political departments of the national government will rarely intrude upon the residual powers of the states. So we may assume that the Court would seldom have occasion to nullify a national law that might be the source of controversy. From another perspective, as we have also seen, he seems to judge the Court's record—and that of the political branches, too—by the degree to which its decisions have been "sustained by the sense of the nation."[76] Put another way, we may say that he evidenced some concern about the degree to which the Court's decisions fell within the boundaries of what can be termed the settled consensus of the common constituents as manifested over time in the political branches of the system, both state and national. For this reason, the question whether the Court's opinion *should* take precedence over this developed consensus is not easy to answer. Suppose, for instance, that Marshall in *McCulloch v. Maryland* had declared the national bank unconstitutional on the same grounds originally advanced by Representative Madison. What might the later Madison have said about such a decision in light of the reasons he advanced for his switch on the bank issue? Which decision, that of the common constituents expressed over time or that of the Court, would he have accepted as authoritative?

Leaving these and like questions to one side, we do know how he felt the state-national issues would be settled in practice. Consonant with his more general republican theory, he writes that "it is not probable that the Supreme Court would long be indulged in a career of usurpation opposed to the decided opinions and policy of the Legislature." Nor did he believe "Congress, seconded by Judicial Power" could, "without some change in the character of the nation, succeed in *durable* violations of the rights and authorities of the States." "But, what," he asks, "is to control Congress when backed and even pushed on by a majority of

---

[75]Elliot, IV, 549.
[76]Letter to Edward Everett, August 28, 1830. *Writings,* IX, 397.

their Constituents?'' His answer: ''Nothing within the pale of the Constitution but sound arguments and conciliatory expostulation addressed both to Congress and to their Constituents.''[77]

Madison's positions on this critical issue would lead us to believe that we must differentiate between theory and practice. In practice, as he remarks, the people acting through Congress will prevail, we may presume, because of the republican nature of the system (it will move where the greater ''weight'' carries it) and the central constitutional role of the Congress. At the level of constitutional theory he is somewhat ambiguous. He mentions amendments; a ''tribunal,'' the Supreme Court as it turns out; ''common constituents,'' (which would ''square'' the practical with the theoretical); a firm ''consensus,'' such as that which formed around the legitimacy of the national bank; and ''interposition.'' In no instance does he suggest that the states, save as they participate in the amendment or interposition processes, should have any say in the final resolution of disputes between the two jurisdictions. This is understandable. But, the role he suggests for national institutions—i.e., the Congress and the Supreme Court—as potential referees is not free from theoretical difficulties, since they can also be considered parties to the disputes or controversies they are called upon to settle. Nevertheless, as we see from his discussion of the Alien and Sedition Acts in particular, he seems to believe that the most effective remedy for encroachments by the national government is to be had through distinctly political processes at the national level, that is, through an appeal to the common constituents who will bring Congress back into line. ''In the last resort'' he writes in *The Federalist*: ''a remedy [for usurpation of powers by the national government] must be obtained from the people, who can, by the election of more faithful representatives, annul the acts of the usurpers'' (44:233).

MADISON: PROPONENT OF CONSENSUAL PROCESSES

As the foregoing should clearly indicate, there would seem to be insurmountable difficulties associated with rendering Madison's views on federalism consistent. They do not seem to fit into a coherent whole. Of course, we should hardly expect to find too much by way of consistency between his nationalist and postnationalist stages. But we do find some consistency, which is not altogether insignificant. We have already noted, for instance, that his conception of the foundations of the Union, though unnecessarily obscure in places, remains the same throughout and so, too, does his view of the role of the individual states in resolving federal disputes. His position regarding the ''general welfare'' clause does not change from that he set forth in *The Federalist* during his nationalist phase, though in practice he did deviate from it. And, it would be fair to say, he

---

[77]Letter to Spencer Roane, May 6, 1821. *Writings,* IX, 58–59.

was consistent throughout in his opposition to constitutional constructions that would, in effect, render the system consolidated or unitary.

Madison's real difficulties arise when he takes upon himself the defense of divided sovereignty. While this notion, as we have seen, runs through both stages of his thought, we perceive the problems it raises in terms of theoretical consistency most clearly in the second phase. Specifically, during his "shifting" period, Madison sought to justify divided sovereignty by pointing out the detrimental effects consolidation would have on values such as liberty, justice, and individual rights;[78] that is, on grounds that scarcely fit well with his extended republic theory to which he adhered throughout his life. Moreover, he never faces up to the difficulty that emerges in *The Federalist*: how viable can a system of divided sovereignty be when the national government is charged with the responsibility of providing for the common defense? Can the states, in other words, really possess "inviolable" portions of sovereignty without depriving the nation of its capacity for self-preservation?

But perhaps the greatest difficult encountered in Madison's thought is this: while he defends divided sovereignty, he does not provide us much by the way of transmissible rules and principles for the resolution of disputes between the national and state authorities. To be sure, he addresses this problem, but his answers do vary. Yet, in fairness to Madison and others who have wrestled with this issue, we should hardly have expected him to provide us with clear-cut or definitive answers. Today, even with the benefit of over two hundred years of experience, we still are no closer than Madison to formulating any such principles or standards. Indeed, if we take recent decades as our measure, we seem to have retrogressed: we still cling to the principle of federalism built upon Madison's notion of "divided sovereignty"—if, that is, we are to believe our American government textbooks—but in decision-making circles at the national level, concern about the states' portion of sovereignty, a matter of enormous concern for Madison, is clearly on the wane.

In the last analysis, the search for such rules and principles would appear to be futile. But this very futility is, in our judgment, the profoundest lesson to be derived from Madison's teachings on federalism; namely, we are forced to rely upon our own best resources for resolving jurisdictional disputes. Put otherwise, while the Constitution more or less forces us into resolving these conflicts, it does

---

[78]In the Virginia Report, he declares that an "inevitable result . . . of a consolidation of the states into one sovereignty would be to transform the republican system of the United States into a monarchy." Elliot, IV, 553. In his "Notes on Nullification" he maintains, "It becomes all . . . who are friends of a Government based on free principles to reflect, that by denying the possibility of a system partly federal and partly consolidated, and who would convert ours into one either wholly federal or wholly consolidated, in neither of which forms have individual rights, public order, and external safety, been all duly maintained, they aim a deadly blow at the last hope of true liberty on the face of the Earth." *Writings,* IX, 606.

not provide us with rules or principles for doing so. We are left to our own devices, within, of course, the general boundaries provided by the Constitution.

Now Madison does not leave us completely in the dark over how we should go about settling the perennial disputes over the "line." At the very least he identifies, either expressly or by clear implication, conditions or processes that are important for a satisfactory resolution of differences over the proper boundaries. The most important of these would seem to be those that hold out the prospect of insuring a stable consensus—a consensus that differs from others that emerge from our political processes because a wider and more fundamental complex of considerations and values must necessarily come into play. For instance, the participants are obliged to address themselves at some point to the constitutional issues involved and whatever consensus does emerge cannot be crafted in terms so broad as to have the effect of abrogating the constitutional principle that stands at the heart of the controversy.[79]

Still another aspect of this consensus would be its acceptance by the states. In this regard, Madison seemed to envision the states not only playing a role in shaping the view of the common constituents, but also in setting the broad limits within which the consensus would have to come to rest. Put otherwise, the views of the states would have to be taken very seriously because state reactions, even those far less extreme than Madison pictures in *The Federalist*, could well have an adverse effect on the implementation of national policy. Indeed, we can well imagine, given the terms in which Madison writes, that what a majority of common constituents want might have to be severely modified or even abandoned in the face of potential opposition by several states, particularly those in a contiguous geographical area. Thus, the stable consensus comprises something more than just the majority of the common constituents; in many instances, it also has to embody the attitudes that find expression through the agencies of the states.

To the extent that these observations conform with Madison's general approach—and we think they do—then we may say that he looked, in the main, to the distinctly political processes for setting the boundaries between national and state authority. This seems evident enough because only through the give-and-take of these processes can there be any guarantee or assurance that the outcome does represent a genuine consensus. Obviously, the Supreme Court, given its isolation from the actual give-and-take of politics, is ill-suited to take into account the various forces that must be accommodated to achieve a lasting consensus. What is more, the very nature of the judicial processes precludes measuring the relative intensities of the competing parties.

In saying this, we recognize that another view or interpretation of Madison's position is arguable; namely, he meant for the boundaries to be set by the Court over time, not through the consensual processes described above. In this view,

---

[79]Here we are speaking of a "consensus" not unlike that which he perceived for the support of domestic manufactures and the incorporation of a national bank.

which prevails today, the Court's decisions would be final and binding unless modified or overturned by a constitutional amendment. There is, as we have seen, some evidence to support this interpretation. Aside from his recurrence in his later years to the solution of an impartial "tribunal," originally set forth in Federalist 39, he does seem to hold to the proposition that there are fixed boundaries—as distinct from the "floating" or changing boundaries provided through the consensual process—that ought to be secured by the courts. Indeed, the language used in Federalist 39 would suggest as much: the controversies between the two relatively distinct "spheres" of jurisdiction can be settled impartially by recourse to "the rules of the Constitution."

While arguable, this interpretation, in the last analysis, is probably not tenable for a number of reasons and considerations we have already examined. The so-called "rules of the Constitution" are certainly not so evident or clear as Madison would seem to have us believe. Moreover, this interpretation leaves no room for the standard he sets forth at other places in his writings, namely, the degree to which decisions by the Court and Congress are "sustained by the predominant sense of the nation." And very much related to this, we would have to ignore or dismiss his remarks about the consensual processes that brought about his reversal of judgment on the bank issue. To this we may add another consideration not at all alien to Madison's more general views: reliance on the Court could well produce an inflexibility that might seriously impair the national government in meeting its constitutional obligations; or, if not that, the flouting of the Court's decisions by the political arms would, on any showing, undermine popular confidence in the system.

Finally, in this connection, as we have intimated, the answers that Madison provides for resolving state-national cleavages—the "consensus" and "Court"—are not so incompatible as they might seem. Certainly, in the consensual solution, the Court would have a significant role to play. It would, among other things, have to interpret the relevant provision of the national laws in controversies arising from their implementation. In many instances, of course, it would have some discretion in fitting the terms of the law to the specific circumstances or in determining the "intent" of Congress. In this fashion, at what might be called the "tactical" level, it would have a decided input in adjusting the boundaries between the two jurisdictions. In its most important functions, providing for the uniform interpretation of national laws and insuring that state laws do not contravene national laws or authority, the Court would also have an input. In other words, it is easy to conceive of many circumstances where the Court would act in the capacity Madison ascribes to it in Federalist 39 without having to concede that it is the final arbiter, short of recourse to amendment, with regard to the proper division of powers.

What is beyond dispute is that, no matter what interpretation we lend to Madison's thoughts, there is an insurmountable gulf between them and the more controversial of our current practices regarding state-national relations. We need not go into great detail on this matter to realize that Madison's views cannot conceivably be construed to embrace the virtual abrogation of the federal principle through the Court's unilateral interpretation of the Fourteenth Amendment, which has deprived the states of authority over concerns that had long been regarded as well within their domain. To put this matter in its starkest terms, our present situation represents a violation of one of Madison's most fundamental political principles. In addition to its judicial function, which the Court exercises when it declares state laws, practices, or actions unconstitutional, it has, to an alarming degree, assumed the legislative function by fashioning remedies for the states' presumed "shortcomings." Hence, in Madison's terms, what we are witnessing is a judicial tyranny, a tyranny in which no regard is shown for either the substantive or procedural concerns evident in Madison's thinking.[80]

Madison's views on federalism also help us to understand why the Court's behavior in recent decades is causing unrest and tensions in American society; namely, its intrusions into the states' domain simply are not in accord with "predominant sense of the nation." Rather, they bear all the earmarks of being the product of an ideology. Put another way, it is difficult to believe that the substance of the major decisions of the Court in recent decades—e.g., those relating to prayer, busing, and abortion—would ever have been enacted into law. But, above all, this situation illustrates the unsettling and even disastrous consequences that flow from a doctrinaire approach—one that necessarily eschews consensual processes because it holds to the fiction that the answers are to be "discovered" in the Constitution.

Madison, we should note by way of concluding, understandably perceived the dangers to his system of divided sovereignty residing in a change in the state of mind of the common constituents concerning state-national relations—a change that would manifest itself in Congress and eventually result in greater consolidation. The situation today is quite different: because of the Fourteenth Amendment and the opportunities its language opens up, it is the Court, not the common constituents or Congress, that is the "culprit." Of course, Madison did not believe the Court would assume such a role. In his estimation "whatever may be the latitude of Jurisdiction assumed by the Judicial Power of the U.S. it is less formidable to the reserved sovereignty of the States than the latitude of power which it

---

[80]It was axiomatic for the Framers that the union of any two powers—legislative, executive, or judicial—would represent tyranny or the breakdown of the "rule of law." That is why the Massachusetts Constitution of 1780 declares: "In the government of the Commonwealth, the legislative department shall never exercise the executive and judicial powers, or either of them: The executive shall never exercise the legislative and judicial powers, or either of them: The judicial shall never exercise the legislative and executive powers, or either of them: to the end it may be a government of laws not of men." *The Popular Sources of Political Authority: Documents on the Massachusetts Constitution of 1780,* ed. Oscar and Mary Handlin (Cambridge: Harvard University Press, 1966), 337–38. That Madison shared this view is clear from his discussion of the separation of powers in essays 47 through 51. See in this regard chapter 3 above.

has assigned to the National Legislature.''[81] But he was not at a loss about what to do if the Court did play such a role: ''Such is the plastic faculty of legislation, that notwithstanding the firm tenure which judges have on their offices, they can by various regulations be kept or reduced within the paths of duty; more especially with the aid of their amenability to the Legislative tribunal in the form of impeachment.'' Moreover, as we have pointed out, he thought it unlikely that the Court ''would long be indulged in a career of usurpation to the decided opinions and policy of the Legislature.''[82]

That Madison's solutions today are regarded as nothing less than heretical in some quarters—a fact that helps to account for the helplessness of the political arms to restrict or otherwise control the Court—indicates the extent to which the Constitution, its character and operations, is now conceived of in terms totally foreign to Madison's. Consequently, what many today conceive of as the problem of federalism—i.e., the gradual erosion of the states' residual authority—is, in fact, but a manifestation of a more basic problem that concerns the character of the regime established by the Constitution.

---

[81]Letter to Spencer Roane, May 6, 1821. *Writings,* IX, 57.
[82]Ibid., 58.

5

The Supreme Court, Judicial Review, and Federalist 78

INTRODUCTORY NOTE

We come at last to the principle of limited government, which, as I indicated at the outset, involves the belief that there are things that government ought not to do, that there are limits to the rightful authority of government. Of course, any contemporary discussion of this principle in the American context leads straightway to a description of the role and function of the Supreme Court and the Bill of Rights, a fact that merely reflects the extent to which the new constitutional morality has taken hold. As I indicated in my previous discussions of Federalist 10 and the principle of separation of powers, the Framers' solutions to the problems of majority factions and tyranny were of a markedly different character. The full dimensions of this difference and its relationship to the new morality, however, can be most effectively presented at this point by way of introducing the following selection which deals with Hamilton's defense of judicial review.

As a point of departure, I think it must be conceded that the "logic" of our Constitution calls for judicial review. Hamilton, in arguing "that the Constitution ought to be the standard of construction for the laws, and that wherever there is an evident opposition, the laws ought to give place to the Constitution," points out that "this doctrine is not deducible from any circumstance peculiar to the plan of [the] convention, but from the general theory of a limited Constitution." But should it fall to the courts to determine whether there is an "evident" conflict between the law and the Constitution? Again the answer seems clear enough: unless we are prepared to argue that the Congress should be the judge of the extent of its constitutional powers which would be tantamount to arguing for an unlimited constitution, the task must fall to the judiciary. Certainly, to borrow another argument from Hamilton, we should hardly expect "that the men who had infringed the Constitution in the character of legislators would be disposed to repair the breach in the character of judges" (81:417).

As sensible and moderate as this position might seem, Hamilton's position was attacked by certain Antifederalists who argued that this doctrine would provide an opening for the judiciary to usurp almost unlimited power. "Brutus" was among the more forceful in his attack: "They [the courts] will give the sense of every article of the constitution that may from time to time come before them. And in their decisions they will not confine themselves to any fixed or established rules, but will determine, according to what appears to them, the reason and spirit of the constitution. The opinions of the supreme court, whatever they may be, will have the force of law; because there is no power provided in the constitution that can correct their errors, or control their adjudications. From this court there is no appeal."* Over the years Brutus's contentions have gained credibility from the parallel charge that Hamilton wanted a strong judiciary to protect the privileged from the rampaging majorities. Indeed, an enduring revisionist theme, shared by some conservatives as well, is that the Court was designed to be the final bastion against majorities intent upon regulating property rights. In this regard, it is commonly noted that when the Court, after its turnabout in the mid-1930s, no longer could be counted upon to perform this function, conservatives and liberals switched sides on its relative virtues.

Be that as it may, what is important to note is that Hamilton was apparently quite sensitive to Brutus's charges. He responds in part by noting that "there is not a syllable in the plan under consideration which *directly* empowers the national courts to construe the laws according to the spirit of the Constitution, or which gives them any greater latitude in this respect than may be claimed by the courts of every State" (81:416–17). He points out that Brutus's argument can be employed against "every constitution that attempts to set bounds to the legislative discretion" (81:417). He regards the charge that the judiciary might encroach upon the legislative authority as without solid foundation: "Particular misconstructions and contraventions of the will of the legislature may now and then happen; but they can never be so extensive as to amount to an inconvenience, or in any sensible degree to affect the order of the political system." This he "infers with certainty from the general nature of the judicial power, from the objects to which it relates, from the manner in which it is exercised, from its comparative weakness, and from its total incapacity to support its usurpations by force." And, as if this were not enough, he adds that the power of impeachment and removal by itself provides "complete security" against such judicial encroachments (81:418).

Hamilton's observations should make one wonder about certain commonplace assumptions regarding the role that the Framers wanted the courts to play. But, in my mind, the decisive factor, the one that above all casts doubts on the revisionists' interpretation, is Hamilton's opposition to a bill of rights. More precisely, it is the way in which he couches his rather strong objections to a bill of rights; for what seems clear is that Hamilton's lines of argument, and his entire attitude towards rights, would have been substantially different if he had wanted the Court to assume a major, if not decisive, role. Without rights, this is to say, the Court is without the wherewithal to usurp the legislative power or to transform itself into the most powerful branch. So much, I believe, can be seen by asking what the status of the Court today would be without a bill of rights.

What Hamilton does say against a bill of rights is interesting not only from this perspective but also in providing us with an overview of the character of the regime established by the Constitution. Bills of rights, he observes, historically have been "stipulations between kings and their subjects, abridgements of prerogative in favor of privilege, reservations of rights not surrendered to the prince." As such, he argues, "they have no application to constitutions, professedly founded upon the power of the people and executed by their immediate representatives and servants. Here, in strictness, the

---

The Antifederalist Papers, ed. Morton Borden (East Lansing: Michigan State University Press, 1965), 228.

people surrender nothing; and as they retain everything they have no need of particular reservations." And, in this vein, he insists that the ordination and establishment of the Constitution by "WE, THE PEOPLE . . . is a better recognition of popular rights than volumes of those aphorisms which make the principal figure in several of our State bills of rights and which would sound much better in a treatise of ethics than in a constitution of government" (84:443).

Hamilton maintains, moreover, that a bill of rights, "in the sense and to the extent in which they are contended for" by the Antifederalists, would not only be "unnecessary," but also might prove "dangerous." And his argument here is not what we might expect, namely, that the enumeration of some rights would disparage those not enumerated. Rather, using "liberty of the press" for purposes of illustration, he believes that restrictions on government "would furnish, to men disposed to usurp, a plausible pretense, for claiming that power." "They might," he believes, "urge with a semblance of reason that the Constitution ought not to be charged with the absurdity of providing against the abuse of an authority which was not given, and that the provisions against restraining the liberty of the press afforded a clear implication that a power to prescribe proper regulations concerning it was intended to be vested in the national government" (84:444).

Nor was Hamilton unmindful of the difficulties associated in defining rights. "What," he asks, "is the liberty of the press? Who can give it any definition which would not leave the utmost latitude for evasion?" Because any such definition is, in his judgment, "impracticable," the security for the liberty of the press is not to be found in "whatever fine declarations may be inserted in any constitution respecting it"; rather, he maintains, its preservation "depend[s] on public opinion, and on the general spirit of the people and of the government." These, he continues, are the "only solid basis of all our rights" (84:444).

Now these are hardly the words of one who would look to the Court to protect property rights or, more importantly, of one who envisioned the Court playing a predominant role in our constitutional system. We should take care to note in this respect that his argument is based upon a fundamental proposition that there is a basic incompatibility between the notion of an expansive bill of rights and the principle of republicanism. Hence, he leaves no room—as well he might have, had he been so inclined—for a change of heart on the issue of rights. For instance, he might have taken a "wait and see" attitude on this matter that would not have foreclosed the future incorporation of those rights that, according to the revisionists, he presumably wanted to protect. That he did not do so is telling.

At the heart of the new constitutional morality stand the twin pillars of judicial supremacy and rights, the more fundamental of which is rights because without them the avenues for judicial supremacy would not be open, not at least under the guise of republicanism or constitutionalism. But clearly ours is not a "rights tradition" in the sense the American Civil Liberties Union (ACLU), most academics, and the modern courts would have us believe. And even the adoption of the Bill of Rights soon after ratification does not alter this fact, for how else could Madison, its "father," see fit to declare that these rights could not "endanger the beauty of the Government in any one important feature, even in the eyes of its most sanguine admirers"?** And, in all of this, there is true irony because the Antifederalists, who championed the cause of a bill of rights, sought to limit the authority of the national government vis-à-vis the states. At that time they were unable to

---

**The Annals of Congress, 1st Congress, 1st Session, April 8, 1789, 441.

secure the passage of amendments that would effectively limit the national government, and today it is the application of the Bill of Rights through the Fourteenth Amendment that has served to further nationalize our system.

The nationalization of the Bill of Rights via the due process clause of the Fourteenth Amendment obviously involves all of the pitfalls to which Hamilton refers; even more so, if we regard the due process clause as in a class by itself because of its "indefiniteness," which has allowed the courts to expand or contract it over the decades. Moreover, in this process, as the following essay will indicate, the Court has abandoned every single guideline that Hamilton set forth for the proper exercise of judicial review. Thus, it is no wonder that the Court stands at the center of so much controversy. Nor is it any wonder, given its potential to effectuate sweeping changes under the guise of protecting and advancing our constitutional rights, that the proponents of the new morality serve as its apologists.

THE SUPREME COURT, JUDICIAL REVIEW, AND FEDERALIST 78

The Supreme Court's role, status, and power within our constitutional framework have been so thoroughly explored over the decades that it is futile to attempt a listing of the major books and articles dealing with this subject.[1] And, one is left to ask, is there anything more to be said about the Court and the various stances individuals throughout our history have taken toward it, particularly with respect to the matter of judicial review? Our feeling is that (a) there *is* something new to say about the Court and its role in our system, and (b) a good deal of admittedly fine scholarship has tended to divert our attention from those questions we should be asking about the Court and its power of judicial review.

JUDICIAL REVIEW AND THE FRAMERS' INTENT

Our first contention is that we have to clear away a good deal of the underbrush that inevitably surrounds discussions concerning the Court. Much of this so-called "underbrush" deals with the questions whether the Court is actually a weather vane of public morality or opinion; the "goodness" or "badness" of its decisions; the various philosophies justices have brought to the Court and expounded in their decisions; the impact of Court decisions (that is, whether we really get around to obeying certain of its decisions); or what the system would be like if the Court were divested of its presumed power to nullify state and national laws that contravene the basic laws as set forth in the Constitution. These and like concerns are, to be sure, important and bear upon the central questions of what direction the Court will take, the degree of confidence the population places in the Court's decisions, and its general relationship to the other branches of our national government. And some of them are admittedly important because they involve us in fundamental partisan issues of the day or an era as, for example,

---

[1] An annotated bibliography of the leading and most salient works dealing with these matters is to be found in Charles S. Hyneman's *The Supreme Court on Trial* (New York: Atherton Press, 1963).

Roosevelt's court-packing proposal, the fights over the nominations of Carswell and Haynsworth, the movement to impeach Justice Douglas, the Southern resistance to the Court's integration rulings, and the myriad of Warren Court decisions relating to the rights of the accused in criminal processes. While these disputes have tended to focus upon a number of considerations concerning the proper rule of the Court, they have, for the most part, only tangentially addressed themselves to the basic issues surrounding the Court and its powers. Perhaps this is to be accounted for by ''shifting alliances'' on partisan issues, where observers of the Court are one day its friends and the next its enemies. Underlying these controversies and the arguments of the adversaries, however, there seems to be an unarticulated premise, to wit, that the Court should exercise judicial review. The disputes, in other words, have been largely tactical in nature. There is ample room to question the motives of the participants in assuming the positions they do because in practically all such episodes political interests of the highest order were at stake. This point, we believe, is well known and hardly needs extensive documentation here.

Most serious scholars of the Court are well aware of this practice. As a result, it would seem they have tried to probe further into the basic question of whether the Supreme Court was ever intended to be involved in such disputes. More specifically, we have developed a growing body of scholarship that has attempted to determine whether judicial review was or was not intended to be vested with the Supreme Court by those who drafted the Constitution. The sheer bulk of such endeavors precludes detailed analysis here. Generally speaking, however, the focus of such inquiries concerning the intent of the Framers has been threefold:

1. What evidence exists to show that the state or colonial courts did invalidate legislative actions? To what extent can one say that this was an accepted practice and well understood by the people? Conversely, to what degree can such practices on the part of the Court be considered mere aberrations of such insignificant proportions that scarcely any heed was paid to them, and that, far from being a generally acknowledged power of the courts, they are to be viewed as deviations from the generally held views concerning judicial power?

2. What did the Framers of the Constitution think about judicial review? What do the proceedings at Philadelphia, transcribed in various notes, tell us about this issue? What did those who participated in the Convention privately think about the matter of judicial review as revealed by their correspondence with others?

3. What does the Constitution say, either expressly or implicitly, about the judicial powers? More exactly, does the Constitution logically require that the power of review be vested with the judiciary?

Two important observations are called for regarding these inquiries. First, one might well ask, what difference does it make what the intentions of the Framers were or what the people regarded as the proper function of the judiciary? Why try to settle the matter through the approaches outlined above? Why can't we, the people of today, make these decisions for ourselves independent of reasoning about what the Constitution logically requires or what the Framers and their forebears might have believed? This question can best be answered by asking another: if it can be shown that judicial review was not intended or even considered and rejected, on what conceivable grounds can the Court claim this power? Moreover, how can the Court obligate those affected by its exercise of this power to obey its rulings? Of course, in asking such a question one is implicitly utilizing the contract framework and its corollary of consent (tacit or express) in determining the boundaries and nature of obligation. Is such an approach, we can ask, fair? Does it "stack" the cards one way or the other in the seemingly endless controversies surrounding the role and function of the Court? The answer to this must be an emphatic "no," and for the following reasons:

1. The Constitution, after all is said and done, can be viewed as a contract of the most fundamental sort, specifying as it does the institutions and powers of government. As such it is a binding document until such time as it is changed through the prescribed processes. To argue otherwise would lead to philosophical mayhem.

2. The approach does allow for one to go beyond the Constitution, as many scholars have done, to adduce evidence concerning the customs, prevailing beliefs, and the like that form a backdrop for interpreting the Constitution and the "spirit" with which its provisions are to be interpreted and its institutions are to operate. This is to say that the Constitution itself on many fundamental issues cannot be read independent of the prevailing morality of the time, which, though not expressly articulated in the document, serves to give it a broader meaning, purpose, and moral framework. The contractual approach certainly makes allowances for the introduction of such an overarching morality, which can also lay claim to be of binding force.

3. The neutrality of the approach is attested by the fact that it has been used extensively by those whose views regarding the Court and its powers vary widely. The *approach,* in other words, provides one common ground for the disputants in the controversy.

4. The method is endemic to and well recognized in the judicial process itself, particularly in controversies of similar nature that inevitably arise concerning interpretation of key provisions of the Constitution.

5. To adopt another approach, for reasons that will be spelled out later, involves insurmountable difficulties that seem to defy rational resolution. Indeed, it is when one does depart from the contractual approach that debate about the Court takes on all the attributes of a circle-squaring expedition.

Having said this much, we turn to our second contention: the literature that has sought to determine whether the Court does possess the power of judicial review by studying precedents, the Convention, and the language of the Constitution (those areas cited above) has proved far from conclusive on this point. Most scholars who have approached the subject in the manner outlined above have, in fact, acknowledged as much. They do talk in terms of the preponderant weight of evidence, but they differ markedly on which side of the scales the preponderant weight does fall. This is true of almost every phase of their investigations. One would imagine, for example, that the matter of preconstitutional precedents of judicial review would lend conclusive weight for one side or the other in this dispute. This is far from the case. For example, Charles G. Haines, an exponent of the doctrine of judicial review, claimed that there were eleven decisions by state and colonial courts before 1787 in which the power of judicial review was asserted.[2] This in itself is hardly convincing evidence that judicial review was widely practiced and accepted, but the analyses of these cases by William Crosskey[3] and Brent Bozell,[4] both opponents of judicial review of national legislation, narrow this number to just one. To cite another example, proponents of judicial review contend that by plain inference Articles III and VI of the Constitution grant the power of judicial review to the Court. Yet, not only has the inference been called into serious question, but also the opponents of judicial review contend that the issue, important as it is to an understanding of the national system, would hardly be left to inference; rather, it would have been spelled out in unambiguous terms.[5] In sum, no matter where we look for evidence that would help us understand the nature of the contract in the sense we are speaking of it, the evidence is at best highly inconclusive. This is true of the Convention Debates, the Ratifying Conventions, the State Constitutions, and the utterances and writings of leading political figures of the time. We may surmise that this is one of the reasons much of the scholarship concerned with the Court seems to assume a stance pretty much as follows: "Judicial review whether intended or not is with us." It then proceeds, as we have said, to study the Court from various angles that have nothing to do with the question of its legitimacy within the contractual framework we have outlined above.

To all of this the following should be noted: scholarship in this area, to quote Charles S. Hyneman, "has not laid to rest a widespread suspicion that our judges have taken upon themselves a role which the founders of our constitutional system did not intend them to have."[6] Nor, might we add, is it likely that such a widespread suspicion will ever be laid to rest, for it is inconceivable that after so many decades of careful research any new evidence of sufficient magnitude and authority will be unearthed to settle the controversy. To be sure, old arguments will be rehashed periodically, and an added bit of evidence may be placed on one side of the scale or the other, but, as far as we can see, the question of intent and hence our obligations within our constitutional system as they relate to the judiciary will

---

[2]Among others see Charles G. Haines, *The American Doctrine of Judicial Supremacy* (New York: Russell and Russell, 1959), Ch. 4 and 5. Haines lists the major works of Thayer and Corwin that deal with these cases.

[3]William Crosskey, *Politics and the Constitution in the History of the United States,* (Chicago: University of Chicago Press, 1953), II, Ch. 27.

[4]L. Brent Bozell, *The Warren Revolution* (New Rochelle, New York: Arlington House, 1966), 159–215.

[5]For a discussion of this see among others, Hyneman, Ch. 10; and Alexander Bickel, *The Least Dangerous Branch* (New Haven: Yale University Press, 1962), Ch. 1.

[6]Hyneman, 123.

never be settled. With this in mind, we will approach the matter from another angle, which, one hopes, will put the matter of judicial review and the legitimacy of the Court's powers in another perspective.

FEDERALIST 78 AND JUDICIAL REFORM

Virtually all the literature dealing with the foundations of judicial review touches at one point or another upon Federalist 78, because in this paper the power of judicial review over national legislation is unambiguously affirmed. To be sure, the essay is usually accorded only a lukewarm reception by the modern proponents of judicial activism, since its reasoning will not support the notion of judicial supremacy. Likewise, there is antipathy tòwards this essay on the part of some of those who are most critical of the modern Court, precisely because it does support the doctrine of judicial review that has been used as a stepping stone for judicial aggrandizement. Nevertheless, there is no denying that Federalist 78 clearly constitutes the most authoritative evidence we possess that the Framers intended judicial review. *The Federalist* in which it appears has been accorded quasi-constitutional status even by the courts; that is, it is looked upon, by both its friends and critics, as the best single source we have for understanding the Constitution and its basic principles as it emerged from the Philadelphia Convention. Beyond this, we know from other sources not only that the reasoning of this essay was well known, but also that its assumptions were widely shared. In this connection we cannot help but note the heavy reliance that Marshall in his *Marbury* decision places upon the mode of reasoning employed in this essay. Equally revealing is the fact that Marshall does not bring external evidence to bear in order to support the Court's claim to the power of judicial review. In other words, for one reason or another, he ignores the evidence and other modes of inferential reasoning with which contemporary students wrestle. As Professor Charles Hyneman noted in this regard:

> If, as seems an irresistible conclusion, Marshall was convinced that language in the Constitution did not establish a power of judicial review beyond need for further evidence, one would expect him to inquire next into the announced purposes of those who constructed that document. He gives us no report on the results of that inquiry. Neither in the Marbury opinion nor elsewhere does he tell us what was said about interpretation and enforcement of the Constitution in the Philadelphia convention or in the several state ratifying conventions. The journals of the drafting convention and the notes made by several members of that body on which we rely so heavily today had not been printed at the time of *Marbury v. Madison.* But Marshall may well have had access to much of this knowledge by word of mouth, and it is possible that he obtained by that route a great deal more knowledge about the intentions of the framers than has been available to later scholars. He certainly knew what was said in the Virginia ratifying convention about the

fundamental character of the Constitution and about judicial power under the Constitution, for he was himself a member of that assembly.[7]

We can only conjecture that Marshall found such undertakings inconclusive and sought to plant the roots of judicial review on the strongest possible footing.

We are now prepared to turn our attention to Federalist 78 with an understanding of its critical role in the controversies surrounding judicial review and the power of the Court.

The essay begins by noting the provisions that have been made for the appointment of judges and their tenure or, as Hamilton put it, "to the manner of constituting it [the federal judiciary]." He writes:

> The standard of good behavior for the continuance in office of the judicial magistracy, is certainly one of the most valuable of the modern improvements in the practice of government. In a monarchy it is an excellent barrier to the despotism of the prince; in a republic it is a no less excellent barrier to the encroachments and oppressions of the representative body. And it is the best expedient which can be devised in any government, to secure a steady, upright, and impartial administration of the laws (401).

The following two paragraphs clearly seem designed to allay fears that the judiciary, because of this independence, will pose any danger to the liberties of the people. We are told, among other things, "the judiciary from the nature of its functions, will always be the least dangerous to the political rights of the Constitution; because it will be least in a capacity to annoy or injure them." More: unlike the executive who "holds the sword of the community," and the legislature which "not only commands the purse, but prescribes the rules by which the duties and rights of every citizen are to be regulated," the Courts do not have "FORCE nor WILL, but merely judgment; and must ultimately depend upon the aid of the executive arm even for efficacy of its judgments" (401–2).

Hamilton continues in the same vein in the next paragraph:

> This simple view of the matter suggests several important consequences. It proves incontestably, that the judiciary is beyond comparison the weakest of the three departments of power; that it can never attack with success either of the other two; and that all possible care is requisite to enable it to defend itself against their attacks (402).

Beyond this, he writes:

> though individual oppression may now and then proceed from the courts of justice, the general liberty of the people can never be endangered from that quarter; I mean so long as the judiciary remains truly distinct from both the legislature and the Executive (402).

---

[7]Hyneman, 100–101.

What follows is a reaffirmation that the judicial branch should be as separate from the other branches as possible and constituted so as to resist their encroachments. In sum, the power of the judiciary is "next to nothing" compared with those of the coordinate branches; the people have nothing to fear from this quarter; and the judiciary, because it is so feeble, must be constituted to maintain its independence.

From this point to almost the end of the essay, Hamilton asserts and justifies the power of judicial review:

The complete independence of the courts of justice is particularly essential in a limited Constitution. By a limited Constitution, I understand one which contains certain specified exceptions to the legislative authority; such, for instance, as that it shall pass no bills of attainder, no *ex post facto* laws, and the like. Limitations of this kind can be preserved in practice no other way than through the medium of courts of justice, whose duty it must be to declare all acts contrary to the manifest tenor of the Constitution void. Without this, all the reservations of particular rights or privileges would amount to nothing (402).

Basic to Hamilton's justification is what can be termed the "fundamental law" argument. In essence, this argument is very simple: the Constitution represents the fundamental law and all laws (ordinary legislative acts) that conflict with the fundamental law are null and void. This means explicitly that, "whenever a particular statute contravenes the Constitution, it will be the duty of the judicial tribunals to adhere to the latter and disregard the former" (404). Put another way, "the Constitution ought to be preferred to the statute, the intention of the people to the intention of their agents" (403).

There are, of course, as the above quotations indicate, crucial elements that must be added to this justification. First, it is within the special province of the judiciary to declare laws contrary to the Constitution void:

If it be said that the legislative body are themselves the constitutional judges of their own powers, and that the construction they put upon them is conclusive upon the other departments, it may be answered, that this cannot be the natural presumption, where it is not to be collected from any particular provisions in the Constitution. It is not otherwise to be supposed that the Constitution could intend to enable the representatives of the people to substitute their *will* to that of the constituents. It is far more rational to suppose that the courts were designed to be an intermediate body between the people and the legislature, in order, among other things, to keep the latter within the limits assigned to their authority. The interpretation of the laws is the proper and peculiar province of the courts (403).

Second, as intimated in the above passage, the Court in nullifying legislation does not "suppose a superiority of the judicial to the legislative power. It only supposes that the power of the people is superior to both" (403). And, third, as a corollary of this it must be assumed that the "real," basic, or fundamental, will of the people is to be found in the Constitution. Thus,

> Until the people have, by some solemn and authoritative act, annulled or changed the established form, it is binding upon themselves collectively as well as individually; and no presumption, or even knowledge, of their senti- ments, can warrant their representatives in a departure from it, prior to such an act (405).

We have here in pretty much undiluted form Hamilton's case for judicial re- view, a case that is probably the strongest both in terms of justifying judicial review *and* providing an unambiguous basis for maintaining that it possesses a contractual legitimacy that carries with it a corresponding obligation on the part of individuals and institutions to observe, honor, and obey. To put this latter point in other terms, if we accept Federalist 78 as part of our constitutional system, we have given our consent to judicial review to the degree and the extent it is con- tended for in this essay.

THE LIMITS OF JUDICIAL REVIEW

With this in mind, then, let us take another look at this essay with the following in mind: the fundamental law theory is based in part upon the proposition that the agencies it creates are subordinate to it and must operate within its confines. To quote Hamilton again: "To deny [this proposition] would be to affirm, that the deputy is greater than his principal; that the servant is above his master; that the representatives of the people are superior to the people themselves; that men acting by virtue of powers, may do not only what their powers do not authorize, but what they forbid" (403).

A perfectly logical and reasonable line of inquiry is this: the Court is also, by Hamilton's line of reasoning, subordinate to the Constitution. There can be no question of this because the Court is as much a creature of the Constitution as the Presidency or Congress. What, then, would constitute an unconstitutional act on the part of the judiciary? Specifically, for our purposes, how can we tell when the courts have used their powers, particularly that of judicial review, unconstitutionally?

Hamilton in the following quote seems to recognize that the Court could act unconstitutionally, but he does not fully answer the question at hand:

> It can be of no weight to say that the courts, on the pretence of a repugnancy, may substitute their own pleasure to the constitutional intentions of the leg- islature. This might as well happen in the case of two contradictory statutes; or it might as well happen in every adjudication upon any single statute. The courts must declare the sense of the law; and if they should be disposed to exercise WILL instead of JUDGMENT, the consequence would equally be

the substitution of their pleasure to that of the legislative body. The observation, if it proved anything, would prove that there ought to be no judges distinct from that body (404).

From this passage it seems clear that the Court would be acting *ultra vires* when it uses its power of judicial review to thwart legitimate statutory law. But the key phrase here is that which differentiates WILL from JUDGMENT, and this particular passage tells us very little about how to make such a differentiation. We do know, for starters, this much: the exercise of WILL is within the province of the legislative body. This is consonant with Hamilton's earlier statement in comparing the powers of the Court with those of the executive and legislative bodies—namely, the judiciary has "neither FORCE [the major constitutional power of the executive] nor WILL [the constitutional prerogative of the legislature], but merely judgment." We are safe in concluding that in this context WILL connotes at least a choice among alternatives or goals with the concomitant capacity to achieve, implement, or move toward the attainment of the choice. JUDGMENT would seem to have a more *passive* connotation because implementation or attainment are not so closely associated with it. However, leaving aside active and passive connotations, both JUDGMENT and WILL do involve elements of choice. The exercise of WILL may or may not involve JUDGMENT but merely preference, volition, or desire. In this sense an act of WILL can, and often does, partake of arbitrariness, e.g., choosing among ninety-seven flavors of ice cream, all of which are equally attractive to the consumer. JUDGMENT, in contrast to WILL, is usually brought to bear in the context where the range of choice is far narrower; that is, normally upon a situation, act, or circumstance. JUDGMENT, moreover, is a considered opinion or decision that is the outgrowth of a ratiocinative process in which relevant factors (factors, that is, relevant to the decision in the particular instance) are juxtaposed, assigned priorities, and carefully weighed. Judgments, of course, may vary over an endless variety of matters so that we are inclined to call most judgments opinions; e.g., was Stan Musial a better baseball player than Ted Williams? In some cases, subsequent events may bear out judgments, so that we are entitled to label some judgments "good" and others "bad."

While much more can be said about WILL and JUDGMENT, we have enough before us to explore Federalist 78 with an eye to determining what rules or standards the Court is bound to follow in the exercise of its JUDGMENT, particularly when it voids an act of the legislature. Such rules and standards, we hasten to add, are integral to Hamilton's justification of judicial review, for without them there would be no guides for ascertaining when the Court is acting unconstitutionally, i.e., usurping the legitimate powers of the other branches. These guides and rules, we should also point out, are usually ignored in the literature dealing with judicial review.

First, we might be led to believe that judicial review should be exercised only when Congress violates specific constitutional prohibitions on its powers. The

Court we are told should certainly nullify "bills of attainder" and "*ex post facto* laws and the like." However, in the very next sentence Hamilton seems to open the door for a more expansive role for the Court when he writes:

> Limitations of this kind [bills of attainder, *ex post facto* laws, and the like] can be preserved in practice no other way than through the medium of courts of justice, whose duty it must be to declare all acts contrary to the manifest *tenor* of the Constitution void (402; emphasis added).

The word "tenor" would suggest that the Court can move into realms beyond the specific prohibitions. And later in the essay we find evidence that this might well be the case:

> This independence of the judges is equally requisite to guard the Constitution and the rights of individuals from the effects of those ill humors, which the arts of designing men, or the influence of particular conjunctures, sometimes disseminate among the people themselves, and which, though they speedily give place to better information, and more deliberate reflection, have a tendency, in the meantime, to occasion dangerous innovations in the government, and serious oppressions of the minor party in the community. Though I trust the friends of the proposed Constitution will never concur with its enemies in questioning that fundamental principle of republican government which admits the right of the people to alter or abolish the established Constitution whenever they find it inconsistent with their happiness; yet it is not to be inferred from this principle that the representatives of the people, whenever a momentary inclination happens to lay hold of a majority of the constituents incompatible with the provisions in the existing Constitution would, on that account, be justifiable in a violation of those provisions (404–5).

Yet, even in this passage he sees fit to speak in terms of "momentary" inclinations "incompatible with the provisions in the existing Constitution." And we must be careful not to overlook the use of the word "manifest" when used in connection with the word "tenor." Manifest would certainly seem to mean obvious, clear, and undisputed, thus confining the scope of judicial review. Moreover, "manifest tenor" is used in association with the specific prohibitions placed upon Congress, all of which leads us to believe that the scope of judicial review should be narrow or, more accurately, the Court should nullify only obvious legislative violations of the Constitution.

Second, and very much supportive of this view of the matter, is the following passage taken from that section of the essay in which he justifies judicial review:

> A constitution is, in fact, and must be regarded by the judges, as a fundamental law. It therefore belongs to them to ascertain its meaning as well as the meaning of any particular act proceeding from the legislative body. If there should happen to be an irreconcilable variance between the two, that which has the superior obligation and validity ought, of course, to be preferred (403).

The words "irreconcilable variance" are plain enough and certainly impose a very stringent obligation on the Court before it voids legislation. On this account we find little evidence to support the proposition that Hamilton was in effect bestowing upon the Court a position of supremacy among the three branches.

And a third major factor that bears upon the WILL-JUDGMENT dichotomy is the following: "To avoid an arbitrary discretion in the courts, it is indispensable that they should be bound down by strict rules and precedents which serve to define and point out their duty in every particular case that comes before them" (406). Here the words "indispensable," "bound down," and "strict rules and precedents" are abundantly clear in their meaning and provide still another measure that can be used for the determination whether the judiciary has abandoned JUDGMENT for WILL.

We submit, then, that Federalist 78, when read in its entirety (which means reading it with the problem of WILL and JUDGMENT in the back of our minds), amounts to a perfectly sensible statement with which few, if any, would seriously disagree, given the fact that we have a written charter of government. To note, as Hamilton does, the feebleness and weakness of the judiciary, the fact that it cannot take any "active resolution whatever," that it is to be a passive institution exercising only JUDGMENT, that its powers extend to declaring acts of the legislature unconstitutional only when contrary to the "manifest tenor" of the Constitution (in the sense spelled out above), that it can only use this power when there is an "irreconcilable variance" between the statute and the Constitution, and, finally, that it is "indispensable" that it be "bound down by strict rules and precedents," hardly lends support to the thesis that he sought to vest the judiciary with the kind and degree of powers that modern-day "judicial activists," among others, impute to it. Put otherwise, we have noted that, if judicial review is indeed a part of the contract to which we have given our tacit consent, we must, perforce (as we have argued above) go to Federalist 78 to see the justification for it and to understand its scope as well as the obligations of the Court in exercising this power. When the terms of the contract are broken by the Court, our obligation to respect or obey its power of judicial review is severed, and the other branches of government, principally the Congress, are entitled, nay *obliged,* to use the constitutional means at their disposal to curb, regulate, and control the Court in such a manner as to compel conformance with the terms of the contract. This line of reasoning is but a corollary of the line of reasoning by which the courts lay claim to the power of judicial review. The Court is equally obliged as a creature of the Constitution not to overstep its bounds or exceed its constitutional authority. To argue otherwise would be to say that the Court endorses judicial supremacy.

THE EXTENT OF THE MODERN PROBLEM

A mark of the times is that the foregoing analysis and approach, particularly among most constitutional scholars, seems quaint, antiquated, and overly simplistic. Nobody in his right mind, nowadays, believes that the Court only exercises JUDGMENT or that *stare decisis* is or should be considered a binding principle in litigation. Rather, the Court is looked upon not as the custodian of the Constitution in the sense Hamilton advocated, but more as our moral guardian who will lead us by the hand to the fulfillment of our most cherished ideals, which far more often than not turn out to be those of secular, materialistic liberalism. Critical analyses of the Court usually focus on whether it has moved too fast or too slow in reaching the destined goals in light of the opportunities that present themselves measured against the mood of the public. Mature scholars now find it worthwhile to study fastidiously the written and spoken words of the justices, usually in a vain attempt to squeeze some coherency out of their judicial theories and decisions. Intramural squabbles occur between those who advocate "judicial restraint" and "judicial activism."[8] The legal "realists"—and that they are—have abandoned the idea that there is any such thing as judicial or legal reasoning or, more exactly, that judicial reasoning is what the judges reason. Those nominated for appointment to the Court, as recent history attests, are judged fit or not on the basis of their attitudes towards our most contemporary problems (along with, we might add, how many Harvard or Yale professors will support the nominee, which comes down to pretty much the same thing), a fact that confirms what we already know: the Court is as much a part of the purely political whirl as any other institution of our government.

Despite these confusing views of the Court and its role, one can detect in all of these contemporary disputes a sense of inevitability. If the people, as they are wont to do, drag their feet or protest too much about integration, prayer in the public schools, reapportionment, or like matters, the mood seems to prevail that the Court should "wait out" the storm before taking another quantum leap in the "proper" direction. How many times have we been told: "The Warren Court blazed a trail in the areas of civil rights and liberties. Subsequent Courts will have to consolidate these gains before moving ahead"?

What can account for this tangled situation and the direction the Court has taken and is taking? Perhaps the most important factor was the adoption of the Bill of Rights, which has served to provide a colorable pretext for the expansion of judicial powers. It may be that Hamilton envisioned this in Federalist 84, where he argued against the addition of any rights to the original constitution. But we do know now that Madison's prophecy in the first Congress that the Bill of Rights would not alter the fundamental structure or nature of the original Constitution was wrong. And the Fourteenth Amendment with its "equal protection" and "due process" clauses, as we all know, has been used as a device by the Court to "nationalize" rights, a task the Court has taken on with fervor and relish.

---

[8]That is, squabbles in the sense that both camps accept wide judicial powers but vary as to the wisdom of employing them in this or that case.

But the expansion of judicial power could not have come about save for the transformation in the entire nature of our public discourse. People tend more and more to think in terms of rights, so much so that the situation has become outlandish. We hear now of the right to read rapidly, the right to die, the right to live, the right to have good teachers, the right to know, and so forth. Such a mode of thinking induces one to use rights as the basis for appeals to the judiciary for redress of grievances, real or imagined, a function that the Court willingly assumed. What is ironic is that Hamilton's justification for judicial review served as the basis for legitimizing this assumption of power. But, in this process, soon forgotten were the restrictions and qualifications that were also an integral part of his argument. Totally arbitrary interpretations of virtually every right specified in the Constitution and chief clauses of the Fourteenth Amendment have time and again been used to invalidate state and national legislation, thereby jettisoning the "irreconcilable variance" rule. Motives and intentions were attributed to the drafters of the Bill of Rights and the Fourteenth Amendment to achieve the desired decisions and results. With this the "manifest tenor" injunction went out the window. The Court and its supporters began to harp on the familiar themes of "changing times" and "complex society" and the Court's responsibility to meet the demands of the twentieth century. Thus the "strict precedent" admonition vanished.

Hamilton's theory also served the judiciary in dismantling his very own proposition that the judiciary can take "no active resolution whatever." His theory, whatever else one might say about it, does lend dignity and meaningful purpose to the judiciary. Banking on this, but seemingly oblivious to Hamilton's restrictive injunctions, the Court gradually assumed its present status and power which are, to say the least, well beyond those envisioned by Hamilton. On more than one occasion we have seen frustrated Presidents on national television tell the American people in effect: "The Court has spoken and we must, whether we like it or not, obey the Constitution." It is not at all uncommon to hear high-ranking administrators and congressmen, when faced with a particular difficulty, declare that "the matter will have to be settled by the courts." In sum, the Court now has, particularly in the areas of integration and reapportionment, not only invalidated state legislation and state constitutional provisions, but set up standards with which they must comply. And, because of the new morality concerning the sanctity of the Court, there is no one, not even the President, to say it "nay." To do so would probably create a political turmoil of immense proportions.

Our point is not the simple one: we confess that we are dismayed that the "manifest tenor" of the Constitution has been interpreted to mean that children can no longer say voluntary prayers in public schools because to allow such a practice we would vault over some allegoric "high wall"; that this manifest tenor dictates that the states cannot, even if a majority of their citizens so desire, base their legislatures on any other representational principles than "one man, one vote"; that somehow manifest tenor means that the life of the unborn begins at three months and one day; or that the Constitution manifestly dictates that children should be carted from one neighborhood to another in order to achieve the "proper" racial balance as determined by the courts.

No, we repeat, this is not our point. Rather, our point is that the Court has itself violated the manifest tenor of the Constitution and it has done so in these and like cases by failing to observe the injunctions that Hamilton set forth.

Yet, as we have said, the Hamiltonian theory may seem quaint and outdated. Its restoration, we fully realize, is now next to impossible. But at least it possesses the virtue and dignity of resting upon sound philosophic and moral grounds, characteristics notably lacking in the fatuous, but currently fashionable theories that strive to justify judicial usurpation of power in the name of democracy.

6

Due Process, Liberty, and the Fifth Amendment: Original Intent

INTRODUCTORY NOTE

This chapter illustrates a highly significant dimension of the way in which the Court, principally in this century and at an accelerating rate in recent decades, has assumed the enormous powers that render Publius's teachings in Federalist 78 virtually obsolete. What follows might be considered a case study that traces one critical dimension of the transition from the Founders' Court, pictured by Publius as the weakest and least dangerous of the branches, to the modern Court, arguably the most important and powerful branch of government. More specifically, we deal with the matter of substantive due process. But we do so only after examining the historical understanding of due process in the English and American traditions, as well as the meaning accorded liberty in the context of due process. Our investigation also touches upon the Fourteenth Amendment and the question of incorporation; that is, the application of the provisions in the national Bill of Rights to the states via the due process clause of the Fourteenth Amendment. Bearing in mind this range of concerns, let me turn by way of introduction to certain issues that I think deserve emphasis.

As, no doubt, many instructors of American government can attest, few things are more difficult than trying to explain ''substantive due process'' to students. The difficulty, from my perspective at least, resides in trying to explain the move from process to substance, from the how to the what—a shift implied in the term itself and explicit in its application. One must somehow provide intermediate assumptions or postulates, derived from the ordinary or ''common sense'' understanding of due process, that serve to join or link substance to process in a reasonable fashion. To put this another way, most individuals readily comprehend the notion of due process; they have an intuitive understanding of the term, even though they may lack knowledge of its specific requirements. But this intuitive understanding by itself does not embrace or suggest the necessary linkage.

On this score, I must confess that some of my difficulties in trying to convey the meaning of substantive due process flow from my own inability to grasp the connection. For reasons that will be spelled out in this chapter, I remain unconvinced by the conventional argument advanced to justify the Court's use of substantive due process, which

139

runs roughly as follows: The "Madisonian problem" (providing for republican government free from the ravages of majority factions) is not completely solved by the multiplicity and diversity of interests, representation, and institutional processes that assure delay and deliberation. Despite these protections, minorities are still victimized by unjust, oppressive, partial, or just plain stupid laws that are properly enacted but do not violate any specific provision of the Constitution. The "perfection" of the system, thus, consists in giving to the judiciary the power to invalidate such laws.

The attentive student will remember that, while acknowledging in Federalist 78 and elsewhere that laws of this type might indeed find their way onto the statute books, Publius stops short of arguing that the Court possesses the authority to nullify such laws. One reason for this is apparent to those who have a coherent understanding of the system; namely, such a "cure" could well turn out to be worse than the disease since it would grant enormous discretionary powers to the judiciary. In any event, such a remedy for factions could hardly be called "republican," the only kind of remedy, Publius insists, consistent with the overarching principles of the proposed system (10:46).

The easy rejoinder to this observation is that the Fifth Amendment, with its "due process" clause, was added after the adoption of the Constitution and that, in spite of these reservations, it was intended to "perfect" the Philadelphia Constitution. In these terms the issue comes down to whether the due process clause was intended or designed to allow for judicial control over the legislature in the manner suggested in the argument above.

Now this concern readily lends itself to historical research for resolution, and most of what follows in this chapter deals with the development and traditional understanding of due process. In this endeavor, my primary concern is to determine whether the historical record and intentions would bear out the modern notions of substantive due process. I do so primarily with regard to the Fifth Amendment's due process clause, but my findings go well beyond this.

Here, by way of introduction to this historical analysis, a few comments relative to the broader theoretical concerns that arise from the conventional argument advanced for substantive due process are called for. In defending substantive due process, as I have remarked, it is fashionable to speak of legislatures passing unreasonable, evil, and oppressive laws, laws that are offensive to our sense of justice or decency. Now this argument— at least in the abstract—presupposes that there is a fundamental agreement on a wide range of values so that, for example, the conditions that constitute injustice can be readily discerned. Indeed, I would argue that it is precisely this presumption that renders the argument so appealing to many. But if there is such a consensus over right and wrong, just and unjust, why would the representatives act contrary to these consensual norms? On what grounds are we justified in assuming that legislative bodies, consisting of individuals elected by and accountable to the people, would be inclined to pass laws of this character?* To believe, as judicial activists are wont to do, that legislatures are in constant need of judicial oversight because of their propensities to pass unjust and oppressive laws clearly brings into serious question the underlying justifications for republican government and suggests that, if it is justice we seek, perhaps some other form of government would be more suitable.

---

*We should not forget in this connection how the *reflexive* principle, which results from the separation of powers, militates against oppressive, partial, or unjust laws.

The fact is that in the American system the unreasonableness or wickedness of legisla-tion contested on due process grounds is never so clear-cut as the arguments for substan-tive due process assume, and this is precisely because legislative bodies simply are not inclined to act in an arbitrary and unreasonable manner contrary to the prevailing values of the society. Instead, what we normally find in cases of dispute are competing values, with the Court in its exercise of substantive due process giving priority to one set of values over another. And when the Court rejects the decision of the legislature, the pre-sumption must be that the Court possesses knowledge of a finer, more elevated sense of justice, a special knowledge not accessible to the ordinary citizens or their representatives.

Naturally questions arise relative to the Court's elevated sense of justice: What is its source and substance? What renders it superior to the conceptions of the people or the legislators? How precisely do legal training and practice or judicial experience provide such a refined and special insight into justice and the good? Just to ask these questions, in my judgment, is sufficient to indicate that the doctrine of substantive due process rests on extremely feeble foundations. And my view is borne out by looking at the uneven record of the Court in those instances where it has seen fit to overturn legislation on substantive due process grounds, beginning with its first excursion into this area, the Dred Scott case. That is to say, there is no reason to believe that the justices have ruled on the basis of a coherent, well-developed, refined, and enduring sense of justice; rather, most of their major decisions in recent decades are informed by and conform with the values articulated by the more ''enlightened'' sectors of the community—e.g., law school deans and profes-sors, the editorial views of the ''respectable'' press and its minions—presumably preoc-cupied with realizing ''social justice.''

To nullify or veto legislation on due process grounds, though scarcely justifiable on our showing, is the lesser of the evils associated with the Court's use of substantive due process. As our final chapter will make clear, the Court has moved well beyond simply declaring legislative acts null and void; it has assumed legislative powers by reading into the ''liberty'' component of due process such rights as ''the right of privacy'' that here-tofore has never existed, and then specifying in detailed fashion what the states must do to protect or advance these rights. This practice again raises questions about the source of the Court's special insight into matters of rights and justice, this time at an even more fundamental level. How is it that the Court can see more clearly than the legislature into the requirements of justice and what it demands by way of public policy? And what is to prevent it from using this power for unjust or oppressive ends?

In sum, as we noted at the outset of this book, the Court has moved to a new plateau of power; one that places it on a level above the legislature in our system. This move clearly represents a drastic departure from the original design and the intentions of the Framers, and it is safe to say that the Constitution surely would never have been ratified if it had been understood that judicial powers could be employed in this fashion.

I think the substance of what follows in this chapter will show why it is that due process was never intended to be a limitation on the legislatures; its entire history, even through the ratification of the Fourteenth Amendment, demonstrates that it was intended as a limitation primarily on the judiciary and, to some extent, on the executive branch. It is somewhat ironic how the due process clause was turned on its head to provide the basis for judicial oversight of legislative actions.

With respect to ''liberty'' in the due process clause, I must emphasize that its meaning was clearly understood in terms of the ends or purposes of due process. Liberty was most relevant to due process in criminal cases and, as a consequence, it was defined in common law in terms of confinement, or a limitation on the movement of an individual. In brief, an individual could not be jailed without due process of law. Yet, I should remark in this connection about a matter I do not take up in this book: towards the end of the nineteenth century, for reasons that are not fully known, liberty came to have a broader and broader meaning. Liberty is now so broadly defined that it can serve as a justification for new rights whenever a majority of the Court is so inclined. This expanded conception did not gain official recognition until the *Gitlow* decision in 1925. Today, as we know, this "new" liberty, as the distinguished constitutional historian, Charles Warren, dubbed it, stands virtually unchallenged.

Finally, the developments traced in this chapter show another dimension of the inroads made by the progressivist morality with its emphasis on ends, even to the extent of undermining the legitimate republican processes spelled out in the Constitution. This entire process, as we shall see in the final chapter, culminates in the infamous *Roe v. Wade* (1973) decision.

DUE PROCESS, LIBERTY, AND THE FIFTH AMENDMENT: ORIGINAL INTENT

In the decades immediately preceding the convening of the first Congress in 1789, Americans were engaged in an examination of the meaning and nature of liberty with an intensity and thoroughness that have few, if any, parallels in history. From the early 1760s to the Declaration of Independence, the colonists sought to find justifications for their opposition to Great Britain's policies towards the colonies, policies that they increasingly came to regard as oppressive and tyrannical. These justifications, which were premised on the value of protecting and advancing liberty, necessarily involved an examination of the relationships that should exist between ruler and ruled. They also entailed an examination from various perspectives concerning the foundations, power, and role of legitimate government, as well as the meaning and substance of liberty.[1]

Having gained independence, Americans then had to undertake the necessary and critical task of founding governments that would avoid the tyranny and oppression they had known. Moreover, these governments had to conform with the

---

[1]The standard primary works of this era—the deliberations at the Constitutional Convention, *The Federalist*, the ratification debates, Antifederalist writings, among others—are only the tip of a huge body of relevant literature. For a more complete picture see "Suggestions for Further Reading" later in this book, particularly the edited works of Charles S. Hyneman and Donald S. Lutz, Bernard Bailyn, Oscar and Mary Handlin, Herbert Storing, Philip B. Kurland and Ralph Lerner, and Bernard Schwartz.

There are a number of secondary works, based upon primary materials, that endeavor to convey the prevailing political thoughts of the period in a systematic fashion. Among these are: Bernard Bailyn, *The Ideological Origins of the American Revolution* (Cambridge: Harvard University Press, 1967); Clinton Rossiter, *Seedtime of the Republic* (New York: Harcourt, Brace, and Company, 1953); Gordon Wood, *The Creation of the American Republic, 1776–1787* (Chapel Hill: University of North Carolina Press, 1969); John Phillip Reid, *The Concept of Liberty in the Age of the American Revolution* (Chicago: University of Chicago Press, 1988).

very standards and principles of legitimate government that had been used to judge the character of British rule. But there was a complication associated with this endeavor. The genius of the American people was avowedly "republican," so that now rights and liberties had to be understood and protected, not in the context of the people versus a tyrannical king, but in one where the people themselves were ultimately sovereign.[2] Their failure to adapt to this altered political environment in the new state constitutions, evident to many at the time,[3] prompted even further inquiry into the content and nature of liberty and how it might best be preserved without sacrificing popular self-government.

Both of these phases of development were marked by a theoretical tension that has manifested itself subsequently in our political tradition and that is mirrored in the long-standing controversy over the meaning and scope of "due process" and the kind of "liberty" it protects. There are those who view the yearnings of our revolutionary period as a struggle for transcendent "rights," who believe that the better part of our tradition has been a constant quest to achieve the noble and lofty ends associated with that period.[4] These ends would, of course, include the self-evident "equality" of the Declaration of Independence, as well as "life, liberty,

---

[2]That this created a different political landscape that created new problems for securing liberty—problems that the new constitution makers had not proven particularly adept in handling—is manifest from Madison's remarks to this point in *The Federalist*. In essay 48 he writes, "they [the American people] seem never to have turned their eyes from the danger, to liberty, from the overgrown and all-grasping prerogative of an hereditary magistrate, supported and fortified by an hereditary branch of the legislative authority. They seem never to have recollected the danger from legislative usurpation, which, by assembling all power in the same hands, must lead to the same tyranny as is threatened by executive usurpations." *The Federalist*, 255–56.

Later, in introducing his bill of rights, he amends this position: "In our government it is, perhaps, less necessary to guard against the abuse in the Executive Department than any other, because it is not the stronger branch of the system, but the weaker. It therefore must be levelled against the Legislative, for it is the most powerful and most likely to be abused, because it is under the least control. Hence, so far as a declaration of rights can tend to prevent the exercise of undue power, it cannot be doubted but such declaration is proper. But I confess that I do conceive, that in a Government modified like this of the United States, the great danger lies rather in the abuse of the community than in the Legislative body. The prescriptions in favor of liberty ought to be levelled against that quarter where the greatest danger lies, namely, that which possesses the highest prerogative power. But this is not found in either the Executive or Legislative departments of Government, but in the body of the people, operating by the majority against the minority." *The Annals of Congress*, 1st Congress, 1st Session, April 8, 1789, 437.

[3]Jefferson, for example, was most critical of the Virginia Constitution on a number of grounds, particularly its lack of effective barriers to legislative encroachment on the other branches. See his *Notes on the State of Virginia*, ed. William Peden (New York: W.W. Norton, 1954), 110–29. Madison was alarmed not only by the mutability of state laws, but by "the aggressions of interested majorities on the rights of minorities and of individuals" as well. Letter to George Washington, April 16, 1787. *The Writings of James Madison*, ed. Gaillard Hunt, 9 vols. (New York: G.P. Putnam's Sons, 1900–1910), II, 345.

[4]This view has found expression in the populist/progressive interpretations of the American experience that first appeared in the earlier part of this century. As I have pointed out in the introduction, these interpretations are basically "ends" or "results" oriented.

and pursuit of happiness.'' At a more mundane level, they would also include, albeit in a more modern and expansive form, those derived from the British tradition and inscribed in its most fundamental documents—the Magna Carta, the Petition of Right, and the Bill of Rights.

There are those who interpret the British political experience and the American tradition from a markedly different perspective. Briefly put, they view British history in terms of a continuous struggle for popular government, for self-government rather than rule by a tyrannical monarch. And they look upon the American evolution largely from this same perspective.[5] Thus, it is not at all surprising that, in arguing against a bill of rights, Alexander Hamilton could declare in *The Federalist* that the ''WE, THE PEOPLE'' of the Constitution's preamble is a ''better recognition of popular rights than volumes of those aphorisms which make the principal figure in several of our State bills of right'' (84:443). Here Hamilton is echoing the view, implicit in the Declaration of Independence, that the most basic right of a people is self-government.

In theory the tension is evident: Popular or republican government and rights do not, on occasion, mix very well. Majorities may encroach upon rights, and rights can serve to inhibit majorities. But the tension in the American experience is a concrete and practical one. That is, understanding its origin and nature, as well as the terms in which it is manifest, involves examining not only our history, but the history of England as well. For example, any effort to determine the original meanings of ''liberty'' and ''due process'' (the two, for reasons that will become apparent later, cannot be entirely separated) involves asking questions that can be answered only by recourse to history. Then, too, differences over the meaning and applicability of these terms in the American context arise from other concerns. To begin with, are English rights, which evolved from grants or concessions by the crown, appropriate for a republican regime?[6] To what extent, for instance, can these rights be incorporated into the American system without seriously undermining the republican principle? To what extent can we legitimately

---

[5]Hamilton, Madison, and Jay, on the basis of their contributions to *The Federalist*, can be placed in this category. Interesting in this connection are Madison's remarks: ''The first question that offers itself is, whether the general form and aspect of the government be strictly republican? It is evident that no other form would be reconcilable with the genius of the people of America; with the fundamental principles of the revolution; or with that honorable determination, which animates every votary of freedom, to rest all our political experiments on the capacity of mankind for self-government'' (39:194).

[6]As Hamilton observed in *The Federalist*: ''It has been several times truly remarked that bills of rights are, in their origin, stipulations between kings and their subjects, abridgements of prerogative in favor of privilege, reservations of rights not surrendered to the prince. Such was MAGNA CHARTA, obtained by the barons, sword in hand, from King John. Such was the subsequent confirmation of that charter by subsequent princes. Such was the *petition of right* assented to by Charles the First in the beginning of his reign. Such, also, was the Declaration of Right presented by the Lords and Commons to the Prince of Orange in 1688, and afterwards thrown into the form of an act of Parliament called the Bill of Rights'' (84:443).

read constitutionalism, in the sense of a fundamental law that controls and limits government, into the British tradition? The relevance of these and like controversies in fixing the original meaning of "due process" and "liberty" will also be apparent in due course.

Beyond concerns of this nature is another that relates principally to the essence and nature of liberty as it was understood at the time of Founding and the place of due process within this understanding. More specifically, from the historical context from which it evolved, what can be said about the role of due process with respect to liberty? Was its function intended to be a limited one; that is, to guarantee against abuses in only well-defined and restricted areas of the ruler/ruled relationship or, conversely, was it meant to apply to this relationship in a more comprehensive manner, constituting a standard, so to speak, against which many, if not most, actions of the rulers should be judged? Likewise, in what sense was the word "liberty" used in the Fifth Amendment? Concretely, was it used in a narrow sense (e.g., freedom from confinement) or a broad sense to embrace the elements of a wider conception of liberty?

There is, to put these concerns in a slightly different context, a reciprocal relationship between "due process" and "liberty." If, for instance, liberty is interpreted expansively—beyond, say, just the absence of physical restraint to encompass the elements of modern civil libertarianism—then the meaning of due process must also broaden to embrace new tests or standards to determine what processes of regulation relative to these liberties is "due."[7] Or, "due process" might be interpreted to contain inherent concepts or principles—"justice," "fairness," "reasonability," "equal protection"—that by themselves would expand the range of liberties to be protected by "due process."[8]

We can most profitably explore these and related matters by first surveying the meanings and concepts of liberty that prevailed at the time of Founding. As we shall see when we later turn to the English experience, "due process," in an important sense, is a derivative from the widely accepted understanding of liberty and its essential attributes. With this background or overview, we can then examine "due process," its meaning and its place within this generally accepted understanding of liberty. This should enable us to understand the sense in which

---

[7] In this connection, John Hart Ely's *Democracy and Distrust* (Cambridge: Harvard University Press, 1980) comes immediately to mind. In an important sense this widely acclaimed work is an attempt to set forth standards for "due process of lawmaking."

[8] For example, the notion of due process as "intended to secure the individual from the arbitrary exercise of the powers of government, unrestrained by the established principles of private rights and distributive justice" advanced by Justice William Johnson in 1819 (*Bank of Columbia v. Okely*, 17 U.S. [4 Wheat.] 235) would clearly expand the scope of liberty to be protected by due process. Quoted in Raoul Berger, " 'Law of the Land' Reconsidered," in *Selected Writings on the Constitution* (Cumberland, Virginia: James River Press, 1987), 134. Hereafter cited as *Selected Writings*. Rodney Mott's work, *Due Process of Law* (New York: De Capo Press, 1973), first published in 1926, is the *locus classicus* for the position that "due process" ("law of the land") authorized the courts from colonial times forward to strike down laws as "unreasonable" or "arbitrary."

"liberty" and "due process" were joined in the Fifth Amendment and the meaning attached to both.

LIBERTY: AN OVERVIEW

During the founding period—for our immediate purposes, that period running from approximately 1760 to the adoption of the Constitution—liberty, and its character and scope, was almost always discussed in the social compact or contract framework of thinking. There are a number of plausible reasons why this framework enjoyed such popularity, not the least of them being that such compacts—far from being mere theoretical fictions or abstractions—were a real part of the American tradition, dating back to the Mayflower Compact in 1620.[9] Consequently, the social contract approach, set forth systematically by serious political thinkers such as John Locke, fit in with the American experience. What is more—and a matter of some importance for an understanding of the roots of our Bill of Rights—William Blackstone in his *Commentaries*[10] was able to superimpose the contractarian approach upon the British common law tradition and the rights contained therein. Indeed, Blackstone was able to place these rights and liberties into a social contract context consonant with republican government.

Not all these social contract theories were exactly alike. But they all contained, in one form or another, the same basic elements—a state of nature, laws of nature, the consent of the governed, and some form of contract. They were also alike with regard to the ends of the government established by the contract, namely, life, liberty, and property. The second paragraph of the Declaration of Independence with its emphasis on the "Governments deriving their just powers from the consent of the governed" and holding "Life, Liberty, and the pursuit of Happiness" to be "unalienable Rights" succinctly summarizes the prevailing thought.[11] As

---

[9]Indeed, from the perspective of one student, modern American constitutionalism emerges from the numerous covenants, compacts, and charters that date back into antiquity. Certainly a goodly part of the American political tradition is caught up with the numerous compacts, voluntarily entered into, that set forth the terms for self-government among the colonists. See Donald S. Lutz, *The Origins of American Constitutionalism* (Baton Rouge: Louisiana State University Press, 1988).

[10]*Commentaries on the Laws of England.* Published in four volumes between 1765 and 1769, this work was widely read in the colonies. For an excellent analysis of the impact of Blackstone's *Commentaries* during the founding period, see Dennis Nolan, "Sir William Blackstone and the New Republic," *Political Science Reviewer* 6 (1976), 283–324.

[11]Questions have arisen as to why Jefferson substituted "pursuit of Happiness" for "property," the term generally employed in describing natural rights. One answer may be found by reference to Section 2 of the Virginia Declaration of Rights adopted June 12, 1776. It reads: "That all men are by nature equally free and independent, and have certain inherent rights, of which, when they enter into a state of society, they cannot, by any compact, deprive or divest their posterity; namely, the enjoyment of life and liberty, with the means of acquiring and possessing property, and pursuing and obtaining happiness." *The Founders' Constitution*, ed. Philip B. Kurland and Ralph Lerner, 5 vols. (Chicago: University of Chicago Press, 1987), I, 6. Hereafter cited as *Founders' Constitution*. In other words, Jefferson's formulation can be looked upon as a shorthand statement that merges

Jefferson was to write some fifty years after the fact, he intended that the Declaration be "an expression of the American mind." "All its authority," he continued, "rests then on the harmonizing sentiments of the day, whether expressed in conversation, in letters, printed essays, or in the elementary books of public right, as Aristotle, Cicero, Locke, Sidney, etc."[12]

If we probe a bit further into contract theory, we come to see the relationship between liberty and law. The following is a fairly typical picture of the state of nature encountered in the literature of this period: "In a state of nature, or where men are under no civil government, God has given to every one liberty to pursue his own happiness in whatever way, and by whatever means he pleases, without asking the consent or consulting the inclination of any other man, provided he keeps within the bounds of the law of nature. Within these bounds, he may govern his actions, and dispose of his property and person, as he thinks proper. Nor has any man, or any number of men, a right to restrain him in the exercise of this liberty, or punish, or call him to account for using it. This however is not a state of licentiousness, for the law of nature which bounds this liberty, forbids all injustice and wickedness, allows no man to injure another in his person or property, or to destroy his own life."[13]

This view of a conception of the state of nature corresponds in most particulars with the one that seemed to prevail at the time of Founding. It also prompts a

---

property rights with liberty. This merger, of course, does take place later in our constitutional history. On how this came to pass see Edward S. Corwin, *Liberty against Government* (Baton Rouge: Louisiana State University Press, 1948). See in particular chapter 3, "Liberty into Property before the Civil War." Corwin here deals extensively with the development of the "due process" clause of the Fifth Amendment.

[12]Letter to Henry Lee, May 8, 1825, in *The Works of Thomas Jefferson*, ed. Paul L. Ford, 12 vols. (New York: G. P. Putnam's Sons, 1905), XII, 409. Many have commented on the parallel between the Declaration and John Locke's language in his *Second Treatise of Government*. See John Locke, *Two Treatises of Government*, ed. Peter Laslett (Cambridge: Cambridge University Press, 1967). Hereafter cited as *The Second Treatise*. Jefferson writes of "Life, Liberty, and the pursuit of Happiness" and Locke of "life, liberty, and estate." The phrase "pursuit of Happiness" would seem to be more inclusive than "estate" in the sense that it could well embrace the liberty to acquire and use property within the limits of the law.

But, on this issue, see Philip A. Hamburger, "Natural Rights, Natural Law, and American Constitution," *Yale Law Review* 102 (1991), 914–15. Hamburger notes that America of the founding era possessed "highly generalized notions" of natural rights extracted from "the varying ideas espoused by Locke, Sidney and other European writers." Most Americans, he writes, "only became familiar with—or only retained—a relatively simple approach abstracted from the details of the foreign treatises. This simplified, generalized theory that Americans often learned in school, they repeated and had reinforced in sermons and secular political arguments. It is hardly surprising, therefore, that large numbers of Americans spoke about government, liberty and constitutional law on the basis of some shared assumptions about natural rights and the state of nature."

[13]Simeon Howard, "A Sermon Preached to the Ancient and Honorable Artillery Company in Boston" (1773) in *American Political Writing during the Founding Era, 1760–1805*, ed. Charles S. Hyneman and Donald S. Lutz, 2 vols. (Indianapolis: Liberty Fund, 1983), I, 187. Hereafter cited as *American Political Writing*.

serious question: Why would individuals ever consent to leave the state of nature to join together into a civil society? Why would reasonable men give up the relatively absolute liberty of the state of nature and opt for a more restrictive civil society? The answers invariably belie an idyllic state of nature marked by community, peace, and universal obedience to the natural law. If we take Locke's account, which seems to embrace those set forth in the political commentaries of the founding era, civil society necessarily comes into being because of the "influence of unruly passions," the disposition of some "to violate" or encroach "upon the liberty of others," and the "superior power of bad men" to injure the "*weak*," "without the means of security or redress."[14]

In sum, by this account, disobedience to the laws of nature leads to injustice and therewith diminishes liberty in the state of nature. But this is only the manifestation of a more basic difficulty. In the last analysis, the incapacity of men to settle disputes according the precepts of the natural law in the state of nature poses the fundamental problem. As Locke points out, the reason why men must quit the state of nature arises from the equality that allows each "*the Executive Power* of the Law of Nature.*" This renders "Men . . . Judges in their own Cases" which, in turn, leads to "partiality and violence." Not only will "Self-love . . . make men partial to themselves and their Friends," but their "Ill Nature, Passion and Revenge will carry them too far in punishing others." "*Civil Government*," Locke concedes, "is the proper Remedy for the Inconveniences of the State of Nature"; that is, more exactly, for the "Confusion and Disorder" that arise from men judging of their own causes.[15]

In the vocabulary of the founding era, by quitting the state of nature men traded their "natural liberty" for "civil" or "political liberty," a trade that was widely regarded as a bargain. James Wilson in his Lectures on the Law,[16] certainly the most extensive and systematic treatment by any of our Founding Fathers relating to foundations of government, put this commonly shared belief in measured and restrained terms: "It will, I think, be found, that wise and good government . . .

---

[14]Ibid. In this respect, we might note in passing, until a relatively recent date, it was customary for students of political thought to stress the differences between Locke's state of nature, which was depicted as relatively tranquil, with that drawn by Hobbes in his *Leviathan*, a "war" of all against all wherein the life of the individual is "short," "nasty," and "brutish." Recent scholarship questions whether any such distinction can be made; that is, whether the "inconvenience" of Locke's state of nature does not in reality amount to the very conditions depicted by Hobbes.

[15]*The Second Treatise*, Ch. 2, Sect. 13.

[16]These lectures, thirty-five in all and in various stages of completion, deal with a variety of legal matters such as the nature and types of crime; the duties of judges, juries, and attorneys; and, most significantly, the origins, nature, and purposes of government. They were delivered at the College of Philadelphia (now the University of Pennsylvania) in the winter of 1790–91. Wilson's various business ventures—he was one of the great land speculators of this era—and his duties on the Supreme Court as an Associate Justice did not allow him time to continue his lecture series or even to put all of the lectures into a final and polished form. The lectures, however, comprise the bulk of what we have from the pen of Wilson.

instead of contracting, enlarges as well as secures the exercise of the natural liberty of man; and what I say of his natural liberty, I mean to extend . . . to all his other natural rights.''[17] Others, particularly those who approached this issue from a Christian perspective, argued that true liberty could only be had through civil law. Aside from arguing that civil law properly enforced by ''civil magistrates'' was necessary to curb men's ''unbridled lusts'' and to preserve the ''public safety,'' they emphasized the need for an orderly, predictable, and uniform application of laws that would encourage the promotion of ''good''; protect the ''liberties and privileges'' derived from the natural, God-given laws; and permit individuals freely to choose their pursuits, ''consistent with the public good.''[18]

ESCAPE FROM ARBITRARINESS: THE LINK BETWEEN THEORY AND PRACTICE

These observations are significant because they point to what is not only a precondition or *sine qua non* of liberty, but also one of its core ingredients. This is to say, natural liberty was not regarded as ''true'' or ''real'' liberty because of the uncertain and unpredictable application of the laws of nature in the state of nature. Moreover, an arbitrariness characterized the application of natural laws, particularly in those situations where individuals were allowed to judge their own cause.

To put this otherwise, at the time of the Founding there was almost universal acceptance of Montesquieu's teachings concerning liberty and its character. ''Liberty,'' he wrote, ''is a right of doing whatever the laws permit, and if a citizen could do what they forbid he would be no longer possessed of liberty, because all his fellow-citizens would have the same power.''[19] Aside from the fact that this stipulation carries with it certain important presumptions—e.g., that the laws must be duly enacted and known—its very terms deny that liberty could exist in a state of nature where individuals violate the laws of nature whenever it suits their interests. But, perhaps more to the point in this respect is Montesquieu's association of ''political liberty'' with the subject's ''tranquility of mind'' that arises ''from the opinion each person has of his safety.'' For this liberty to exist, he insists, ''it is requisite the government be so constituted as one man need not be afraid of another.''[20]

---

[17] *The Works of James Wilson*, ed. Robert G. McCloskey (Cambridge: Harvard University Press, 1956), II, 586–87.

[18] Samuel West, ''On the Right to Rebel Against Government'' (1776) in *American Political Writing*, I, 415.

[19] *The Spirit of the Laws,* trans. Anne M. Cohler (New York: Cambridge University Press, 1989), Ch. 11, Sect. 3. Of course this definition must be read in context; that is, on the presumption that the regime is bent upon legislating in accordance with the precepts of the natural law. Not all accepted this definition without reservations. Theophilus Parsons, for example, modified it to read: ''political liberty is the right every man in the state has, to do whatever is not prohibited by laws, TO WHICH HE HAS GIVEN HIS CONSENT.'' *American Political Writing*, I, 488.

[20] Ibid., Sect. 6.

It is hardly surprising, then, that one proposition that emerges with unmistakable clarity from the thought of this era is that liberty and arbitrariness are incompatible with one another, that where arbitrariness prevails, "tyranny" is to be found. Indeed, it would be difficult to exaggerate the extent to which the absence of arbitrariness was considered to be the essence of liberty and a requisite for a *legitimate* government. The concern of those during the founding period was not, of course, that of moving out of a state of nature into a civil society in order to escape the arbitrariness associated with the exercise of "natural liberty." Rather, the critical problem—as Montesquieu's observations suggest—was how to fashion institutions and processes that would avoid the arbitrariness that was the bane of liberty. As Locke asked plaintively: can government be the "remedy" for the arbitrariness found in the state of nature when "one Man commanding a multitude, has the Liberty to be Judge in his own Case, and may do to all his Subjects whatever he pleases, without the least liberty to any one to question or controle those who Execute his Pleasure?"[21] Thus, with many others, Locke saw that leaving the state of nature was not by itself a cure for the problem of tyranny; an absolute monarchy scarcely constituted any improvement over this natural state. Clearly, his views on this score were influenced by the arbitrary and capricious rule associated with absolute monarchy, the very conditions that had prompted the development of rights and privileges in the common law.

The concern to avoid arbitrary government evidences itself at different levels during the founding period, if only because it had also been part of our experience as well during the colonial period. At the highest level, that involving the basic constitutional structures and powers, concerted efforts were made to provide for a "government of law, not of men," a fact that accounts for the virtually universal acceptance of the separation of powers principle. Article 30 of the Massachusetts Constitution of 1780, part of a preamble of sorts setting forth the rights and liberties of the people, explicitly draws the connection between the separation of powers and a government of laws. "In the government of this Commonwealth," it declares, "the legislative department shall never exercise the executive and judicial powers, or either of them. The executive shall never exercise the legislative and judicial powers, or either of them. The judicial shall never exercise the

---

[21]Ch. 13. To repeat and emphasize a point that we made in chapter 3, Locke brings up a point here that Aristotle had explored in his *Politics*. For Aristotle there were true and perverted forms of government, classified according to the source of sovereignty—the one, the few, the many. The pure or good form of rule by the one was, according to Aristotle's classification, monarchy; the corrupted, tyranny. Thus he linked tyranny with rule by one, the most severe form of which involved "a single person [governing] men, who are all his peers or superiors, without any form of responsibility, and with a view to his own advantage rather than that of his subjects. It is thus a rule of force; and no freeman will voluntary endure such a system." *Politics*, trans. Benjamin Jowett (New York: Modern Library, 1943), Bk. 4, Ch. 11. Locke, however, believed that tyranny existed where such arbitrary authority was exercised by the "one or many." *The Second Treatise*, Ch. 18, Sect. 201. Locke's more expansive view prevailed because the essence of tyranny was thought to consist of arbitrary control over others, whether this control was exercised by one, a few, or many.

legislative and executive powers, or either of them: to the end it may be a government of laws and not of men.''[22]

Certain essays in *The Federalist* manifest the depth of the Founders' concern to provide a "government of law," as well as the relationship between this goal and the separation of powers. In Federalist 47, Madison's most general discussion of the separation of powers, he sets out to show that the critics of the proposed Constitution are mistaken in their view that it provides for a dangerous blending of powers. Yet, he confesses at once that if the critics were correct "no further arguments would be necessary to inspire a universal reprobation of the system." And his reasons for this he makes clear. Of the separation of powers, he writes, "No political truth is certainly of greater intrinsic value, or is stamped with the authority of more enlightened patrons of liberty." He declares, without any qualifications, that the accumulation of the legislative, executive, and judicial powers "in the same hands, whether of one, a few, or many . . . may justly be pronounced the very definition of tyranny" (47:249).

The equation of the concentration of powers with tyranny is revealing. In Madison's definition the mere existence or condition of such a concentration, by itself—quite apart from *how* or for *what ends* the powers are used—constitutes tyranny. Whether the powers are used oppressively or benevolently has no bearing on whether tyranny exists; their concentration alone is sufficient because such a condition would, in effect, establish a master/slave relationship with the ruled subject to arbitrary and capricious commands of the rulers.[23] He quotes from

---

[22]*Founders' Constitution*, I, 13–14. In this connection it should be remarked that separation of powers was a feature of the constitutions of all but two states (Rhode Island and Connecticut) at the time of ratification. In four of these nine states there was a constitutional declaration similar to that of the Massachusetts Constitution concerning the need for separation of the branches. In addition, three of the last four states to ratify the Constitution—Virginia, Rhode Island, and North Carolina— recommended an amendment specifying that "the legislative, executive, and judiciary powers of Government should be separate and distinct." *Documents Illustrative of the Formation of the Union of the American States*, ed. Charles C. Tansill (Washington, D.C.: Government Printing Office, 1927), 1028–29, 1045, and 1053. Hereafter cited as *Documents Illustrative*.

[23]James Fenimore Cooper, in the following excerpt, points up why the mere potentiality of arbitrary and capricious rule was considered inimical to liberty. "A slave holder in Virginia is the master of two slaves: to one he grants his liberty, with the means to go to a town in a free state. The other accompanies his old associate clandestinely. In this town, they engage their services, voluntarily, to a common master, who assigns to them equal shares in the same labor, paying them the same wages. In time, the master learns their situation, but, being an indulgent man, he allows the slave to retain his present situation. In all material things, these brothers are equal—they labor together, receive the same wages, and eat of the same food. Yet one is bond, and the other free, since it is in the power of the master, or his heir, or of his assignee, at any time, to reclaim the service of the one who was not legally manumitted and reduce him again to the condition of slavery. One of these brothers is the master of his own acts, while the other, though temporarily enjoying the same privileges, holds them subject to the will of a superior." *The American Democrat* (Indianapolis: Liberty Fund, 1981), 56.

Cooper's illustration reveals why many colonists believed that they were slaves because of their subordinate relationship to Great Britain. As Stephen Hopkins put it in 1764, "those who are governed at the will of another, or of others, and whose property may be taken from them by taxes or

Montesquieu to the effect that where the executive and legislative powers are joined "there can be no liberty, because apprehensions may arise lest *the same* monarch or senate should *enact* tyrannical laws to *execute* them in a tyrannical manner." Where the judicial power is united with the legislative, "the life and liberty of the subject would be exposed to arbitrary control, for *the judge* would then be the *legislator*." Similarly, if the judicial and executive powers are united, "*the judge* might behave with all the violence of *an oppressor*" (47:251). In sum, and quite in keeping with the teachings of Montesquieu, Locke, and Aristotle (to name but a few), Madison regarded tyranny as a condition or state of affairs in which the ruled may be subject to arbitrary control by the rulers. The relationship between rulers and ruled in a system with a consolidation of powers is the same as that of masters to slaves in the sense that both the rulers and masters possess total and arbitrary authority over their subjects. And, though a ruler possessed of legislative, executive, and judicial powers may govern benevolently, this does not alter the condition of tyranny any more than a master by treating his slaves in a thoroughly enlightened manner abrogates the condition of slavery.

Now aside from providing for the rule of law, the separation of powers was viewed as a protection against legislative bodies' passing oppressive laws. Because the administration of the laws would be the responsibility of an independent executive, the legislators—as well as their families, friends, and political allies—would be obliged to conform to the provisions of the law. This fact alone, it was believed, would serve as a powerful deterrent against the legislators' passing oppressive laws.[24] Madison makes this very point in Federalist 57 when he writes that a restraint upon the House's passing "oppressive measures" is that its members "can make no law which will not have its full operation on themselves and their friends, as well as on the great mass of the society." And he cautions, should "the vigilant and manly spirit which actuates the people of America—a spirit which nourishes freedom, and in return is nourished by it . . . ever be so far debased as to tolerate a law not obligatory on the legislature, as well as on the people, the people will be prepared to tolerate anything but liberty" (57:296–97).

---

otherwise without their own consent and against their will, are in the miserable condition of slaves." *American Political Writing*, I, 46.

Garry Wills argues, in much this same vein, that the constitutional separation was aimed at making the rulers accountable to the law, a condition that had to be met in order to render the Constitution legitimate. See his *Explaining America* (Garden City, New York: Doubleday, 1981), particularly chapter 12.

[24]To comprehend the importance attached to this "reflexive" principle, we need only recur again to the Virginia Declaration of Rights. Section 5 reads: "That the Legislative and Executive powers of the States should be separate and distinct from the Judicative; and, that the members of the two first may be restrained from oppression, by feeling and participating the burdens of the people, they should, at fixed periods, be reduced to a private state, return into that body from which they were originally taken, and the vacancies be supplied by frequent, certain, and regular elections." *The Roots of the Bill of Rights*, ed. Bernard Schwartz, 5 vols. (New York: Chelsea House, 1971), II, 235. Hereafter cited as *Roots*.

LIBERTY AND DUE PROCESS: THE ENGLISH LEGACY

While the Founders were certainly inventive and looked to the failings of the state governments for lessons on how to avoid both tyranny and oppression, they were also very familiar with the English experience and the "rights" of Englishmen found in the common law, especially those that were intended to eliminate the arbitrariness that Locke and Montesquieu feared. That the colonists from the very outset considered themselves under protection of British law is evident from the Virginia Charter of 1606 which provided that the colonists and their descendants "shall have and enjoy all Liberties, Franchises and Immunities within any of our other Dominions, to all intents and purposes, as if they had been abiding and born within this our Realm of England or any other of our said Dominions."[25] Similar language is to be found in all the charters that followed, the last being the Georgia charter in 1732.[26] These provisions constitute one of the reasons that, in their disputes with the mother country prior to the revolution, the colonists could use provisions and principles of the common law and Parliamentary statutes to support their positions against the Crown.

To understand the nature of these rights and privileges, as well as the influence of the British legacy on the Founding Fathers, we must begin with the Magna Carta and, in particular, chapter 39 of its 1215 version.[27] In modernized form this chapter reads: "No freeman shall be arrested, or detained in prison, or deprived of his freehold, or outlawed, or banished, or in any way molested; and we will not set forth against him, nor send against him, unless by the lawful judgment of his peers and [or] by the law of this land."[28] After two reissues in 1217 and 1225, this provision and chapter 40 ("To no one will we sell, to no one will we refuse or delay, right or justice") were merged into chapter 29 of the "official" version of the Magna Carta put on the statute books in 1297 by Edward I. While these provisions are universally regarded as the most significant portions of the original charter, chapter 20 (amercement "according to degree of offense") and chapter

---

[25]Ibid., I, 59–60.

[26]The second resolution of the First Continental Congress in 1774 asserted that "our ancestors, who first settled these colonies, were at the time of their emigration from the mother country, entitled to all the rights, liberties, and immunities of free and natural-born subjects, within the realm of England." *Roots*, I, 216.

[27]The 1215 version of the Magna Carta underwent unofficial revisions involving additions and deletions in 1216 and 1217. It was officially promulgated in 1225 by Henry III. While the 1225 version is the "official" one, the 1215 version is the one most frequently referred to in scholarly writings. Chapter 39 of the 1215 manuscript became chapter 29 in the official version.

[28]McKechnie's translation in "Source Materials" in Roscoe Pound, *The Development of Constitutional Guarantees of Liberty* (New Haven: Yale University Press, 1957), 123. Hereafter cited as "Source Materials." The latter part of this provision ("unless by the lawful judgment of his peers and by the law of the land") reads in Latin: *nisi per legale judicium parium suorum vel per legem terrae*. Dispute has arisen over whether *vel* is to be translated "and," "or," or "and/or." Many of the colonial charters and state constitutions, as we will see below, incorporated this chapter verbatim and, in virtually every instance, used "or."

28 (compensation for taking "corn or other chattels") do embody principles that are articulated later in more expansive form.

Clearly the chief provisions of chapter 39 were intended to promote the conditions of liberty that we have discussed above. In fact, the very objective was to curb the arbitrary and capricious actions of King John (presumably as well as future monarchs) that had resulted in punishment without recourse to processes, such as proper notification, hearing, or judicial judgment, which were part of the common law or of customs so deeply embedded and so well understood as to enjoy the status of law. What is more, as Raoul Berger points out, "judicial judgment" tacitly assumes an "antecedent law . . . the violation of which" gives rise to such judgment. Thus, chapter 39 tacitly embraces the Roman maxim that "no person shall be punished except in pursuance of a statute which fixes a penalty for criminal behavior." In this way, chapter 39 plays a key role in subordinating the king to the laws.[29]

Largely through the efforts and writings of Edward Coke, the Magna Carta and its provisions, particularly chapter 39, have played a central role in both British and American constitutional development. Coke must be credited with advancing the notion that the Magna Carta constituted a fundamental English law whose provisions, amplified by judicial interpretations, served as a restraint on the king's prerogatives. Coke must also be credited with supplanting the phrase "law of the land," found in chapter 39 of the original Magna Carta, with the more modern expression "due process of law."[30] In his *Second Institute*—a commentary on the Magna Carta published after his death by order of the House of Commons in 1642—Coke amplified the meaning of chapter 39. He maintained that since the time of Edward III (1355) "the true sense and exposition" of the phrase "by the law of the land" has been equated with "due process of law." Such he derived from the statute enacted by Parliament under Edward III which provided "that no man be taken, imprisoned, or put out of his free-hold without process of the law; that is, by indictment or presentment of good and lawfull men, where such deeds be done in due manner, or by writ originall of the common law." The same statute declared moreover that "No man of what state or condition he be, shall be put out of his lands or tenements, nor taken, nor imprisoned, nor disinherited, nor put to death, without he be brought to answer by due process of law" wherein "due process of law" is taken to mean "due process of the common law."[31]

Coke's views found expression in the Petition of Right (1628), which was forced upon Charles I by Parliament to curb the royal prerogative by prohibiting

---

[29]Berger, *Selected Writings*, 127.

[30]Though we will discuss this matter later, it is important to note that Coke's equation of "law of the land" with "due process" is not entirely justifiable. As Raoul Berger, citing the researches of C.B. Adams and Charles McIlwain, points out, the term "law of the land" was used to ensure that the barons could be punished only for violation of known statutes, not at the mere will or whim of the King. Berger, *Selected Writings*, 127–28.

[31]"Source Materials," 153.

arbitrary imprisonment, taxation without consent, misuse of martial law, and the unauthorized billeting of soldiers and sailors. Sections 3 and 4 of its provisions, however, are the most theoretically significant. Section 3 expressly invokes the provisions of chapter 39 of the Magna Carta against these practices, while the fourth section sets forth Coke's reformulation of the "law of the land" clause found therein by declaring "That no man of what estate or condition that he be, should be put out of his land or tenements, nor taken nor imprisoned, nor disinherited, nor put to death without being brought to answer by due process of law."[32] In Coke's commentary on the Magna Carta in his *Second Institute*,[33] especially that on chapter 29 of the 1297 version (the original chapter 39), are to be found accepted principles and practices of due process—indictment by grand jury, trial by "law of the land," and habeas corpus.

Aside from the fact that Coke's "due process" and its application were clearly designed to curb the arbitrary powers of the monarch—and this in keeping with the essence of liberty as it was understood at the time of our Founding—two other matters warrant our attention, particularly in light of subsequent developments. First, as we have already noted, Coke's substitution of "due process of law" for "law of the land" that we find in the Petition of Right did not take hold on this side of the Atlantic. This fact is of considerable significance because, to anticipate a bit what follows, this "law of the land" phraseology eventually provided a plausible opening for the argument that there were fundamental laws—well beyond any associated with mere procedures—that, though not expressly set forth in the Constitution, serve to limit the scope of legitimate lawmaking authority. Put another way, "law of the land," far more readily than "due process," opens up avenues for extensive claims against the state on any number of grounds: e.g., that "the law of the land" embodied in the Magna Carta is derived from "right reason" or from "natural law" that endows it with a status superior to that of ordinary law; that there is an "animating spirit" behind "the law of the land" that constitutes a standard for judging the validity of ordinary statutes.[34] "Law of the land" has, in fact, been interpreted in this manner in the American context, originally to protect "vested rights."[35] And, while Coke's equation of "due process" and "law of the land" might have originally served to inhibit any such line

---

[32]*Roots*, I, 20.

[33]The second of a four-volume *Institutes of the Laws of England* published by order of Parliament in 1641. The *Second Institute* includes a commentary on the provisions of the Magna Carta, the 1297 version.

[34]See our discussion below on the *Declaration and Resolves* of the First Continental Congress to see how the Magna Carta and the rights derived from it are merged with the natural "rights" that flow from contractual mode of thinking.

[35]For developments very similar to this, see Edward Corwin, *Liberty Against Government*. Corwin sees this development springing from Locke's *Second Treatise*. However, contrary to what Corwin contends, Locke did not advocate limited majority rule or the protection of "rights." For the most exhaustive work on this subject see Willmoore Kendall, *John Locke and Majority Rule* (Champaign-Urbana: University of Illinois Press, 1940).

of development, the equation eventually proved useful because whatever fell under the scope of "law of the land"—including, of course, liberties of various kinds—could, on the authority of Coke, be squeezed back into "due process."[36]

We shall have occasion to analyze in greater detail the distinctions between "due process" and "law of the land" when considering the meaning of the due process clause in the Fifth Amendment and its relationship to other provisions in the Bill of Rights.

Our second observation is this: leaving the "due process"/"law of the land" equation to one side—as well as the question whether such an equation is entirely legitimate—Coke subscribed to the proposition that the Magna Carta embodied fundamental law; that its provision did limit sovereign authority, including Parliament. As a member of Parliament in his battle against Charles I, he would declare:

> I know that prerogative is part of the law, but sovereign power is no Parliamentary word; in my opinion, it weakens Magna Carta and all our statutes; for they are absolute without any saving of sovereign power. And shall we now add to it, we shall weaken the foundation of the Law, and then the building must need fall; take we heed what we yield unto—Magna Carta is such a Fellow he will have no Sovereign.[37]

In this connection, his opinion in Bonham's case, nullifying an act of Parliament, is usually cited. In this instance, however, Coke made no reference to the Magna Carta, relying instead on "common right and reason" which he closely associates with the common law.[38]

It would be wrong, however, to believe that Coke's notions about fundamental law (in the sense he meant) and "common right and reason" as a limitation on Parliament were widely shared either in Great Britain or the colonies. To be sure, in Lechmere's case (1761), James Otis cites and employs Coke's reasoning to

---

[36]Coke sought judicial enforcement of rights and liberties by reference to fundamental law and reason. That he thought "due process" important to this enforcement—save as it provided for certain modes of procedure, principally in criminal cases—is not at all clear. That is, whereas in recent decades "due process" is a critical element in much of our modern judicial enforcement of substantive rights, Coke did not seem to look upon it in a fashion suitable for this function. This could account for the fact that he narrowed "law of the land" down to "due process."

A firmer justification for an extensive judicial protection of rights within Coke's theory is clearly to be found in his references to "fundamental law" and to "common right and reason." Put otherwise, Coke would probably not place such enormous reliance on "due process of law" to serve the ends of judicial control over the substance of legislation because, in his mind, significant as it was, the term had a narrow and specialized meaning and function.

[37]Quoted in A. E. Dick Howard, *The Road from Runnymede* (Charlottesville, Virginia: University of Virginia Press, 1967), 120.

[38]"And it appears in our books that in many cases, the common law will controul acts of Parliament, and sometimes adjudge them to be utterly void: for when an act of Parliament is against common right and reason, or repugnant, or impossible to be performed, the common law will controul it, and adjudge such act to be void." "Source Materials," 173.

argue that the Parliamentary act authorizing the use of Writs of Assistance was null and void, contrary to the fundamental principles of the Magna Carta and English constitutional practice.[39] Yet Otis's position is remembered precisely because it was relatively novel in this era.

What is more, within the confines of the British constitutional framework as it was generally understood after the Glorious Revolution of 1688, Parliament was considered supreme. Blackstone, whose *Commentaries* in the later part of the founding era had supplanted Coke's *Second Institute*, declared that "The Power and jurisdiction of Parliament" was "transcendent and paramount." "It hath sovereign and uncontrollable authority," he wrote, "in making, confirming, enlarging, restraining, abrogating, repealing, reviving, and expounding of laws, concerning matters of all possible denominations, ecclesiastical, or temporal, civil, military maritime, or criminal; this being the place where that absolute despotic power, which must in all government reside somewhere, is entrusted by the constitution of these kingdoms." "True it is," he observed, "that what the parliament doth, no authority upon earth can undo."[40]

What is interesting in this connection is the *Declaration and Resolves* of the First Continental Congress which we have already had occasion to allude to. Because Parliament was recognized as supreme, the colonists had to find grounds to question its legitimacy by using a standard outside of the British constitutional framework. These grounds are set forth at the outset of this document and contain elements of social contract thought such as the "immutable law of nature" and the claim that the colonists are entitled to "life, liberty, & property" of which they cannot be deprived "without their consent."[41] What is notable here is the three-tier claim of the colonists that blends together this transcendent "natural law" with the common law rights and those derived from the Magna Carta, as well as the colonial charters and compacts. That is, the rights they claim are adduced from "the immutable laws of nature, the principles of the English constitution, and the several charters or compacts."[42]

---

[39]"Source Materials," 184–85. John Adams summarizes Otis's position in the Lechmere Case (1761): "As to act of Parliament. An Act against the Constitution is void: an Act against natural Equity is void." *Roots*, I, 183. This, it can be argued, goes well beyond what Coke declared in Bonham's case. Narrowly interpreted, Coke declared in Bonham that it is contrary to right or reason that a party should be judge of its own cause. This argument, it should be emphasized, differs from the one that gained considerable currency during the pre-Revolutionary period to the effect that Parliament possessed no legitimate authority to pass laws for the colonies—that the relationship between the Parliament and colonies was that of master to slave, since Parliament did not have the consent of the colonists to legislate for them. This argument is caught up in the expression "no taxation without representation" and does not really touch upon the fundamental doctrine of legislative supremacy challenged by Otis.

[40]William Blackstone, *Commentaries on the Laws of England* (Chicago: University of Chicago Press, 1979), Bk. I, Ch. 2, Sect. III.

[41]*Roots*, I, 216.

[42]Ibid.

This is an interesting linkage because it unites the theoretically oriented contract approach with the more down-to-earth common law evolution as a grounding for rights, a linkage that was to be expected given the dual nature of thinking about the sources of rights and privileges. Perhaps more important, this approach "sanctifies" the common law rights; it gives them a higher law status, not an unimportant transmutation in light of later developments we will discuss.

Now the issue raised by this mode of thinking ultimately goes beyond the question of Parliamentary supremacy and the arguments posed by Otis. The colonists certainly did have a good case in arguing (as they did in the *Declaration and Resolves* and elsewhere[43]) that taxation without representation was clearly contrary to established English constitutional practice. But this—and, of course, the more general argument that any legislation without colonial representation violated the colonists' liberties and privileges—posed a more fundamental concern, namely, whether the British constitutional framework could ever insure the liberties and rights of the colonists. They raised the issue, that is, whether the colonists could ever enjoy liberty under the authority of Parliament or whether separation with self-government was the only feasible solution. In short, this protest and others brought into question the very legitimacy of the relationship between the colonists and Great Britain within the framework of the British constitution.[44]

LAW OF THE LAND: THE AMERICAN EXPERIENCE

The substance and full impact of the English heritage can be seen by turning to the American colonial experience. First, in this endeavor, we cannot help but see that Coke's teachings had an enormous impact on colonial thinking.[45] Coke's influence is most evident in William Penn's *The Excellent Privilege of Liberty and Property Being the Birth-Right of the Free-Born Subjects of England* (1687). This publication, intended to acquaint the citizens of Pennsylvania with their liberties, presents a commentary on the Magna Carta that derives almost entirely, albeit indirectly,[46] from Coke's *Second Institute*. Its introductory paragraphs are

---

[43]See especially *The Rights of the Colonists and a List of Infringements and Violations of Rights* which first appeared in Massachusetts in 1772. *Roots*, I, 200.

[44]On the use and effectiveness of these arguments see John Phillip Reid, *The Concept of Liberty in the Age of the American Revolution*, chapter 11.

[45]See *The Road from Runnymede*, chapter 6, for a survey of the most commonly used law sources during the colonial period. As Howard comments by way of conclusion to this chapter: "It was Coke which the colonial writers cited, and which the colonial courts relied on, far more than any other authority. It was natural that the colonial lawyer should put this same tradition to work in defense of his rights in the years before the Revolution. It was because he had learned the lessons of the common law so well that the American was able to use the Magna Carta and Coke and the other precedents so effectively in arguing the colonial case against England" (132).

[46]Penn's commentary on the Magna Carta was lifted from Henry Care's *English Liberties* which, in turn, relied very heavily on Coke's elaboration.

by themselves noteworthy for indicating both the ends and scope of English liberty as it was understood at this time. "In *France*, and other nations," Penn remarks, "the mere will of the Prince is law, his word takes off any man's head, imposeth taxes, or seizes any man's estate, when, how and as often as he lists; and if one be accused, or but so much as suspected of any crime, he may either presently execute him, or banish, or imprison him at pleasure; or if he will be so gracious as to proceed by form of their laws, if any two villains will but swear against the poor party, his life is gone; nay, if there be no witness, yet he may be put on the rack, the tortures whereof make many an innocent person confess himself guilty, and then, with seeming justice, is executed."[47]

Penn immediately contrasts this situation to the one that prevails in England where "the Law is both the measure and the bound of every Subject's duty and allegiance, each man having a Fundamental Right born with him, as to freedom of his person and property in his estate, which he cannot be deprived of, but either by his consent, or some crime, for which the law has imposed such a penalty or forfeiture." In this vein he goes on to point out that the "Kings take a solemn oath . . . to observe and cause the laws to be kept" and that the judges are bound "to do equal Law and Right to all the King's Subjects, rich and poor, and not to delay any person of Common Right."[48]

Still another characteristic of the American colonial experience involved setting forth in some detail "laws of the land," primarily with regard to judicial and executive processes. The Concessions and Agreements of West New Jersey (1677) is particularly notable among the early charters in presenting a collation and refinement of the Magna Carta's guarantees. For example, its chapter XVII provided "That no Proprietor, freeholder or inhabitant of the said Province of West New Jersey, shall be deprived or condemned of life, limb, liberty, estate property or any wayes hurt in his or their privileges, freedoms or franchises upon any account whatsoever, without a due tryal, and judgment passed by twelve good and lawful men of his neighbourhood first had: And that in all causes to be tryed and in all tryals, the person or persons arraigned may except against any of the said neighbourhood, without any reason rendered (not exceeding thirty five) and in case of any valid reason alleged, against every person nominated for that service."[49] Other chapters specify additional elements of a "due tryal." Chapter XIX provided that there be "three Justices or Commissioners who shall sitt with the twelve men of the Neighbourhood with them to heare all causes and to assist the said twelve men . . . in case of Law." But the justices or commissioners were bound to the "Judgment as they shall receive from" the jurors, "in whom only the Judgment resides, and not otherwise."[50]

---

[47]*Founders' Constitution*, I, 432.
[48]Ibid.
[49]*Roots*, I, 127.
[50]Ibid., 128.

In the ensuing decades to the time of the adoption of the Constitution, these procedural guarantees were refined and expanded. The provisions of the more elaborate state constitutions adopted soon after the Declaration of Independence illustrate the extent of this development. The Massachusetts Constitution of 1780, for instance, provided, ''No subject shall be held to answer for any crimes or offence, until the same is fully and plainly, substantially, and formally, described to him; or be compelled to accuse, or furnish evidence against himself. And every subject shall have a right to produce all proofs that may be favorable to him; to meet the witnesses against him face to face, and to be fully heard in his defence by himself, or his counsel, at his election.''[51] Article IX of the Pennsylvania Declaration of Rights, drafted four years before its Massachusetts counterpart, fixed upon the same procedural guarantees in only slightly different language: ''That in all prosecution for criminal offences, a man hath a right to be heard by himself and his council, to demand the cause and nature of his accusation, to be confronted with the witnesses, to call for evidence in his favour, and a speedy public trial, by an impartial jury of the country, without the unanimous consent of which jury he cannot be found guilty; nor can he be compelled to give evidence against himself.''[52]

There are other similarities between the bills or declarations of rights of the states that followed upon the Declaration of Independence. In fact, as the Pennsylvania provision cited immediately above would suggest, the more extensive listings contained those provisions that were later incorporated in the national Bill of Rights—compensation for property taken for public use, provision against unreasonable searches and seizures, the right to bear arms, protection against cruel and unusual punishment, and trial by jury in criminal cases. What is apparent in all of these bills of rights to one degree or another, however, is the influence of rights, principles, and procedures that had evolved in the English experience over the centuries and whose development was traceable to the Magna Carta.

The West New Jersey agreement raises another highly significant question that, as we shall see, bears upon the matter of the drafters' intentions regarding the due process clause of the Fifth Amendment, as well as the more general controversy surrounding the constitutional scope of judicial authority to limit legislative power. The agreement, that is to say, expressly declares that fundamental laws such as those cited above pose limitations on legislative authority. Chapter XIII declares ''THAT the common law or fundamental rights and privileges of West New Jersey, are individually agreed upon by the Proprietors and freeholders thereof, to be the foundation of the government, which is not be altered by the Legislative authority, or free Assembly hereafter mentioned and constituted, but that the said Legislative authority is constituted according to these fundamentals, to make such laws as agree with, and maintain the said fundamentals, and to make

---

[51]Ibid., II, 342.
[52]Ibid., II, 235.

no laws that in the least contradict, differ or vary from the said fundamentals, under what pretence or allegation soever.'' The next chapter endeavors to put some teeth in this provision with the following warning: ''BUT if it so happen that any person or persons of the said General Assembly, shall therein designedly, willfully, and maliciously, move or excite any to move, any matter or thing what-soever, that contradicts or any ways subverts, any fundamentals of the said laws in the Constitution of the government of this Province, it being proved by seven honest and reputable persons, he or they shall be proceeded against as traitors to the said government.''[53]

With the West New Jersey charter we have an early example of constitutional-ism, American style; that is, the notion of a ''fundamental law'' that cannot be altered or abridged by the institutions created by this fundamental law. By the time Publius writes, he can speak of a ''distinction . . . well understood in Amer-ica,'' and not so well understood elsewhere, ''between a Constitution established by the people and unalterable by the government, and a law established by the government and alterable by the government'' (53:277).[54]

Limitations of this nature on legislative authority to alter the modes of proce-dure in criminal (or, for that matter, civil cases) was far from universal. The exceptions are not hard to come by.[55] The Massachusetts Body of Liberties prom-ulgated in 1641—a year before the publication of Coke's *Second Institute*—con-tained many of the guarantees that had over the centuries evolved from the Magna Carta and the common law. Among the *Rights Rules and Liberties con-cerning Juditiall proceedings* is the right to a hearing in all criminal cases; punish-ment proportionate to the crime; and protection against double jeopardy, self-incrimination, and punishment ''inhumane Barbarous or cruel.''[56] But these are statutory guarantees against, let us take great care to note, the judiciary—guarantees that can be enlarged, changed, or modified by the legislative body. The feeling prevailed, it would seem, that the people were ultimately the best safeguard of the common law procedures. Such a view finds expression in the very first article which embraces chapter 39 of the Magna Carta: ''No mans life shall be taken away, no mans honour or good name shall be stayned, no mans person shall be arrested, restrayned, banished, dismembred, nor any wayes pun-ished, no man shall be deprived of his wife or children, no mans goods or estaite shall be taken away from him, nor any way indammaged under colour of law or

---

[53]Ibid., I, 126.

[54]Of course, Publius is to use this concept of constitutionalism to justify a very limited form of judicial review in Federalist 78.

[55]In fact, Publius in arguing against the addition of a bill of rights was quick to point out that the common law rights contained in the New York State Constitution were ''subject 'to such alterations and provisions as the legislature shall from time to time make concerning the same.' '' As such, he pointed out, ''They are therefore at any moment liable to repeal by the ordinary legislative power, and . . . have no constitutional sanction'' (84:442–43).

[56]*Roots*, I, 76, 77.

Countenance of Authoritie, unlesse it be by vertue or equitie of some expresse law of the Country waranting the same, established by a generall Court and sufficiently published."[57]

The restatement of chapter 39 of the original Magna Carta—the use of "law of the land," rather than Coke's reformulation, "due process"—was customary in the colonial charters and in the later state constitutions. In the Virginia Bill of Rights, adopted even before the Declaration, we find in Section 8 "that no man be deprived of his liberty except by law of the land, or the judgment of his peers."[58] Article XXI of the Maryland Declaration of Rights corresponds even more closely to the original Magna Carta formulation: "That no freeman ought to be taken, or imprisoned, or disseized of his freehold, liberties, or privileges, or outlawed, or exiled, or in any manner destroyed, or deprived of his life, liberty, or property, but by the judgment of his peers, or by the law of the land."[59] This article concludes, "And no subject shall be arrested, imprisoned, despoiled, or deprived of his property, immunity, or privileges, put out of the protection of the law, exiled, or deprived of his life, liberty, or estate, but by the judgment of his peers, or the law of the land."[60] Connecticut, interestingly enough, in its 1776 Declaration of Rights, reverts to the language of the Massachusetts Body of Liberties: "No Man's Honor or good Name shall be stained: No Man's Person shall be arrested, restrained, banished, dismembered, nor any Ways punished: No Man shall be deprived of his Wife or Children: No Man's Goods or Estate shall be taken away from him, nor any Way indamaged under the Colour of Law, or Countenance or Authority: unless clearly warranted by the Laws of this State."[61]

We even find this formulation used in perhaps the most significant document enacted under the Articles of Confederation, the Northwest Ordinance. Article II of this Ordinance—which, it is of some significance to note, was passed in July 1787 at a time when the Philadelphia Convention was hammering out the Great Compromise that made possible the Constitution—provides: "The inhabitants of the said territory shall always be entitled to the benefits of the writs of *habeas corpus*, and of the trial by jury . . . and of judicial proceedings according to the course of the common law. . . . no cruel and unusual punishment shall be inflicted. No man shall be deprived of his liberty or property, but by the judgment of his peers, or the law of the land."[62]

---

[57]Ibid., I, 72.

[58]Ibid., II, 235.

[59]Ibid., II, 282.

[60]Ibid., I, 242. Article XV of the New Hampshire bill of rights is identical to the Massachusetts provision just quoted.

[61]Ibid., II, 290. This is also a significant provision because it serves to undermine the claim that "law of the land" referred to some supra-constitutional laws or principles. On the contrary, this mode of expression supports the view that the "law of the land"—as used in all the states, save Georgia, Delaware, Rhode Island, New Jersey, and New Hampshire—meant the law of the state.

[62]Ibid., II, 395.

The "law of the land" provision was generally understood to mean the laws of the colonies or states. And save as certain guarantees were made of the fundamental law or constitution, such as we found in the West New Jersey agreement, it was understood that the legislatures had discretion.[63] In fact, "law of the land" provisions, as the foregoing discussion makes clear, had the effect of limiting the judiciary. And this was so whether the "laws" were "fundamental," possessing constitutional status, or not. But, as we shall see, in turning to the Fifth Amendment's due process clause, the modern understanding, as articulated by the Supreme Court in relatively recent decades, turns this accepted view on its head.

THE FIFTH AMENDMENT: LIBERTY AND DUE PROCESS

The debate over the provisions that now constitute the Bill of Rights was neither extensive nor particularly informative. On June 8, 1789, Madison set forth those amendments that in his view would be "proper" for the Congress to recommend to the state legislatures. These recommendations were presented in nine major sections, each section constituting an amendment that was to be inserted or incorporated into the Constitution, not added to it. In all, the amendments embraced nineteen major distinct areas of rights that, when broken down into particulars, contained thirty-two specific rights. Thirty of these rights were mentioned at one point or another in the amendments recommended by the state ratifying conventions.[64]

Of the nine sections of Madison's proposal, the fourth was by far the longest and most involved. It was to be inserted into the Constitution in Article I, Section 9, between clauses 2 and 3 (i.e., between the protection of habeas corpus and the prohibition on bills of attainder and ex post facto laws). In it can be found most of the rights and provisions that now constitute the Bill of Rights, ranging from freedom of religion and press to the equivalent of what is now the Ninth Amendment. The sixth paragraph of this section, reads: "No person shall be subject, except in cases of impeachment, to more than one punishment or one trial for the same offence; nor shall be compelled to be a witness against himself; nor be deprived of life, liberty, or property, without due process of law; nor be obliged to relinquish his property, where it may be necessary for public use, without a just

---

[63]For a thorough examination of the prevailing views see Berger, *Selected Writings*. Rodney Mott fails to provide any convincing evidence to the contrary, despite his contention that the clauses in question legitimated the expansion of judicial powers over the legislatures. Indeed, as Berger points out, even on Mott's own showing it was understood that "law of the land" imposed restraints on the judiciary, while allowing for legislative discretion.

[64]Edward Dumbauld, *The Bill of Rights and What It Means Today* (Norman: University of Oklahoma Press, 1957), 36–37. To put matters this way is misleading in one respect. The hard core advocates of a bill of rights wanted one that would significantly weaken the national government. See text below.

compensation.''[65] This paragraph was reformulated principally by the Senate into what is now the Fifth Amendment; the only significant change resulting from the House consideration concerned the confinement of the self-incrimination privilege to criminal cases.

Later, in the ninth paragraph, certain procedures in criminal cases were spelled out in terms very similar to the existing Sixth Amendment: ''In all criminal prosecutions, the accused shall enjoy the right to a speedy and public trial, to be informed of the cause and nature of the accusation, to be confronted with his accusers, and the witnesses against him; to have a compulsory process for obtaining witnesses in his favor; and to have the assistance of counsel for his defence.''[66]

While the Fifth Amendment would seem to flow as matter of course from the British and American traditions outlined above, controversies have arisen over the precise meaning of the ''due process'' clause, controversies that bear upon the question whether both procedural and substantive ''rights'' and ''protections'' should be read into ''due process'' or ''liberty.'' These issues are somewhat interrelated and, as we have indicated above, arise out of Coke's approach to the Magna Carta and its status in the English tradition.

Law of the Land and Due Process. As we have already had occasion to remark, it is very doubtful that ''due process'' can be equated with ''law of the land'' on the grounds that ''law of the land'' embraces more than ''due process.'' Raoul Berger musters several leading authorities to this effect, and the careful research of Keith Jurow would certainly seem to bear him out.[67] As we noted earlier, Berger argues that the expression ''law of the land'' embraces something more than the ''mere mode of trial.'' Citing Charles McIlwain, he contends that the ''law of the land'' phrase ''was . . . employed in a wider sense, *i.e.*, a trial in accordance with the 'law of the land.' '' On McIlwain's showing, according to Berger, ''the chief grievance of the barons was the king's seizure of their persons without first convicting them of some offense in his curia''; that is, with the lack of process, not with the abuse of process. Berger concurs with McIlwain's conclusion that ''lawful judgment of his peers''—the companion phrase to ''law of the land''—was to ''preclude attacks 'except *after* a *judgment* obtained in the

---

[65]*The Annals of Congress*, 1st Congress, 1st Session, April 8, 1789, 434.

[66]Ibid., 445.

[67]Keith Jurow has intensively examined the origins, usage, and meaning of the term ''due process'' in the English tradition. Here we can only state the conclusions of his exhaustive and careful study that may well account for the fact that ''due process'' was never equated with ''law of the land'' on this side of the Atlantic. ''It can be said that despite the attempt by Coke to define 'per legem terrae' in chapter twenty-nine of Magna Carta as 'due process of law,' the two clauses never meant the same thing in English law. Unlike the term 'by the law of the land,' an ambiguous phrase over whose meaning Englishmen argued for centuries and spilled a considerable amount of blood, the term 'due process of law' and the word 'process' were always used in the most precise and consistent way.'' ''Untimely Thoughts: A Reconsideration of the Origins of Due Process of Law,'' *American Journal of Legal History* 19 (1975), 277–78.

ordinary course, *i.e.*, by a judicium parium.' '' And these proceedings, as we have pointed out, presuppose an antecedent law.[68]

The important point in this account, however, is that, given its origins, the expression "law of the land" as it was used in the colonial charters and state constitutions was not intended to limit the legislatures; instead, the expression "law of the land" embraces the laws duly enacted by the legislature that apply to executive and judicial proceedings. One of the clearest expressions of this view is that of Attorney General Haywood of North Carolina in speaking to the status of the "law of the land" provision in the North Carolina Constitution in 1792. He defines this provision as "a law for the people of North Carolina, made or adopted by themselves by the intervention of their own Legislature."[69] He points out that at that time "the *lex terrae* of North Carolina" consisted "partly of the common law, partly of customs, partly of the acts of the British Parliament received and enforced here, and partly of the acts passed by our own Legislature." But, in his view, the legislature was free to modify or eliminate the other elements of the *lex terrae*—in other words, and contrary to what was being urged by others, the *lex terrae* provision posed no limitation on the authority of the legislature. And, in so doing, he emphasizes the absurdity that inheres in regarding the "law of the land" clause as a limitation on legislative authority.

> It would contradict the very spirit of the Constitution, which in establishing a republican form of government must have been inevitably led to foresee the great alteration that the new state of things would make necessary in the great fabric of the common law; they must have intended such changes therein by the legislative power as would more perfectly adapt it to the genius of that species of government, many of the maxims of which are so diametrically opposed to all those of the common law which have any view towards the support of the kingly power or that of the nobles. Such a construction would destroy all legislative power whatsoever, except that of making laws in addition to the common law, and for cases not provided for by that law. It would lop off the whole body of the statute law at one stroke, and leave us in the most miserable condition that can well be imagined.[70]

"All capital punishments," he continued, "ordained by the statute law for murder, rape, arson, etc., would be done away, and every malignant passion of the human heart let loose to roam through the land, unbridled by fear, and free from all manner of restraint except those very ineffectual ones the common law imposes."[71]

---

[68]Berger, *Selected Writings*, 127.
[69]*Founders' Constitution*, V, 316.
[70]Ibid.
[71]Ibid.

This position, it would appear, was widely accepted before the adoption of the Constitution.[72] But it was challenged—and sometimes successfully—by those who regarded "law of the land" as a limitation on legislative authority, particularly with regard to the regulation of property. The development of the notion of vested property rights, in large part traceable to viewing the "law of the land" provisions in the state constitutions as limiting the legislatures,[73] can be seen in an 1805 decision by the North Carolina Supreme Court that effectively turned the earlier view of "law of the land" on its head.[74] In this case the majority expressly rejects the "insistence" that "the term, 'law of the land,' does not impose any restrictions on the Legislature, who are capable of making the law of the land" and that, moreover, the provision "was only intended to prevent abuses" on the part of the executive and judicial branches.[75] To this contention, the Court responds:

> It is evident the framers of the Constitution intended the provision as a restraint upon some branch of the Government, either the executive, legislative, or judicial. To suppose it applicable to the executive would be absurd on account of the limited powers conferred on that officer; and from the subjects enumerated in that clause, no danger could be apprehended from the Executive Department, that being entrusted with the exercise of no powers by which the principles thereby intended to be secured could be affected. To apply to the judiciary would, if possible, be still more idle, if the Legislature can make the "*law of the land.*" For the judiciary are only to expound and enforce the law, and have no discretionary powers enabling them to judge of the propriety or impropriety of laws. They are bound, whether agreeable to their ideas of justice or not, to carry into effect the acts of the Legislature as far as they are binding and do not contravene the Constitution.[76]

It concludes from this that the "clause is applicable to the Legislature alone, and

---

[72]This is evidenced by the state courts' decisions, which, according to Charles G. Haines, provided state precedents for judicial review. See his *The American Doctrine of Judicial Supremacy* (New York: Russell and Russell, 1959), Ch. 5. For an analysis of these cases, see Berger, *Selected Writings*, 134–37.

Aside from the provisions in the Massachusetts Body of Liberties and the Fundamental Orders of Connecticut regarding the protection of life, liberty, and property in the absence of specific laws noted in the text above, the New York Charter of Liberties and Privileges leaves no doubt on this score. "Noe freeman shall be taken and imprisoned or be disseized of his freehold or Libertye or free Customes or be outlawed or Exiled or any other wayes destroyed nor shall be passed upon adjudged or condemned But by the Lawfull Judgment of his peers and by the Law of this province." *Roots*, I, 165.

[73]This development is examined in some detail by Edward Corwin in *Liberty Against Government*.

[74]*Trustees of the University of North Carolina v. Foy*, 1 Mur. 58 (N.C. 1805).

[75]*Founders' Constitution*, V, 325.

[76]Ibid.

was intended as a restraint on their acts (and to presume otherwise is to render this article a dead letter).''[77]

While this mode of interpretation rendered the ''law of the land'' clauses in the state constitutions an avenue through which the courts could limit legislative authority in the domain of property ''rights,''[78] it also provided the grounds upon which the courts could eventually scrutinize the constitutionality of legislation that touched upon ''liberty.''[79] In this fashion, the authority of the judiciary was greatly expanded, a rather paradoxical development in light of the fact that the ''law of the land'' clause recognized and enshrined legislative supremacy and was designed as a control upon the executive and judicial branches.

In any event, the national Bill of Rights lacked any ''law of the land'' clause; instead the Fifth Amendment provided for ''due process'' of law. This fact is somewhat surprising in light of the universal use of ''law of the land'' in the state constitutions and declarations of rights at the time the Fifth was drafted. It is even more surprising because only one state ratifying convention (New York), in setting forth recommendations for rights to be incorporated into or added onto the Constitution, used the term ''due process.'' This recommendation read: ''That no person ought to be taken imprisoned or disseised of his freehold, or be exiled or deprived of his Privileges, Franchises, Life, Liberty or Property but by due process of law.''[80] The Virginia proposal provided: ''That no freeman ought to be taken, imprisoned, or disseised of his freehold, liberties, privileges or franchises, or outlawed exiled, or in any manner destroyed or deprived of his life, liberty or property but by the law of the land.''[81] The North Carolina recommendation was identical save that it provided ''but by trial by jury, or by the law of the land.''[82] The minority report of the Pennsylvania ratifying convention, while leaving out ''life'' and ''property,'' conformed very closely to the wording in most of the state constitutions, ''no man be deprived of his liberty, except by the law of the land or the judgment of his peers.''[83] All of these specific proposals were located among other provisions relating to trials and prosecutions, provisions which, for the most part, were mere restatements of common law guarantees such as the right to demand ''the cause and nature'' of the accusation, a ''fair and speedy trial,''

---

[77]Ibid.

[78]Chancellor Kent of New York is perhaps the best-known jurist to advance this position in his writings and opinions. See Corwin, *Liberty Against Government*, Ch. 3.

[79]As Corwin notes, in the later part of the nineteenth century the state courts began to take up the cause of ''liberty of pursuit'' which soon became ''liberty of contract.'' See Corwin, *Liberty Against Government*, Ch. 5. Of course, as we know, it was a short step from the use of the due process clause of the Fourteenth Amendment to protect economic liberty to the protection of civil and political liberties through the ''incorporation'' of the First Amendment.

[80]*Documents Illustrative*, 1035.

[81]Ibid., 1029.

[82]Ibid., 1046.

[83]*Roots*, III, 665.

and protection against self-incrimination. This placement would strongly support the proposition that the "liberty" protected by the Fifth Amendment was a personal liberty that conformed with Blackstone's definition, "the power of locomotion, of changing situation, or removing one's powers on to whatsoever place one's own inclination may direct, without imprisonment or restraint."[84]

Nevertheless, as we have remarked, Coke's equation of "due process" and "law of the land" eventually comes into play to provide the basis for a more expansive view of liberty and due process. In 1856, after Justice Curtis equated the "law of the land" with "due process" on the authority of Coke's *Second Institute*,[85] the national judiciary had unwittingly embraced the framework of reasoning that would now allow it to use "due process" at the national level to limit Congress in the same way as some state courts had used the "law of the land" clauses to curb the state legislatures. The full effect of this particular decision and the potential it held for the expansion of judicial power, however, were not felt until the adoption of the Fourteenth Amendment and the eventual interpretation of its "due process" clause as an extension of and in conformity with the tenor and spirit of certain expansive interpretations given to states' "law of the land" clauses.[86]

Due Process, Intent, and Redundancy. Questions of another nature have surrounded the scope of the due process clause of the Fifth Amendment. If it is

---

[84]Blackstone's *Commentaries*, Bk. I, Ch. 1, Sect. II. After exhaustive research, Charles E. Shattuck concludes that Blackstone's definition was widely accepted both here and in England. His conclusions from these findings are interesting: "As regards the tendency to give the clause a broad interpretation, and at least to include within the term 'liberty' the right to follow any lawful calling, natural and reasonable as such a construction may at first glance appear, it seems, upon examination, to have little real foundation either in history or principle. The use of the term 'civil' to denote the ordinary substantive rights, other than life and property, which every citizen has, and constantly exercises in his daily life, is of recent origin, probably not extending back farther than the War of the Rebellion, and a construction of the term 'liberty' making it coextensive with 'civil rights' in that limited sense of the term 'civil,' seems to be unhistorical and arbitrary." "The True Meaning of the Term 'Liberty' in Those Clauses in the Federal and State Constitutions Which Protect 'Life, Liberty, and Property,' " *Harvard Law Review* 4 (1891), 391–92. The thrust of these observations accords with the findings of Jurow, "Untimely Thoughts . . . ."

[85]See his majority opinion in *Murray's Lessee v. Hoboken Land and Improvement Co.*, 59 U.S. 272 (1856). Of course, Curtis was obliged to explain why the drafters of the Fifth Amendment did not conform with the practice of the day and use the "law of the land" phraseology. He argues that since the Sixth Amendment provided for trial by jury in criminal cases—which he took to be the equivalent of the phrase "trial by his peers," traditionally the other half of the constitutional protection—to have used "law of the land" by itself might have been misleading.

[86]If there be any doubts on this score, a look at Harlan's dissenting opinion in *Hurtado v. California* (110 U.S. 516 [1884]) ought to dispel them. In his dissent, he presents the basic framework of reasoning that is ultimately to prevail regarding the meaning of the "due process" clause of the Fourteenth Amendment, a mode of thinking indispensable to the process of "incorporation." Here we see most clearly how the assimilation of the substantive version of "law of the land" and "due process" has over the decades led to a new and expanded conception of the protected "liberty."

viewed, as many are wont to do, expansively, as including at a minimum all the procedural guarantees found in the Bill of Rights, then serious problems arise. Specifically, if we accept this expansive view, then we must be prepared to explain why the drafters expressly provided for "due process" as well as indictment by grand jury and protection against double jeopardy and self-incrimination in the same amendment. Why, in other words, this redundancy, if indeed they clearly understood "due process" to embrace these other common law rights? What is more, the Sixth Amendment guarantees trial by jury in criminal cases, along with a series of other "rights" that are, in the main, taken from the common law. Why, again, this redundancy? In sum, on its face, this would seem to amount to an unnecessary and double protection of "due process," a needless redundancy that we should be very hesitant to attribute to the drafters of these amendments in the absence of compelling reasons.

This difficulty, of course, does not arise if we take the traditional, narrow view of "due process." Clearly if the drafters conceived of "due process" in terms of its essential principles—notice and hearing—then they surely would have realized that any number of processes or procedures could satisfy its requirements. If this is the case, we can see why they would have felt constrained to provide for indictment by grand jury since this process, while it conformed with the demands of "due process," was not one of its indispensable elements. And, if this was the case with indictment by grand jury, which had traditionally been so closely associated with due process, then it most certainly explains why other provisions of the Bill of Rights—e.g., no cruel or unusual punishment and protection against self-incrimination and double jeopardy—also were not considered inherently necessary for due process. Such an interpretation would follow from the reasoning of Justice Stanley Matthews in *Hurtado v. California* (1884) that adheres to the common-sense injunction against interpreting any part of the Constitution, especially the provisions of key amendments, as superfluous.[87]

But William Crosskey offers another interpretation of "due process" that derives from the fact that the "presentment or indictment by grand jury" provision of the Fifth Amendment was known to be an element of Coke's definition of due process, "indictment and presentment of good and lawful men, and trial and conviction in consequence."[88] This redundancy, he holds, "mandatorily require[s]" that a different meaning be given to "due process" as it is used in the

---

[87]As Charles Warren points out, up to 1923 this view was substantially held with regard to the "due process" of the Fourteenth Amendment. "While the Court had indulged in . . . general statements about 'fundamental rights' guaranteed by the Fourteenth Amendment, it had actually only recognized a few rights as comprised in the term 'liberty,' in addition to freedom from restraint of the person." "The New 'Liberty' under the Fourteenth Amendment," *Harvard Law Review* 39 (1926), 453–54.

[88]William W. Crosskey, *Politics and the Constitution in the History of the United States*, (Chicago: University of Chicago Press, 1953), II, 1104. Hereafter cited as Crosskey.

Fifth Amendment. What is equally certain to Crosskey is that the phrase cannot be read in such an expansive fashion as to embrace the whole range of the common law procedures relating to criminal procedures. Beyond the fact that such an interpretation would render the specification of common law rights stipulated in the Bill of Rights superfluous, it would serve to prevent Congress from making any changes whatever in the common law procedures. Improvements or corrections of such procedures would, using this view of its meaning, require constitutional amendments.

Crosskey holds that "the phrase 'due process of law' . . . simply means 'the appropriate process of law' *in a general way* and contemplates various sub-categories of 'propriety' thereunder."[89] Such an interpretation, he believes, "completely fits the entire documentary context."[90] On his showing, the Fourth, Fifth, Sixth, Seventh, and Eighth Amendments provide "specific guarantees" to "particular phases" of the legal processes with which "due process," traditionally understood, was intimately associated in the common law.

The "sub-categories of 'propriety' " to which Crosskey refers actually serve to illustrate the role of the "due process" clause. The first category of "due process" consists of those processes marked out in the various amendments of the Bill of Rights. These fixed, constitutionally defined process guarantees are, he points out, of "two kinds: those that prescribe particular elements of Common Law 'process' and those that enjoin modes of 'process,' as to particular matters, which the framers of the amendments regarded as desirable, even though the Common Law did *not* require them."[91] But wide-ranging as these processes are, they do not cover all the phases or aspects of process. The "due process" clause of the Fifth Amendment, thus, is intended to apply primarily to those phases of the legal processes or concerns involving "life, liberty, and property" not specifically dealt with by the relevant procedural guarantees in the Bill of Rights.

At this juncture, in effect, Crosskey's analysis comes around to join with that of those who take the "narrow" view of "due process." More exactly, the "due process" of the Fifth Amendment would require "fair" and "appropriate" processes in all cases involving "life, liberty, and property." The test of "fairness" and "appropriateness" of the processes would, according to Crosskey, "first come down to whether the 'process' at issue in a particular case is one *un*forbidden by the Constitution." Beyond this a second-level test would be whether the procedures are "supported by 'applicable' precedents at Common Law" at the

---

[89]Ibid., II, 1105.

[90]Ibid., II, 1106.

[91]Ibid., II, 1106. This is the juncture at which Crosskey would part company with Berger, or so it seems. Berger would argue, I believe, that no specific requirement of process could be read from the common law. Thus, the response to Crosskey's position would be that the procedural guarantees in the Bill of Rights, including indictment by grand jury, were put into the Constitution precisely to secure their status by making them part of the fundamental law. Crosskey would buy this view only with regard to certain non-mandatory provisions of the common law.

time the Fifth Amendment was adopted. Finally, if a process is unforbidden by the Constitution, but without precedent in the common law, then the "due process" clause of the Fifth Amendment requires that it meet standards of "reasonableness" and "fairness."[92]

The practical difference between the "narrow" view of the "due process" clause of the Fifth Amendment—such as that endorsed in *Hurtado*—and Crosskey's comes down to what can legitimately be "incorporated" and applied to the states via the "due process" clause of the Fourteenth Amendment.[93] But to the question whether "due process" of the Fifth Amendment expands the powers of the courts, both are in substantial agreement. Berger concludes that it is a "perversion of 'due process' or of the 'law of the land' to apply either for the judicial overthrow of legislation,"[94] and Crosskey asserts that "if the words of the clause ["due process" of the Fifth Amendment] are heeded, there is, of course, no right to review the substantive acts of Congress at all."[95] Both see the "due process" provision as placing a requirement or limitation primarily on the courts "because," as Crosskey remarks, "the subject of 'appropriate legal process' relates directly and especially to the proper discharge of the judicial functions."[96] And both can see the courts' discretionary role in nullifying acts of Congress under the "due process" clause as very confined; namely, that of judging the "appropriateness" or "reasonability" of the procedures Congress might stipulate that are, to use Crosskey's framework, "*un*forbidden" by the Constitution but lack common law precedents.[97]

To this point we have not dealt with the meaning of "liberty" as that word is used in the "due process" clause. Our discussion of "due process" (and "law of the land") renders the nature of "liberty" protected fairly obvious. No matter how we interpret "due process," narrowly or expansively, the focus is clearly on judicial processes, particularly in criminal cases. Consequently, the English and American uses of "liberty" in the context of "due process," up to and well beyond the Founding, clearly support Blackstone's definition of "due process"

---

[92]Ibid., II, 1107.

[93]We offer it as our opinion that, despite what Crosskey contends, the result reached in *Hurtado* is correct, though we would use a slightly different mode of reasoning. In our view, the drafters may very well have viewed "due process" as having a "core" meaning beyond and somewhat independent of those processes and provisions that had been associated with its realization. To use an analogy, the meaning of "efficiency" is not entirely caught up with any of those processes—e.g., routine, elimination of waste, dedication to work—that serve as a means to its maximization. The means may best be comprehended in light of the end—be that end "due process" or "efficiency"—but the means fall far short, individually or collectively, of fully conveying the entire character or meaning of the end.

[94]Berger, *Selected Writings*, 147.

[95]Crosskey, II, 1107.

[96]Ibid.

[97]The courts would also have the responsibility of determining whether the procedures specified by Congress had common precedent. Of course, aside from this, the courts would have the responsibility to enforce the provisions of the amendments.

"liberty," i.e., an individual's freedom of movement. Nor can "due process," on either of these approaches, be stretched to embrace a wider or more comprehensive view of liberty that would give the courts considerable latitude in reviewing the constitutionality of legislation. For example, despite the differences between the "narrow" and "broad" conceptions of what "due process" was understood to embody at the time of Founding, both would hold that the liberties contained in the First Amendment were not among those for which its guarantees were intended.[98]

SUBSTANTIVE DUE PROCESS

These views of due process and liberty clearly do not correspond with the notions of due process and liberty advanced by our courts in recent decades. And the question thus arises: could it be that both views are too constrictive? That neither one captures the full intentions of the drafters, intentions that support and justify the current, more expansive, conceptions of "liberty" and "due process"?

The answer, for reasons of a different character, would clearly seem to be "no." To see why the answer seems so clear, let us first turn to certain important elements of the Framers' political thinking. To begin with, and this is often overlooked, the Framers did not place a great reliance on the courts to preserve liberties or to protect minority rights.[99] We have already pointed out how they relied upon the separation of powers to provide for rule of law and to protect against arbitrary and capricious rule, the essence of tyranny. As for the problem of oppressive or factious majorities, Madison's prescription—fully set forth in *The Federalist*, his letters, and comment to the Philadelphia Convention—is the extended republic with a multiplicity and diversity of interests. In his view, this

---

[98]Charles Warren, among others, offers a compelling reason for this conclusion. "It is unquestionable that when the First Congress adopted the Fifth Amendment and inserted the Due Process Clause, they took it directly from the then existing State Constitutions, and they took it with the meaning it then bore. And there is convincing evidence that 'liberty' in the Fifth Amendment was not intended to include civil rights like the right of free speech. For those rights were expressly protected against violation by Congress in the First Amendment, which provided that 'Congress shall make no laws . . . abridging the freedom of speech.' If 'liberty' included the right of free speech, then the Due Process Clause of the Fifth Amendment must be construed as if it read: 'No person shall be deprived of . . . . freedom of speech . . . without due process of law.' It is hardly conceivable that the framers of that Amendment, having already provided in the First Amendment an *absolute prohibition* on Congress to take away certain rights, would in the Fifth Amendment, declare or imply that Congress *might* take away the same rights by due process of law. Equally unlikely is it, that the rights of life, liberty or property which might be taken by due process should include rights which prior provisions of the Amendment absolutely forbade Congress or the Federal Government to take away under any circumstances." "The New 'Liberty' . . . ," 440–41.

[99]We should not forget in this connection that the Philadelphia Constitution contained no bill of rights, as we understand these rights today. The Convention, each state voting as a unit, unanimously rejected the idea of putting in a bill of rights. For this reason among many others, it is doubtful that the participants believed the courts would play much of a role in preventing either tyranny or oppressive majority rule.

multiplicity and diversity would render a combination of a majority around interests detrimental to the rights of individuals or minorities highly unlikely. Indeed, at the very end of Federalist 10, the most widely read and cited of these essays, he writes: "In the extent and proper structure of the Union, therefore, we behold a republican remedy for the diseases most incident to republican government" (48). Later, in Federalist 51, he reiterates this basic proposition: "in the extended republic of the United States, and among the great variety of interests, parties, and sects which it embraces, a coalition of a majority of the whole society could seldom take place on any other principles than those of justice and the general good" (269). In fact, in this same essay, he specifically rejects the notion that a "will in the community independent of the majority" can or should protect minorities. "This, at best," he observes, "is but a precarious security; because a power independent of the society may as well espouse the unjust views of the major as the rightful interests of the minor party, and may possibly be turned against both parties" (268).

These considerations may seem only tangentially related to the questions surrounding the scope of "due process" and its relationship to "liberty." Yet, they bear directly upon these matters. In Federalist 48 at the start of his discussion of how the separation of the branches provided for in the Constitution can be maintained, Madison felt it necessary to reorient his readers to the political context in which they lived. The "danger" to their "liberty," he informs them, is no longer to be found in the "overgrown and all-grasping prerogative of an hereditary magistrate, supported and fortified by an hereditary branch of the legislative authority." Instead, in a "representative republic," he warns, they "ought to indulge all their jealousy and exhaust all their precaution" against the legislative authority because it is "inspired by a supposed influence over the people with an intrepid confidence in its own strength" and "everywhere extending the sphere of its activity and drawing all power into its tempestuous vortex" (255–56). In other words, in republics the legislative assemblies possessed the potential to be the counterparts of the tyrannical monarchs in the British tradition. To prevent the realization of this potential is the very reason that the Framers divided the legislature in two, provided for life tenure for judges, and equipped the president with the veto power. But their solution provided for more than this. To recur to the "reflexive" principle, it provided as well that the legislators, like other citizens, would be subject to the laws they enacted. As a consequence, those of the founding era could place a good deal of confidence in the legislature—that, for instance, its members would not deny due process, if only because they, their family, friends, or political supporters might very well have to pay the consequences. Or, to put this another way, the Founders had no substantial reason to fear that legislative bodies would pass laws that would randomly operate to deprive individuals of the protection of due process. To do so would probably result in self-inflicted injustice.

Still another fact that speaks against the proposition that the drafters of the Fifth Amendment held to the more expansive conception of "liberty" and "due process'' adopted by the courts in recent decades is, simply, the absence of any extended discussion or debate over the terms of the Fifth Amendment in the House of Representatives at the time the Bill of Rights was proposed.[100] If ''due process'' was considered a general authorization for the courts to substitute their will for that of the legislature on substantive matters of policy or if ''liberty'' was conceived of as embracing far more than simply the absence of physical restraint, then it is utterly inconceivable that there would not have been extended debate.[101] In our view, it is simply preposterous to believe that the drafters of the Fifth Amendment shared anything resembling the modern progressive notions of ''liberty'' and ''due process.''

What is more, Madison, in proposing the Bill of Rights, uses a ''there is something to gain, nothing to lose'' line of argument.

> I believe every gentleman will readily admit that nothing is in contemplation, so far as I have mentioned, that can endanger the beauty of the Government in any one important feature, even in the eyes of its most sanguine admirers. I have proposed nothing that does not appear to me as proper in itself, or eligible as patronized by a respectable number of our fellow-citizens; and if we can make the Constitution better in the opinion of those who are opposed to it, without weakening its frame or abridging its usefulness in the judgment

---

[100] A survey of the debates and proceedings in the House reflects the speed with which the representatives moved in considering the chief provision of the Bill of Rights. Madison, who headed the select committee of the House to winnow the various proposals in order to come up with a draft bill of rights for consideration by the House, reported to the Committee of the Whole on August 13, 1789. By August 18, the Committee of the Whole concluded its deliberations. Since August 16 was a Sunday, only four days were devoted to a consideration of the select committee proposals. Moreover, approximately half of this time was devoted to debates over the form that the amendments should take, the proper size of the House of Representatives, law relating to compensation of legislators, and the right of the people to instruct their representatives. Actually, fewer than two days were devoted to a discussion of those provisions that, in one form or another, constitute the present Bill of Rights. While there was further consideration of these provisions by the full House August 19–22, most of this period was taken up turning back the amendment of the Antifederalists designed to weaken the national government.

While there is no record of the Senate debates, we do know that it considered and changed the seventeen articles that composed the House version between September 2 and 9. For an overview of the differences between the House and Senate versions, as well as the compromises between them, see Edward Dumbauld, *The Bill of Rights*, 44–49.

[101] Such intentions would have been almost totally at odds with both the common understanding of the role of the institutions under the Constitution and the prevailing political beliefs of the time. While Hamilton sets forth the basis for judicial review in Federalist 78, at the same time he points out the need for judicial tenure during good behavior because the judiciary is ''incontestably . . . the weakest of the three branches . . . . and that all possible care is requisite to enable it to defend itself against'' attacks by the other branches. He quotes approvingly from Montesquieu to the effect that, compared with the other branches, the ''JUDICIARY is next to nothing.'' He notes that the courts ''have no influence over either the sword or the purse, no direction either of the strength or of the wealth of society, and can take no active resolution whatever'' (402).

of those who are attached to it, we can act the part of wise and liberal men to make such alterations as shall produce that effect.[102]

In this connection, we should remark, Madison is generally credited with simultaneously removing the issue of a bill of rights from the political arena, while, at the same time, fending off the Antifederalist proposals that would have considerably weakened the national government.

Finally, none of the renowned commentators on the Constitution between the time of founding and the Civil War ascribed to "due process" or "liberty" a meaning different from the one that they had in the common law tradition. Justice Joseph Story in his *Commentaries* sees fit to treat of the Fifth Amendment in book III in his chapter on the "Judiciary—Organization and Powers," rather than in a later chapter on "Amendments to the Constitution," a fact that tends to affirm that the "due process" clause imposed an obligation or requirement primarily on the judiciary. In any event, he devotes only one paragraph to the "due process" clause:

> The other part of the clause [the Fifth Amendment] is but an enlargement of the language of the magna carta . . . neither will we pass upon him, or condemn him, but by the lawful judgment of his peers, or by the law of the land. Lord Coke says, that these latter words, . . . by law of the land, . . . mean by due process of law, that is, without due presentment or indictment, and being brought in to answer thereto by due process of the common law. So that this clause in effect affirms the right of trial according to the process and proceedings of the common law.[103]

To be sure, in this account, he does not take up certain of the questions raised by Crosskey such as the range of Congressional discretion in prescribing procedures that are "*un*forbidden" by the Constitution. Nevertheless, it is unmistakable that Story did not see any great shift in the meaning of "due process" or "liberty" from that traditionally attached to them in the common law.

William Rawle's views on the "due process" clause are interesting because they tend to confirm Crosskey's interpretation. According to Rawle, provisions of the Fifth Amendment that precede the "due process" clause—e.g., indictment by grand jury, protection against double jeopardy—as well as provisions of the Sixth

---

[102] *The Annals of Congress*, 1st Congress, 1st Session, April 8, 1789, 441. It is also clear from the record that the Antifederalists did not particularly embrace the proposals advanced by Madison because they did not go far enough in curbing the national government in relation to the states. For instance, the Antifederalists in the first Congress wanted the word "expressly" inserted into what is now the Tenth Amendment so that it would read: "The powers not *expressly* delegated to the United States by the Constitution, nor prohibited by it to the states, are reserved to the States respectively, or to the people."

[103] Joseph Story, *Commentaries on the Constitution*, 3 vols. (Boston: Hilliard, Gray and Co., 1833), III, §1783.

and Eighth Amendments, guarantee "that *no one can be deprived of life, liberty, or property, without due process of law.*"[104] As he sees it, the "due process" clause is redundant; it is repeated, he informs us, because "it exhibits the summary of the whole, and the anxiety that it should never be forgotten."[105] But, again, Rawle interprets the clause in the context of its common law origins and operations; he attributes to it no meaning beyond that of providing for established common law guarantees, primarily in criminal proceedings.

Chancellor James Kent in his discussion of "personal security and personal liberty," after a brief history of colonial and state provisions related thereto, observes: "It may be received as a self-evident proposition, universally understood and acknowledged throughout this country, that no person can be taken, or imprisoned, or disseised of his freehold, or liberties, or estate, or exiled, or condemned, or deprived of life, liberty, or property, unless by the law of the land, or the judgment of his peers." And like Story, he takes care to note that "*by law of the land*, as used in *magna carta*, . . . are understood to mean due process of law, that is, by indictment or presentment of good and lawful men; and this, says Lord Coke, is the true sense and exposition of those words."[106] What is more, in his discussion of "personal liberty" and "the privilege of *habeas corpus*," Kent makes it abundantly clear that the "liberty" of the "due process" clause relates to "restraint" or "imprisonment" in keeping with Blackstone's definition.[107]

In sum, the commentaries on the "due process" clause are not extensive—a good indication that the clause was not intended to allow the courts wide discretionary latitude over substantive legislation. Otherwise, it is safe to assume, they would have dwelt on the nature and scope of this new discretionary power so markedly alien to the republican spirit of the times. Equally compelling evidence that the "due process" clause was not intended to bestow new and unparalleled powers on the courts is the fact that all the commentators deal with "due process" and "liberty" in the context of the common law heritage that we have surveyed in this chapter. That this understanding was shared by a majority of the Supreme Court in the two cases to come before it involving the "due process" clause prior to the Civil War hardly comes as a surprise.[108] We can say that, with deviations here and there at the state level regarding property "rights," the prevailing view of "due process" and "liberty" was firmly anchored in the common law tradition. As Charles Warren wrote, "The term 'liberty' in the Due Process Clause was constructed by the State Courts in very few cases. Practically in only one case prior to the Fourteenth Amendment is there any trace of a decision that 'liberty'

---

[104]William Rawle, *A View of the Constitution of the United States* (Philadelphia: H.C. Carey & I. Lea, 1825), 132–33.

[105]Ibid., 133.

[106]James Kent, *Commentaries on American Law* (New York: O. Halsted, 1827), 10.

[107]Ibid., 22.

[108]*Bank of Columbia v. Okely*, 17 U.S. (4 Wheat.) 235 (1819) and *Murray*'s *Lessee v. Hoboken Land Improvement Company*, 59 U.S. 272 (1856).

meant anything more than freedom from physical restraint.''[109] Put otherwise, up to and beyond the Civil War, Hamilton's view of the character and scope of ''due process'' held sway. In speaking before the New York Assembly in 1787, he noted that *''due process''* are words with ''precise technical import'' that apply ''only . . . to the process and proceedings of the courts of justice; they can never be referred to an act of legislature.''[110]

The overwhelming evidence to this effect only serves to highlight questions of the first order that we have barely touched upon in our survey. What can account for the enormous sea-change that has occurred over the meaning and scope of ''liberty'' and ''due process''? To trace this transformation at the theoretical level is possible and we have already indicated the directions any such inquiry might take; how the ''law of the land'' provision could be read to embrace ''fundamental'' laws or precepts that serve to restrain the scope of legislative authority and, then, how this could be subsequently read back into ''due process'' on the basis of Coke's authority. But any such theoretical analysis cannot answer the more significant and intriguing questions. Why, for instance, the eventual acceptance of such tenuous foundations for the exertion of judicial powers well beyond bounds ever anticipated by the Framers? Could it be that, in keeping with Publius's observations about the ''encroaching spirit of power,'' (48:308) ''liberty'' and ''due process'' merely provided the most plausible avenues through which the courts could expand their powers? Or could it be that the courts were only responding to underlying, but significant, ideological changes that call for more expansive interpretations? But, if so, why in many instances has it fallen to the courts, not the legislature, to give effect to the new ideological ends?

Quite aside from the much debated questions whether the courts should be responsive to such ideological changes or whether, instead, they have an obligation to ''stick'' as closely as possible to the letter of the Constitution, the fact that the courts have been responsive to new and expanded conceptions of ''liberty'' and ''due process'' does raise a concern about the general health of the political system bequeathed to us by the Founders. Can it be that our distinctly political branches, principally the Congress, are not responsive to the underlying ideological changes? Can it be that the courts are simply responding to the ''political failures'' of the elected branches? But this leads to the further question, not easily answered—how are we to determine what constitutes a ''political failure''?[111]

---

[109]Charles Warren, ''The New 'Liberty'. . . ,'' 143.

[110]*Founders' Constitution*, V, 313.

[111]The best discussion of this issue that we have encountered is to be found in Charles S. Hyneman, *The Supreme Court on Trial* (New York: Atherton Press, 1963), Ch. 20. Hyneman, an opponent of judicial activism, poses four considerations for answering this question, but the considerations he poses under the first of these indicate the fundamental difficulties of the ''political failure'' argument as grounds for judicial action: ''Can we assume that judicial knowledge, pleadings, and the evidence and argument presented in the course of a trial will provide a better reading of the public mind than the lawmakers can obtain from the unrestrained contacts with the constituents and the forceful demands for attention put on them by people who favor and people who oppose any contemplated

And if we conclude that the courts have only compensated for the political failures of the elected branches, then might not constitutional changes be in order to eliminate the source or sources of these political failures?

These and like questions, we submit, are those that must eventually emerge from any analysis of the original meaning of "liberty" and "due process." And, in turn, they should lead us to an inquiry, not unlike that undertaken by our Founding Fathers, into the relationship between constitutionalism and republicanism.

---

action? Can we assume that the appointed judges, when convinced that they know what the people want, will feel greater compulsion to respond to popular demands than an assembly made up of elected men who must soon win re-election or terminate their service?'' (263)

7

Abortion and the American
Political Crisis

INTRODUCTORY NOTE

While the following and concluding selection was prompted by the Court's abortion decision (*Roe v. Wade*), it draws together much of what I have said about the principles of our older constitutional morality by showing how the operations of the new morality simply supersede them. *Roe v. Wade* and subsequent Court decisions relating to abortion are prime, but by no means the only, examples that can be used to dramatize the extent to which we have abandoned the traditional morality. Beyond this, I attempt to identify what I believe to be the basic theoretical foundations of the new constitutional morality, an effort that necessarily involves going beyond the context of American institutions to a brief examination of modern Western thought.

Nothing has occurred since this piece was written to change the thrust of my argument. However, there are some points that I would emphasize more today and others that I would add. The first of these relates to the fact that there is, indeed, a new constitutional morality; that it is not the figment of the imagination of those who, like myself, do not particularly like to see the Court exercising positive, lawmaking powers and then attaching their pronouncements to some constitutional provision thereby rendering them irreversible through the ordinary political processes. The enormous powers of the Court in this regard are not lost upon some astute observers of our system who now contend that the most important issue at stake in presidential elections is deciding who will fill the vacancies that may arise on the Court. It is entirely conceivable, if not probable, that a President can have more impact on the long-term direction of the nation through his appointments to the Court than he can through the exercise of any other of his constitutional powers or functions. This is one measure of how far the new constitutional morality has taken us from our traditional moorings.

In this respect I would emphasize the dangers inherent in formulating policy in this fashion. The Court as an institution is simply not suited for this task. Unlike the Congress, it has no reliable means to gauge the relative intensity of the interested parties, what the reactions will be to any given pronouncement or, *inter alia,* what obstacles are likely to arise in its execution. And once having embarked on a path, it can pull back or reverse itself only at great cost to its own prestige and the principle of the rule of law. Moreover, leaving aside the legitimacy of these activities, its members are ill equipped for such tasks because legal training scarcely provides the breadth of knowledge in fields such as philosophy, history, the sciences, and social sciences necessary for this mission.

These shortcomings, it is true, might or might not lead to serious consequences. But, taken together with the fact that the Court can act unilaterally, they all point to the potential for the kind of precipitous action that leads to factious policies. To put this another way, the character of the extended republic almost insures prolonged debate and deliberation before the national government can undertake any comprehensive program. And, even with this, as Publius notes, there still is no guarantee that factious majorities might not on occasion prevail. To this issue, Publius speaks in terms of probability; that given the numerous and diverse interests in the republic "seldom" would a factious spirit overtake a majority. But with the Court none of those conditions or factors associated with the extended republic comes into play. In a sense, then, the Court resembles the pure democracy that Madison detested, the more so as ideology grips a majority of its members, because impulse and opportunity for action so readily coincide.

What can be done about this state of affairs? In addition to what I say about this matter in what follows, I am convinced that "judicial self-restraint," which is frequently mentioned as a remedy, simply will not serve the purpose. None of the justices, including those who have advocated this doctrine by way of chastising their activist colleagues, has ever consistently adhered to this doctrine. We cannot expect the judges to abide by this standard any more than we can count on the members of the news media to police themselves when it comes to matters of propriety and national security. And the justices' task is made doubly difficult given the political agenda associated with the new morality, since the temptation arises so frequently to abandon the principle of judicial restraint and strike a blow for "good" over "evil." Nor will the fact that the Court's composition and outlook change—at least that of the majority—over a relatively short period of time (a new justice is appointed on the average of once every 2.5 years or so) serve to keep the Court within its bounds. A change of personnel simply does not go to the heart of the problem. The potential for judicial usurpation remains.

Ultimately, it seems to me, Congress must fashion a permanent remedy either through legislation, or more probably in the form of an amendment.* Limiting the jurisdiction of the Court or recourse to the impeachment process—remedies consonant with the older morality—are at best piecemeal solutions that would provide only temporary relief. The fact is that we look in vain to the Founders for a lasting solution to our problem because, as we have seen from Hamilton's commentary, they simply did not envision the emergence of a new morality that would justify the present role and power of the Court. Put otherwise, impeachment, given their understanding of the system, would be a deterrent and an appropriate remedy for wayward justices precisely because there was a consensus about the proper role of the judiciary. Now, however, thanks to the new morality, this consensus no longer exists and so their remedy is no longer viable. Under the older morality, the justices would never on any consistent basis undertake "active resolution," not so much, we may surmise, because they would be impeached and removed from office, but rather because they understood the role of the Court to be pretty much that described by Hamilton. But, again, thanks to the new morality, this situation no longer obtains.

---

*For the contents of such an amendment see Francis Canavan, "A New Fourteenth Amendment," *Human Life Review* 12 (Winter 1986). Father Canavan's amendment would meet the criteria I set forth here for an effective solution to the problem of judicial supremacy.

What seems clear from this is that, whatever form the remedy takes, its end must be that of effectively delineating the Court's role relative to the other branches. What is also abundantly clear is that the political constellation of forces at this point in history is such that any remedy will be a long time coming. The constitutional crisis to which I refer will be with us for quite some time even though morally and constitutionally monstrous decisions such as *Roe v. Wade* do serve to hasten the day of reckoning.

The solution to the abortion question that I offer, written as it was in 1976, may seem completely outdated to many, if for no other reason than that the political landscape has changed. Now the "right to life" forces have turned the tables and are seeking legislation from a seemingly sympathetic Congress that would codify *Roe v. Wade.* This, I should note in passing, is an interesting development because the move toward legislation derives in part from the realization that *Roe v. Wade* is not sufficient to legitimize abortion "rights," any more than the Dred Scott decision legitimized slavery. Moreover, what is apparent is that Congress, from all indications, is not so sympathetic to abortion "rights" as initially thought; that, contrary to expectation, it would place more restrictions on abortions than the Court.

But be that as it may, my solution is not so outdated as it might seem to be at first glance. In the first place, there is an excellent possibility that resolution of this controversy will, indeed, come through national, not state, regulation. The Court, in effect, has acknowledged that it stepped out of line with its *Roe* decision, all of which strengthens Congress's hand. And once the issue is placed in the political realm for resolution, the pro-lifers will have won a strategic victory of immense significance. Even if the initial legislation caters to the abortionists, subsequent Congresses will have to face enormous pressures to restrict abortion. And unless the nation has lost all of its moral sensibilities, the people will not long endure a policy of abortion on demand that terminates over 1.5 million pregnancies (or about a third of all pregnancies) each year.

Finally, as I argue, Congress should use Section 5 of the Fourteenth Amendment rather than the commerce power in resolving this matter. That it is more sensible to use Section 5 is, I think, readily apparent. Beyond this, though, the Congress would be sending the Court a message, namely, that Congress bears primary responsibility for interpreting the terms of the Fourteenth Amendment.

ABORTION AND THE AMERICAN POLITICAL CRISIS

The abortion controversy mirrors a far wider battle that is taking place in the Western world. The issue clearly involves religious, philosophical, ethical, legal, economic, and, *inter alia,* political considerations of the most fundamental nature, involving the very roots of the Judeo-Christian tradition.[1] But here I mean to note only those aspects of it that clearly pose serious challenges to our own republican institutions and procedures.

---

[1] In the forceful and eloquent words of Malcolm Muggeridge: "We can survive energy crises, inflation, wars, revolution and insurrections, as they have been survived in the past; but if we transgress against the very basis of our mortal existence, become our own gods in our own universe, then we shall surely and deservedly perish from the earth." "What the Abortion Argument is About," *Human Life Review* 1 (Summer 1975), 6.

For the Founding Fathers the central problem of the strengthened national government that they established via the Constitution was this: how could the effects of factions be controlled? For them the word "faction" had a far deeper meaning than we normally attach to it today. It did not refer simply to interest groups in the society, or even to those who had organized to seek change in our political and social structures. Rather, the term referred to those who sought to operate outside the accepted moral and ethical principles that provided the cohesion necessary for the society to operate at all; it connoted a selfish group that sought immediate gratification of its interests at the expense of the long-range interests of the society. These characteristics of faction are embodied in Madison's well-known definition:

> By a faction, I understand a number of citizens, whether amounting to a majority or minority of the whole, who are united and actuated by some common impulse of passion, or of interest, adverse to the rights of other citizens, or to the permanent and aggregate interests of the community (10:43–44).

Factions, of course, could plague any form of government. But it was well recognized, as Madison put it, that factions are the source of the "diseases most incident to republican government" (48), the very form of government that the Constitution embodied. Because the "latent causes of faction are sown in the nature of man" (44), and men possess the liberty to pursue their ends, no matter how selfish or ignoble, factions are necessarily found in abundance in republican forms. Moreover, according to Madison's line of reasoning, it would be both impractical and unwise to take those steps necessary to *eliminate* factions. This would involve the elimination of liberty, an element essential to factions. Yet, to do this would be tantamount to the "annihilation of air . . . because it imparts to fire its destructive agency." Thus, eradicating liberty is too high a price to pay to avoid the ills of faction. To reduce all men to the same interest, another method of eliminating factions, would be impossible because "different opinions will be formed" so long "as the reason of man continues fallible and he is at liberty to exercise it." What is more, to reduce men to the same interests runs counter to the "first object of government," which is to protect the "diversity in the faculties of men" (44).

Here, let us briefly discuss the solution to the problem of factions which Madison, the purported "father" of our Constitution, was foremost in articulating both in the Philadelphia Convention and in *The Federalist*.[2] The very extensiveness of the new republic, a given factor, played a critical role in his thinking. Extensiveness meant that there would be numerous and diverse interests, a condition not to be found in small territorial democracies, and that the people would

---

[2]For a more comprehensive elaboration of Madison's solution see Ch. 2 above.

not make decisions directly. Rather, elected representatives of the people would have to assemble to conduct the affairs of state. These two factors, which are the concomitants of extensiveness, would serve to *control the effects of faction.* How and in what ways? Because, first, in electing representatives, the attention of the people was likely to focus on individuals "whose wisdom may best discern the true interests of the country, and whose patriotism and love of justice will be least likely to sacrifice it to temporary or partial considerations" (47). Thus, factious proposals would stand little chance of success in our national councils of decision making.

Second, the multiplicity and variety of interests would serve to make the task of any faction securing majority support extremely difficult. Factious proposals would seldom "force" themselves into the national political arena. For one thing, among the variety of interests it would be difficult to find a "common motive" for united action, and even if a common motive did exist, extensiveness would make it "difficult for all who feel it to discover their own strength." For another, "where there is a consciousness of unjust or dishonorable purpose, communication is always checked by distrust in proportion to the number whose concurrence is necessary" (48). Beyond this, we may note, any concerted campaign by a factious majority would take time. This would allow the people time to deliberate, so that, unlike pure or direct democracies, there would be far less likelihood that a majority would succumb to unreflective passion and the appeals of a demagogue.

These, in brief, were the factors that Madison felt would operate to control the effects of a majority faction. In his words, in our extended republic "and among the great variety of interests, parties, and sects which it embraces, a coalition of a majority of the whole society could seldom take place on any other principles than those of justice and the general good" (51:269). But if Madison believed that majority factions would seldom rule, he was certain that minority factions would never be able to impose their will on the entire nation. All that he writes concerning the dangers of minority factions is the following:

> If a faction consists of less than a majority, relief is supplied by the republican principle, which enables the majority to defeat its sinister views by regular vote. It may clog the administration, it may convulse the society; but it will be unable to execute and mask its violence under the forms of the Constitution (10:45).

A knowledge of only the essentials of this underlying theory is enough to make the victory of the pro-abortionists by means of a Supreme Court fiat appear incredible. What is evident is that none of the hurdles associated with the extensive republic was even confronted, much less jumped, in their successful "campaign." At no point did the people have the opportunity even to deliberate over an issue of such profound moral and philosophical import. The pro-abortionists had not tasted victory for their position in any such manner in even one of the fifty-one jurisdictions composing the nation. Nor did the elected representatives of the people at any level have any input into that policy that is now national in scope. The evidence is irrefutable: if the American system had operated in a manner even approximating what Madison and the Founders had anticipated, the pro-abortionists would never have achieved a victory of such dimensions.

Clearly the victory for abortion on demand manifests the breakdown of the traditional American political order. It did not cause the breakdown; it is, however, the most vivid and incontrovertible evidence of that collapse. A faction, and a minority faction at that, was able to impose its will upon the entire nation as *constitutionally* binding.[3]

At the political level the explanation for this breakdown is easy to come by. We can best begin by observing that over the last several decades the Supreme Court has increasingly assumed the function of a supreme legislative body. Through its interpretation of the "equal protection" and "due process" clauses of the Fourteenth Amendment, it has increasingly exercised control over matters and concerns that were formerly regarded as within the domain of the states.[4] For instance, through the process generally known as "selective incorporation," it has used these clauses of the Fourteenth Amendment to nationalize the major provisions of the Bill of Rights so that they are now fully applicable to the states. This alone has fundamentally altered our original constitutional ground rules because the Bill of Rights was not intended to apply to the states.[5] On the contrary, it was looked upon as a curb on the powers of the national government vis-à-vis the states.[6] Moreover, and what is more important, the Court's interpretation and use of the Fourteenth Amendment, whether in the process of selective incorporation or scrutinizing state laws to see if they conform with the "equal protection"

---

[3]Most certainly at the time of the Court's decision the pro-abortionists were a minority. As Dean O'Meara puts it: "Not until the recent past did a small but clamorous group begin to agitate for abortion on demand. In *Roe v. Wade* the Court yielded to the pressure of this strident minority." "Abortion: The Court Decides a Non-Case," *Human Life Review* 1 (Fall 1975), 19. Moreover, the polls that purportedly show majority support for abortion have never been worded so as to indicate the full dimensions of the Court's decisions and the practices that they condone.

[4]The relevant section of the Fourteenth Amendment is the first, which reads: "All persons born or naturalized in the United States, and subject to the jurisdiction thereof, are citizens of the United States and the State wherein they reside. No state shall make or enforce any law which shall abridge the privileges and immunities of citizens of the United States; nor shall any State deprive any person of life, liberty, or property, without due process of law, nor deny to any person within its jurisdiction the equal protection of the laws."

[5]Justice Marshall's statement in *Barron v. Baltimore* (1833), 7 Peters (U.S.) 243 is considered definitive on this matter.

[6]This is apparent, for instance, from the controversy surrounding the Alien and Sedition Acts (1798) which prompted the Virginia and Kentucky Resolutions, authored by Madison and Jefferson respectively. The issue at stake was not, as commonly supposed, freedom of speech and press. Rather it was whether the state or national government possessed the power to punish seditious libel. The opponents of the Acts argued that the first amendment precluded any *national* legislation in these areas. See Leonard W. Levy, *Freedom of Speech and Press in Early American History: Legacy of Suppression* (New York: Harper and Row, 1963).

and "due process" clauses, have served to render it an institution of immense powers, far beyond anything dreamt of by the Founding Fathers.

Certain vital issues that in the past evoked controversy concerning the Fourteenth Amendment and its purpose are now, sad to say, regarded as "water under the bridge." For example, it is highly doubtful, to say the least, that the drafters of the Fourteenth Amendment intended that it be used (as it *has* been used) to reduce the states to little more than subordinate principalities under the thumb of the Supreme Court. Rather, common sense, the language of the amendment, and its historical context would strongly suggest that its purpose was to guarantee the newly freed slaves the same due process and equal protection accorded the white citizens of the various states, particularly those that had formerly composed the Confederacy.[7] Nevertheless, as important as this issue may seem in terms of the drift of the American system, it is, as we have said, passé. The course of events and ideological factors seem to preclude serious discussion of this issue today.

Where we do continue to find controversy is in regard to the interpretation the courts have given to the principal clauses of the Fourteenth Amendment, as well as the Bill of Rights. And, more frequently than not, such controversies involve legal mumbo jumbo that makes it difficult to see the forest for the trees. The basic issues involved center around the fundamental principles of our system of government and are best understood in this light. It is not difficult to see that reasonable men will come to a parting of the ways at some point over the meaning of equal protection and due process. Nor is it difficult to see that, if one adopts a liberal or expansive interpretation of these concepts, the way is opened for greater judicial control over the states. Of course, and largely for the same reasons, the Court's interpretation of the Bill of Rights also affects the latitude of state discretion.

Against this background, what is abundantly clear is that modern courts—most especially the Warren Court—have seen fit to read their ideological preferences into the meaning, and hence the requirements, of equal protection, due process, and the Bill of Rights. Long-standing rules of constitutional interpretation were scrapped to advance the goals normally associated with secular liberalism.[8] For the most part, in these endeavors the Court was content to nullify state practices that it deemed inconsistent with its constitutional interpretations. However, with the desegregation cases, the Court took upon itself the authority to enunciate

---

[7]In this regard, it is frequently noted that the very same Congress that passed the Fourteenth Amendment also provided racially separated schools in the District of Columbia. Unquestionably, there is little resemblance between what the framers of the Fourteenth Amendment intended and the various judicial interpretations of it over at least the last sixty years. On this see Charles S. Hyneman, *The Supreme Court on Trial* (New York: Atherton Press, 1963), Ch. 15. See also, Charles Fairman, "Does the Fourteenth Amendment Incorporate the Bill of Rights? The Original Understanding," *Stanford Law Review* 5 (1949–50).

[8]For a detailed and critical analysis of some of the more prominent Warren Court decisions, see L. Brent Bozell, *The Warren Revolution* (New Rochelle, New York: Arlington House, 1966), particularly Section 2, "The Warren Court in the Dock."

positive public policy. In the Warren era it began, in effect, to tell the states: "The laws you have on the books are not only unconstitutional but this is what you must do in order to conform with the Constitution." Now the courts, at every level, are in the business of playing a positive, not negative, role; of commanding specific changes that are presumably the outgrowth of mandates embedded in our constitutional language.[9] Few today, even defenders of the Court, will deny it is legislating. And one has only to look at Boston's Judge Garrity to see clearly the culmination of this process, which comes, in my judgment, to nothing less than judicial tyranny.

In all of this, of course, the Court has far exceeded the role marked out for it by the Founders. Evidence that the Founders intended judicial review is, at best, very scanty. We do find in Alexander Hamilton's Federalist 78 a reasoned argument for judicial review—but of a kind and type totally unlike that which we have described. The Court, Hamilton enjoins, is to follow "strict rules and precedents" (406). The Court's power of judicial review extends only to laws whose provisions violate the "manifest tenor" of the Constitution (402). And, according to Hamilton, it should exercise its veto power over legislation only when there is an "irreconcilable variance" (403) between the provisions of the law and the "manifest tenor" of the Constitution. Finally, Hamilton maintains, the Court should always exercise its "JUDGMENT," not "WILL" (404). The exercise of "WILL" he deemed the particular prerogative of the legislative branch.

To appreciate fully the morality that Hamilton urged upon the Court, as if he knew that even severely limited powers of judicial review would be a matter of intense controversy, we should bear in mind his perception of the relationship of the Court to our other institutions. In this context he writes that the Court is "beyond comparison the weakest of the three departments of power," and the general liberty of the people can never be endangered" (402) by the Court; it possesses neither "FORCE nor WILL, but merely judgment; and must ultimately depend upon the aid of the executive arm even for the efficacy of its judgments;" and, in this vein, the Court "can take no active resolution whatever" (402). In sum, Hamilton takes pains to assure us, we have nothing to fear from the Court, even one vested with the power of judicial review.

Today, of course, Hamilton's conception of the judiciary and its power, as sensible as it is in the context of a limited republican government, is also passé. What we have in its place is a theory of judicial supremacy, a theory that, remarkably enough, is supported by most of our elected leaders, who accept the notion

---

[9]To the best of my knowledge, Charles Hyneman in *The Supreme Court on Trial* (see note 7 above, p. 185) first made this point (pp. 78–80). Also in *Cooper v. Aaron*, 358 U.S. 1 (1958), we find an assertion of judicial power unprecedented in our history, namely, that the Court's interpretation of the Constitution is superior to and binding upon all other branches of government. This cannot be adduced from the language of the Constitution or its recognized principles.

that the Court is the final arbiter as to the meaning of the Constitution. We need not concern ourselves with detailing how it has come to pass that this doctrine has gained ascendancy. What is important are its ramifications. In the first place, we see that, as the Court successfully expands the scope of its domain, the latitude for deliberative self-government diminishes. Put otherwise, matters that were formerly considered to be within the realm of the political processes as outlined above now fall exclusively under judicial control, including both factious and nonfactious matters. Second, this new morality concerning the role of the Court both strains our credulity and serves to thwart our normal political processes.

In sum, the doctrine of judicial supremacy combined with the newly found legislative powers of the Court rests upon the notion that the Court can divine from our Constitution answers to a myriad of perennially perplexing problems— and very small ones as well. The Court seems to be somehow free from the doubts and anxieties that plague mere mortal men when it pretends to answer such questions as: when does life begin? At what stage in the development of the fetus can we say there is "life"? What are the proper structures and processes of our representative institutions? What does representation mean? What ought to be considered in determining the "representative" character of our elected decision-making bodies? How should states finance their schools? What is an equitable tax structure for this purpose? What represents religious intrusion into our publicly financed educational institutions?[10]

NATURAL RIGHTS THEORY AND THE CONSTITUTIONAL DECLINE

Yet this transformation of our basic constitutional division of powers could not have come about unless it had been supported and abetted by a theory, a rationale, or an ideology. Such is demonstrably the case. We are currently witnessing the full effects of a secular, scientific "humanism" that finds it roots in the natural rights philosophy.

While we cannot explore all the aspects of the relationship between the natural rights school of thought and our contemporary *malaise,* certain features do merit our attention. We should note at the outset that the preposterous fiction underlying the natural rights dogma, specifically that of autonomous individuals in a state of nature, reflects a mind-set that regards the state as an artificial but omnipotent construct. Far-reaching consequences flow from this conception. First, let us consider the image of the autonomous individual who is viewed apart from the complex organic whole of society. His duties and responsibilities to others in the order of things are almost nonexistent. Beyond this, the individual becomes a moral

---

[10]For a summary of the concerns over the extent of judicial powers prompted in large part by the abortion decision see "The Power of Our Judges—Are They Going Too Far?" *U.S. News and World Report* (January 19, 1976).

universe unto himself; the rationalism imputed to him is the source of rights. Thus, the individual is not subordinate to any higher or transcendental order not of his own making or derived from his own private stock of reason.[11]

Second, that a state can be born out of the consent of such atomistic individuals also provides us insight into the nature of the resultant political order. The state now becomes the chief repository of reason, itself cut off from any transcendent order or higher moral law. It must, initially at least, build itself on the lowest common denominator of the interests and values of those individuals that compose it. As such it possesses no higher purpose; its actions, laws, and such have as their foundation no more moral force than that which the consenting act of individuals can bestow upon it. It follows that the state, like the individuals composing it, is at sea without a rudder. In this context, to quote the late John Courtney Murray, the state is ''simply an apparatus of compulsion without the moral function of realizing an order of justice; for in this view there is no order of justice antecedent to positive law or contractual agreement.''[12] And this situation leads us straightway into the morass of moral and ethical relativism.

Third, we should note that such a state eventually becomes all-pervasive. In terms of the natural rights theory it is the supreme authority precisely because it can lay a claim, superior to that of any subsidiary associations within the state, to embodying the collective will of all individuals. Consequently, and somewhat paradoxically, while there is a relativism with regard to individual values (the opinions of each autonomous individual are equal), there is an absolutism with respect to the state's function; namely, the full power to enforce the rights that it decrees.

These, we suggest, are the main roots of the secular, scientific humanism that has served to undermine our constitutional order. But to make the picture complete we must deal with certain theoretical developments.

The secularism of the natural rights school bears the characteristics of a religion that has dictated the direction of its modern development.[13] Because there is no transcendent moral order, the chief functions of the state become those of providing for material gratification. Science figures predominantly in this process for two reasons. First, science is the area that is presumably value-free, where, unlike the moral realm, findings, holdings, and the like are free from subjectivism. Thus science provides an objective yardstick in an otherwise relativistic world. Second, insofar as material gratification is the principal end of the state, scientific tech-

---

[11]There is, no doubt, reification involved in the modern uses of natural rights theory. These theories were originally useful in helping to describe in a simplified manner the legal structures and the status of the individual. However, what was originally a purely fictional account constructed for purposes of simplified explanation has, in the last century, increasingly assumed the status of reality. See Sir Henry Maine's *Popular Government* (Indianapolis: Liberty Fund, 1976).

[12]*We Hold These Truths* (New York: Sheed and Ward, 1960), 321.

[13]On this point see John Courtney Murray's ''Law or Prepossessions?'' in *Essays in Constitutional Law,* ed. Robert G. McCloskey (New York: Random House, 1957).

niques can be of use. For instance, crude utilitarianism is a feature of natural rights philosophy, and what could be more natural than the refinement of a "felicific calculus" such as that set forth by Bentham? And this is precisely what has happened. The most recent and exhaustive effort in this direction is Rawls's *A Theory of Justice*,[14] a tedious and rather feeble philosophical defense of the secular welfare state. Understandably, his concern is with "primary goods" and their distribution. Not surprisingly, the primary goods are material goods, and we are led to believe that not only can human wants and needs be determined on a more or less universal basis, but also various levels of need can be established to insure optimum collective or aggregate gratification.

This development assumes great significance because those who "properly" use felicific calculus to meet the evident wants and needs of the people best fulfill the functions of the state. With this we come up against an interesting but logical inversion of the older natural rights philosophy: the best state is not one run by the people without any regard for a transcendent or higher moral law; rather it is one run for the people by those best able to calculate optimum material gratification.

RAMIFICATIONS OF DECLINE: PRESENT AND FUTURE

We know that the vast majority of the American people have never consciously accepted this secular, scientific humanism in the terms we have set it forth. Very few, indeed, have probably ever given much thought to the intellectual and theoretical grounds that seem to dictate the direction of our governmental policies and the changes in our constitutional order. Indeed, probably few are aware of any such direction or shift. But who would deny that the concerted movement in manifestly predictable directions is not guided by a theory or philosophy, no matter how dimly perceived by the general public?[15] The symbols, clichés, slogans, and assumptions of our public discourse make it abundantly obvious to me that we are traveling down the path to oblivion marked out for us by the natural rights theorists.

This account of their theory, sketchy as it is, helps to provide a deeper understanding of what has happened within the American system, as well as the directions it is likely to take. Consider, for instance, only the following:

(a) The elitism spawned by the developments we have traced is a proximate cause for the "realignment" of the intended decision-making authority in our system and of our constitutional rules relative to such decision making. In this context, the Supreme Court is just as capable (probably more so) of making correct calculations as the legislature. After all, legislative deliberation might

---

[14]John Rawls, *A Theory of Justice* (Cambridge: Harvard University Press, 1971).

[15]On this general matter see M. J. Sobran, "The Abortion Sect," *Human Life Review* 1 (Fall 1975).

result in a variety of nonmaterialistic considerations being brought to bear. Moreover, in the last sixty years, the Court's pretense to neutrality finds a warm nesting place among the dogmas of secularism.

(b) The excessive concern for individual rights, apart from the social context in which they are asserted, is also traceable to the natural rights philosophy. The appeal to the state is understandable enough, for, in terms of theory, it is the only agency that is capable of dispensing rights. The result is an omnipotent state busily conferring rights upon individuals without regard to the impact of this on intermediate institutions or associations (the family, churches, schools, voluntary associations, and the like) that are essential for the cohesion of the state. Such intermediate groups have no place in the natural rights philosophy, whose very thrust is, rather, toward homogeneity of the citizens under the all-embracing state.

The process of rights conferral feeds back upon itself. As it tends to break down the intermediary associations, as the individual comes to find nothing between him and the state, the demand for new, more elaborate, and unheard-of rights grows and grows. Little wonder, then, that modern secularist thinking places such emphasis on our Bill of Rights. Yet, our Bill of Rights is essentially negative: it prescribes those things that government should *not* do. Only through such contortions as those we have witnessed in recent decades can the Bill of Rights meet the positive demands of the secularists. But it is doubtful that until the Ninth Amendment[16] is uncorked—something that I believe is imminent—the Bill of Rights will be able to provide the source of all the rights emanating from the secularists. In any event, we can safely predict an expanded role for the Courts in the years ahead.

(c) We can anticipate in the future far more turmoil than we have as yet witnessed within our society. And this no matter whether our constitutional order is restored to its proper moorings of deliberative self-government, or continues on its present path. A restoration would involve severe ''withdrawal'' symptoms for a large part of our population that has grown accustomed to the dispensations of the state, principally the courts. On the other hand, a continuation of the present trend will involve a dragging of feet or disobedience by those who don't like to be ordered about by *fiats* that are *not the product of the deliberate sense of the community.*[17]

---

[16]The Ninth Amendment states: ''The enumeration in the Constitution, of certain rights, shall not be construed to deny or disparage others retained by the people.'' Once it is unleashed there is no limit to what we can expect, given the number and nature of ''rights'' asserted in our society at the present time.

[17]A good deal of the Southern resistance to Court-ordered integration was, in fact, based on the firm conviction that the courts were acting *ultra vires* in their pronouncements. We know of many Southerners who during the 1950s staunchly maintained that they would obey a law passed by Congress but not the edicts of the courts. We may assume that this feeling was widely shared, if we judge by Southern compliance with the civil rights legislation of the 1960s.

Problems and Complexities: Consensual and Political

I have so far focused on certain political and theoretical aspects of our present crises that are highlighted by the abortion controversy, and that indicate quite clearly a breakdown in the American consensus, not merely a breakdown in the consensual process of the political order. A considerable portion of our population, that is to say, knowingly or unknowingly accepts and acts upon a theory that postulates the overriding end of the state to be maximum material gratification, individual or collective. Another sizeable proportion of the population adheres, again knowingly or unknowingly, to an older, but more vigorous and complex tradition that acknowledges a higher moral law. This older tradition, around which there was almost universal consensus at one time in our history, holds that the matter of ''rights'' is a very serious and tricky business once one gets around to acknowledging the complexity of society which is a very fragile organism. It holds that fulfilling the stated purposes of our Preamble—for instance, those of justice, securing the *blessings* of liberty to ourselves and our posterity, and domestic tranquility—is demanding; that there are no a priori answers to be derived from any baseless theory of natural rights for resolving the inevitable conflicts between the values and goods a society cherishes.

At base, then, there is no single solution to the cleavages in our public consensus. All one can do is to expose repeatedly and with clarity the secularists' basic theory and presumptions in the hope that such a shallow and barren philosophy, once exposed, will fade away.

Other matters, admittedly less important but of immediate concern, are involved in the abortion controversy. One such issue comes down to how to rectify the Court's decisions; more specifically, whether recourse should be had to the amendment process. Some antiabortionists hold that such an amendment, taken along with the busing, reapportionment, and prayer amendments, would ''clutter up'' the Constitution with matters not truly of constitutional status and that, moreover, once it becomes common practice to amend the Constitution every time the Court renders an unpopular decision, the stability of the constitutional order would be undermined. Another, and in our view more compelling, argument against the amendment procedure is that such a course of action would signify by clear implication that (a) the Court possessed the power to rule authoritatively on these matters, and (b) the Court's decision represents a correct reading of the Constitution. Else, why amend?

The argument to the effect that the Constitution would somehow be trivialized by the abortion amendment comes with ill grace from the pro-abortionists. Having won their case through the constitutional legerdemain outlined above, they now seek to close off the only possible remedy given the fact the Court has nailed its decision to the Constitution. In the first instance, it was the pro-abortionists and their kin on the Court who closed off all avenues for rectification save that of amendment.

But the theoretical considerations noted above relative to the clear presumptions involved in seeking an amendment are very weighty. To take the amendment route is to accept the liberal secularists' view of the Constitution, its order and processes.[18] We would, in sum, be playing ball in their park and under their rules. And the consequences of this can only be disastrous because their order is, in reality, no order at all: it holds to no principle, save that of imposing its will through processes that pose the least resistance. And that is why we have witnessed in the last several decades the abandonment of federalism in any meaningful sense of that word, a totally outrageous reformulation of the scope of judicial powers, and continued reversals of field with respect to the constitutional powers and prerogatives of the executive. Moreover, we know very well that when it suits their purpose they will once again change the rules.[19]

The case for a "human life amendment" is of course based upon the best of motives and it may seem crass and inhuman to allow these constitutional considerations to preclude a course of action that would put an end once and for all to the ethically monstrous policy of abortion on demand. However, there is another possible remedy that both utilizes our existing constitutional processes and joins the abortion issue with constitutional restoration. Specifically, Section 5 of the Fourteenth Amendment[20] expressly empowers the Congress through legislation to enforce the provisions of that amendment, the most important of which are found in Section 1: "nor shall any State deprive any person of life, liberty, or property without due process of law." Thus, Congress can, through a simple statute, incorporate the provisions of a human life amendment. This would be step one. Having done this, one of two possibilities would present itself. First, the Court might accept the congressional act, thereby abandoning its position. This possibility should not be underestimated, given an expression of congressional feeling and the fact that modern courts have shown a truly ingenious capacity to reverse fields.

The second alternative, of course, is that the Court would declare the congressional act unconstitutional. At this point the congressional recourse must be the

---

[18]In what follows we diverge markedly from the views expressed by Professor John T. Noonan in "A New Constitutional Amendment," *Human Life Review* 1 (Winter 1975). We certainly do not mean to imply that Professor Noonan is a secular liberal.

[19]The views of Arthur S. Miller and Ronald F. Howell best illustrate what we are referring to here. "The role . . . of the Supreme Court in an age of positive government must be that of an active participant in government, assisting in furthering the democratic ideal." And, they continue, "judicial decisions should be gauged by their results and not by either their coincidence with a set of allegedly consistent doctrinal principles or by an impossible reference to neutrality of principle." And, in the realization of the goals associated with secular humanism, they write, "the judiciary has as important a role to play as any other organ of government. Perhaps even more important than the legislature or the executive." "The Myth of Neutrality in Constitutional Adjudication," *University of Chicago Law Review* 27 (1960), 666.

[20]Section 5 reads: "The Congress shall have the power to enforce, by appropriate legislation, the provisions of this article."

impeachment process with the end in mind of clearing the Court of those justices who refuse to budge from their abortion-on-demand position. Here the issues would be joined: is Congress going to allow the Court to persist in a policy that permits the wanton murder of millions, a policy that contravenes Congress's constitutional prescription?

We hasten to add that we do not lightly recommend such a course of action, which would force a constitutional "showdown" of the first order. Such show-downs are to be avoided at almost any cost.[21] But the costs involved in allowing a continuation of the abortion-on-demand policy, by any known ethical standards deserving of the name, scarcely leave any alternative. Moreover, the repeated and successful assaults by the judiciary on our constitutional order, its abortion deci-sions being only among the most recent, must at some point be emphatically turned back. And, while we are under no delusions about the possibilities of achieving success through the means suggested here, the chances of procuring a constitutional amendment are scarcely any better. What is more, to the extent that constitutional action along the lines set forth here is even contemplated—be it only a group of, say, thirty to fifty representatives—the message is bound to be heard by a wider audience; the very terms of the ensuing debate will not only bring into focus the salient issues (moral and constitutional), but also put the pro-abortionists on the defensive and force them to do what is nigh unto impossible for them, namely, to set forth coherently their own moral and constitutional theories.[22]

Finally, in this connection, we must emphasize that the matter of abortion, contrary to what certain antiabortionists might contend, is a national, not a *state* or federal matter.[23] The very nature of the issue involved must preclude even one state permitting abortion on demand, a probable result of any policy that would overturn the Court's decisions only to the extent of returning us to the status quo ante. In this respect, the pro-abortionists have unwittingly performed a service for the antiabortionists: having thrust the issue into the national arena, they have highlighted the need for a remedy that is national in scope. Anything less than this would be a Pyrrhic victory.

This is not to suggest that we should scrap federalism or refuse to recognize the legitimate role of the judiciary in our system of government. Great care must be taken in curbing the Court and in formulating a coherent and prudential theory of

---

[21]Our position on this is set forth in Willmoore Kendall and George W. Carey, *The Basic Symbols of the American Political Tradition* (Baton Rouge: Louisiana State University Press, 1970), Ch. 8.

[22]Aside from this there is the added advantage that legislation would allow for greater flexibility than a constitutional amendment in making needed adjustments as circumstances might require.

While it can be said that legislation does not provide the same security as an amendment, the answer must be that, if the Congress backs a policy of abortion on demand or anything similar to it, there simply is no hope for the republic. If this happens, nothing will save us from our moral degeneration.

[23]For a contrary view see Professor David Louisell, "A Life-Support Amendment," *Human Life Review* 1 (Fall 1975).

state-national relations.[24] These matters clearly call for thought of the highest order. In saying this, we end where we began: the abortion controversy brings into focus the full range of our civilizational, as well as constitutional, crises. That our political order would sanctify abortion on demand as a constitutional right reflects the depth of these crises. And from this we know that the task of restoring our moral and constitutional order will not be easy.

---

[24]In our thinking about these matters, we must not assume a dogmatic stance towards federalism, as if the Founding Fathers had provided us with neat answers to the relative domain of state-national authority. Quite the contrary. They offer no clear-cut answers, but rather depend upon the prudence and good sense of future generations to make reasonable decisions on this matter. See Federalist 37, 39, and 46. See also, George W. Carey, ''Federalism: A Defense of Political Processes'' in *Federalism: Infinite Variety in Theory and Practice,* ed. Valerie Earle (Itasca, Illinois: F.E. Peacock Publishers, 1968). Likewise, we should be most reluctant ever to accept the judicial philosophy of Oliver Wendell Homes, Jr. On this see Walter Berns, ''Oliver Wendell Holmes, Jr.'' in *American Political Thought,* ed. Morton J. Frisch and Richard G. Stevens (New York: Scribner's, 1970).

Suggestions for Further Reading

Students interested in the American political tradition will find an abundance of primary materials, most of which have been put into collections that are readily available. These primary materials are indispensable for a full understanding of many issues and questions that have arisen concerning the origins of our constitutional system, such as: what values were uppermost in the minds of the Founders? What is the relationship between these values and the constitutional forms and processes? What was the intended relationship between the branches of government? What were the anticipated spheres of authority for the state and national governments? At still another level, these materials are important for discovering the sources of the institutions and values that have played an important role in our tradition and for tracing the evolution of these institutions and values over the course of our history.

Among the more important of these collections is *The Records of the Federal Convention of 1787*, edited by Max Farrand, rev. ed., 4 vols. (New Haven: Yale University Press, 1937). This collection contains Madison's notes of the proceedings of the Philadelphia Convention, as well as the partial notes of other delegates, and the correspondence, speeches, and writings of the delegates after the Convention that bear upon the meaning of the Constitution. A new volume that replaces the original fourth volume of Farrand is *Supplement to Max Farrand's the Records of the Federal Convention*, edited by James Hutson (New Haven: Yale University Press, 1988). *The Debates in the Several State Conventions on the Adoption of the Federal Constitution*, edited by Jonathan Elliot, 5 vols. (Philadelphia: J.B. Lippincott Co., 1836), contains notes of the Philadelphia deliberations, important documents relating to constitutional interpretation, and the available debates of the state ratifying conventions. It has been reprinted by the Lippincott Co. (1891) and Burt Franklin (1974). James McClellan and the late M. E. Bradford have produced two volumes (II and III) of a projected seven-volume undertaking to revise and enlarge the original Elliot volumes. Volume II, *The Federal Convention of 1787* (Richmond: James River Press, 1991) offers interesting biographical information on each of the delegates to the Philadelphia Convention. III, *Debates in the Federal Convention of 1787 as Reported by James Madison*, provides an extensive and highly useful index to the Philadelphia deliberations. A widely used one-volume collection of official documents relating to the Philadelphia Convention and its deliberations is *Documents Illustrative of the Formation of the Union of the American States*, edited by Charles C. Tansill (Washington, D.C.: Government Printing Office, 1927).

The Founders' Constitution, edited by Philip B. Kurland and Ralph Lerner, 5 vols. (Chicago: University of Chicago Press, 1987), provides historical materials relating to the major themes of the Constitution, as well as a wide variety of materials that bear upon the meaning of each section of the Constitution and Bill of Rights up to 1835. For an exhaustive survey of the English and colonial sources of the Bill of Rights, see *The Roots of the Bill of Rights*, edited by Bernard Schwartz, 5 vols. (New York: Chelsea House, 1980). The definitive documentary history relating to the formulation and adoption of the Bill of Rights is *Creating the Bill of Rights*, edited by Helen Veit, Kenneth Bowling, and Charles Bickford (Baltimore: Johns Hopkins University Press, 1991).

Colonial charters, early state constitutions, and related documents are found in *The Federal and State Constitutions, Colonial Charters, and Other Organic Laws of the United States of America*, edited by Francis N. Thorpe, 7 vols. (Washington, D.C.: Government Printing Office, 1907). A readily available source of colonial charters, acts, orders, and regulations is *Foundations of Colonial America*, edited by W. Keith Kavenagh, 6 vols. (New York: Chelsea House, 1983). For materials relevant to the revolutionary period and beyond, see *Sources and Documents Illustrating the American Revolution, 1764–1788, and the Formation of the Federal Constitution*, 2nd ed., edited by Samuel Eliot Morison (Oxford University Press, 1965).

Important for understanding the political thinking of those opposed to the adoption of the Constitution is *The Complete Anti-Federalist*, edited by Herbert J. Storing, 7 vols. (Chicago: University of Chicago Press, 1982). Aside from being the most comprehensive collection of Antifederalist writings, Volume I contains a lengthy essay entitled, "What the Anti-Federalists Were For." The best thought of the Antifederalists is also available in single volumes: *The Essential Antifederalist*, edited by W. B. Allen and Gordon Lloyd (Lanham, Maryland: University Press of America, 1985) and *The Anti-Federalist, An Abridgement* (of the Storing edition), edited by Murray Dry (Chicago: University of Chicago Press, 1985).

An interesting collection that highlights the issues dividing the Federalists and Antifederalists during the ratification struggle is *The Debate on the Constitution: Federalist and Antifederalist Speeches, Articles, and Letters During the Struggle over Ratification*, edited by Bernard Bailyn, 2 vols. (New York: Library of America, 1993). For the most extensive collection of political sermons, speeches, and pamphlets of the formative years of the republic, see *American Political Writing during the Founding Era, 1760–1805*, edited by Charles S. Hyneman and Donald S. Lutz, 2 vols. (Indianapolis: Liberty Fund, 1983). Interesting, but far less comprehensive, is *Pamphlets on the Constitution of the United States, 1787–1788*, edited by Paul Leicester Ford (New York: Da Capo Press, 1968).

Many shorter one-volume works present the significant writings of major individuals, primary materials that concern important constitutional issues, and official documents. Comprehensive works of this nature that span our history include: *Documents of American History*, edited by Henry Steele Commager, 7th ed. (New York: Appleton-Century-Crofts, 1963) and *Free Government in the Making*, edited by Alpheus Thomas Mason and Gordon E. Baker (New York: Oxford University Press, 1985). Other edited works contain the writings of notable individuals of the founding period. The American Heritage Series (New York: Liberal Arts Press), under the general editorship of Oskar Priest, has published: *Alexander Hamilton: Selections Representing His Life, His Thought, and His Style*, edited by Bower Aly; *The Political Writings of John Adams*, edited by George A. Peek, Jr.; *The Political Writings of Thomas Jefferson*, edited by Edward Dumbauld; and *Thomas Paine: Common Sense and Other Political Writings*, edited by Nelson F. Adkins. More comprehensive works along these lines are: *George Washington: A Collection*, edited by W. B. Allen (Indianapolis: Liberty Fund, 1988) and *The Mind of the Founder: Sources of the Political Thought of James Madison*, edited by Marvin Meyers (Hanover, New Hampshire: University Press of New England, 1982). The political thought of this era in another domain is found in *Political Sermons of the American Founding Era: 1730–1805*, edited by Ellis Sandoz (Indianapolis: Liberty Fund, 1991).

Debates over the meaning of key provisions of the Constitution in the first Congresses are presented in *A Second Federalist: Congress Creates a Government*, edited by Charles S. Hyneman and George W. Carey (Columbia: University of South Carolina Press, 1967). A very useful one-volume compilation that brings together the entire Congressional debate over the Fourteenth Amendment, as well as over the less controversial Thirteenth and Fifteenth, is *The Reconstruction Amendments' Debates*, edited by Alfred Avins (Richmond: Virginia Commission on Constitutional Government, 1967).

The interpretive literature dealing with the American political tradition has swelled enormously in the last thirty years as historians and political scientists, no longer preoccupied with seeking causes and motivations in the realm of economic and social "forces," have increasingly turned their attention to discovering the values, ideals, and theories that have shaped the foundations of our constitutional order. Differences in emphasis, focus, or approach form the basis for categorizing interpretations, so that it is now customary to speak of schools of thought concerning the theories and values that have shaped our political tradition. The differences between these schools of thought are so significant that some despair of ever achieving scholarly consensus concerning the sources and nature of our constitutional heritage. The reason for this despair should be evident even from our brief survey.

Since the publication of Bernard Bailyn's *The Ideological Origins of the American Revolution* (Cambridge: Harvard University Press, 1967), emphasis has been placed on the role that the values of "classical republicanism" played in the years leading up to and immediately following independence. Two significant works that advance this view in distinct ways are J. G. A. Pocock's *The Machiavellian Moment* (Princeton: Princeton University Press, 1969) and Gordon Wood's *The*

Creation of the American Republic (Chapel Hill: University of North Carolina Press, 1969). Pocock writes of the "Machiavellian moment" in the American tradition that appeared at the time of the Revolution, a moment when the classical republican virtues—e.g., the practice of sublimating individual wants and desires to the common good—prevailed among the citizenry. For his part, Wood sees the abandonment of the classical republican values, which were dominant at the time of the Revolution, with the adoption of the Constitution.

The classical republican approach is, in general, a more elaborate variant of the progressive depiction of our Founding (see the Introduction to this book). One cannot help but note, for example, that classical republicanism clearly bears a very close relationship to the model of French radicalism presented by Vernon L. Parrington, a construct greatly influenced by Rousseau's theories and concepts. Moreover, like the progressive approach, the classical republican portrays the Constitution as a retreat from the loftier and more humane values that inspired the Revolution, paralleling in this regard James Allen Smith's view of the Constitution as a "reactionary" document, designed to thwart the "democratic" aspirations of the people. Both, in other words, advance the proposition that there is a radical discontinuity in the American political tradition.

In two important respects, the classical republicans stand in sharp contrast to those generally known as "Straussians"—students and scholars profoundly influenced, either directly or indirectly, by the teachings of the late Professor Leo Strauss. First, despite differences among Straussians over how Locke's writings should be interpreted, they regard his teachings concerning natural rights and the consent of the governed, rather than the values of classical republicanism, as central to the American Founding. They find these teachings set forth in the Declaration of Independence, particularly the second paragraph whose formulation of rights, "life, liberty, and the pursuit of happiness," closely parallels Locke's "life, liberty, and property." Consequently, some Straussians view our Founding as influenced primarily by "modern" political philosophy, whose ends are not so lofty or ennobling as those set forth in classical thought. For a range of Straussian perspectives on this score, see Thomas Pangle, *The Spirit of Modern Republicanism: The Moral Vision of the American Founders and the Philosophy of Locke* (Chicago: University of Chicago Press, 1988); Harry V. Jaffa, *How to Think about the American Revolution* (Durham, N.C.: Carolina Academic Press, 1978); and certain essays, particularly that by Martin Diamond, in *The Moral Foundations of the American Republic*, 2d ed., edited by Robert H. Horwitz (Charlottesville: University of Virginia Press, 1979). Second, the Straussians view the Constitution teleologically, as an instrument designed to secure and advance the values and principles of the Declaration, particularly equality, inalienable rights, and consent of the governed. In this regard see Walter Berns, *Taking the Constitution Seriously* (New York: Simon and Schuster, 1987) and the collected writings of Martin Diamond, *As Far as Republican Principles Will Admit*, edited by William A. Schambra (Washington, D.C.: AEI Press, 1992).

Scholars who consider the philosophers of the Scottish Enlightenment as the major influence on the founding era form still another school of thought. Garry Wills, in his *Inventing America: Jefferson's Declaration of Independence*, endeavors to show how Scottish thought determined the content and character of the Declaration of Independence through its influence on Jefferson. In *Explaining America: The Federalist* (New York: Doubleday and Co., 1981), a work dedicated to Douglass Adair, Wills argues that both Hamilton and Madison, as authors of *The Federalist*, also reflect this Scottish influence. For the works of Douglass Adair, see *Fame and the Founding Fathers: Essays by Douglass Adair*, edited by Trevor Colbourn (New York: W.W. Norton, 1974).

The most interesting, informative, and heuristic accounts of the foundations of our political tradition, in my judgment, are to be found in works outside these schools of thought, works whose approaches are far more eclectic. This category includes Forrest McDonald's trilogy: *We the People: The Economic Origins of the Constitution* (Chicago: University of Chicago Press, 1958); *E Pluribus Unum: The Formation of the American Republic, 1776–1790* (Indianapolis: Liberty Fund, 1979); and *Novus Ordo Seclorum: The Intellectual Origins of the Constitution* (Lawrence, Kansas: University Press of Kansas, 1985). The final volume evaluates and places in perspective the economic and political theories that shaped the minds of the Framers. Two excellent works that explore the contributions of the classics, Christianity, and medieval thought to our political tradition are Ellis Sandoz, *A Government of Laws: Political Theory, Religion, and the Founding* (Baton Rouge: Louisiana State University Press, 1990) and Russell Kirk, *The Roots of American Order* (La Salle, Illinois: Open Court, 1974).

Other notable works deal primarily with the organic political experiences of Americans in endeavoring to secure self-government with ordered liberty. Among these are: Willmoore Kendall and George W. Carey, *The Basic Symbols of the American Political Tradition* (Baton Rouge: Louisiana State University Press, 1970); Donald Lutz, *The Origins of American Constitutionalism* (Baton Rouge: Louisiana State University Press, 1988); and Andrew C. McLaughlin, *The Foundations of American Constitutionalism* (New York: New York University Press, 1932). The works of M. E. Bradford stress the evolutionary, and distinctly non-ideological, character of our constitutional development: *A Better Guide than Reason: Studies in the American Revolution* (La Salle, Illinois: Sherwood Sugden, 1979) and *Original Intentions: On the Making and Ratification of the United States Constitution* (Athens: University of Georgia Press, 1993). Other approaches, while focusing on the American experience, find the roots of our institutions in Western thought and practice, primarily in the English tradition. James McClellan's *Liberty, Order, and Justice* (Washington, D.C.: Center for Judicial Studies, 1989) is a lucid account of the evolution of our constitutional principles from the English tradition. An earlier and noteworthy effort in this genre is C. Ellis Stevens, *Sources of the Constitution of the United States Considered in Relation to Colonial and English History* (New York: The Macmillan Co., 1929). Also of great interest in this connection are the essays in *Magna Carta: Ancient Constitution and the Anglo-American Tradition of the Rule of Law*, edited by Ellis Sandoz (Columbia: University of Missouri Press, 1993).

Turning to the Supreme Court, there are several books that are critical of its interpretations and activism. These include Christopher Wolfe's *The Rise of Modern Judicial Review: From Constitutional Interpretation to Judge-Made Law* (New York: Basic Books, 1985). Wolfe critically analyzes the arguments of major noninterpretivists, comparing their positions with the traditional view of judicial review. Gary L. McDowell has written two books highly critical of the Court's expanded role and its use of equity powers. See *Curbing the Courts: The Constitution and the Limits of Judicial Power* (Baton Rouge: Louisiana State University Press, 1988) and *Equity and the Constitution: The Supreme Court, Equitable Relief, and the Constitution* (Chicago: University of Chicago Press, 1982). Robert Bork's *Tempting of America: The Political Seduction of the Law* (New York: Free Press, 1990) presents a lucid explanation of the "originalist" position regarding constitutional interpretation. Three works by Raoul Berger deal with the effect of judicial neglect of original intent in critical areas: *The Fourteenth Amendment and the Bill of Rights* (Norman: University of Oklahoma Press, 1989); *Federalism: The Founders' Design* (Norman: University of Oklahoma Press, 1987); and *Government by Judiciary: The Transformation of the Fourteenth Amendment* (Cambridge: Harvard University Press, 1977). L. Brent Bozell's *The Warren Revolution* (New Rochelle, New York: Arlington House, 1966) is one of the first works to challenge the supremacist presumptions of the modern Court. As noted in the text, the pioneering effort in exploring the implications of modern judicial supremacy is Charles S. Hyneman's *The Supreme Court on Trial* (New York: Atherton Press, 1963).

For views that differ significantly from those of the preceding authors regarding the Supreme Court and its role, see Laurence Tribe, *Constitutional Choices* (Cambridge: Harvard University Press, 1985) and Michael Perry, *The Constitution, the Courts, and Human Rights* (New Haven: Yale University Press, 1982).

The Constitutional Convention and its proceedings have been the subject of a number of highly readable works. Among the more popular of these is Clinton Rossiter, *1787: The Grand Convention* (New York: Harcourt, Brace and Co., 1966); Catherine Drinker Bowen, *Miracle at Philadelphia* (Boston: Little, Brown and Co., 1966); and Carl Van Doren, *The Great Rehearsal* (New York: Viking Press, 1948). A shorter work that stresses the frictions and compromises at the Convention is Max Farrand, *The Framing of the Constitution of the United States* (New Haven: Yale University Press, 1913). A scholarly and legalistic work that provides a day-to-day account of the proceedings and traces the origins and meanings of the constitutional provisions is Charles Warren's *The Making of the Constitution* (Boston: Little, Brown and Co., 1937).

Recent works on *The Federalist* include *Securing the Revolution: The Federalist Papers and the American Founding*, edited by Charles R. Kesler (New York: Free Press, 1987). This volume consists of illuminating essays on various aspects of *The Federalist*, principally by Straussians. In *The Political Theory of "The Federalist"* (Chicago: University of Chicago Press, 1984), David F. Epstein focuses on Publius's quest for a republican government and the sources that influenced his thinking. George W. Carey, *The Federalist: Design for a Constitutional Republic* (Urbana: University of Illinois Press, 1989) focuses on Publius's understanding of republicanism, federalism, the separation of powers, and constitutionalism. Of use to students of *The Federalist* is *Concordance to THE FEDERALIST* (Middletown, Connecticut: Wesleyan University Press, 1980) by Thomas F. Engeman, Edward J. Erler, and Thomas B. Hofeller.

Robert A. Rutland, *The Birth of the Bill of Rights* (Chapel Hill: University of North Carolina Press, 1955) traces the development of rights under the post-revolutionary state governments. A book that is somewhat dated but whose appendices are extremely valuable for understanding the character of the rights proposed by the ratifying conventions is Edward Dumbauld's *The Bill of Rights and What It Means Today* (Norman: University of Oklahoma Press, 1957). Insightful and informative essays on the original understanding of the provisions of the Bill of Rights, along with the interpretations given to them today by the modern courts, are contained in *The Bill of Rights: Original Meaning and Current Understanding*, edited by Eugene Hickok (Charlottesville: University of Virginia Press, 1991).

Among the excellent works that historically and analytically explore the principles underlying the American Constitution, see M. J. C. Vile, *Constitutionalism and the Separation of Powers* (Oxford: Clarendon Press, 1967); William B. Gywn, *The Meaning of the Separation of Powers* (New Orleans: Tulane University Press, 1965); S. Rufus Davis, *The Federal Principle: A Journey Through Time in Quest of a Meaning* (Berkeley: University of California Press, 1978); K. C. Wheare, *Federal Government*, 4th ed. (Westport, Connecticut: Greenwood Press, 1980); and *Federalism: Infinite Variety in Theory and Practice*, edited by Valerie Earle (Itasca, Illinois: F. E. Peacock, 1968).

For a more general survey of our constitutional development, see Alfred H. Kelly, Winfred A. Harbison, and Herman Belz, *The American Constitution: Its Origins and Development*, 6th ed. (New York: Norton, 1983) and Andrew C. McLaughlin, *A Constitutional History of the United States* (New York: D. Appleton-Century Co., 1935). Comprehensive works dealing with American political thought include: Charles E. Merriam, *A History of American Political Theories* (New York: The Macmillan Co., 1928); Francis Graham Wilson, *The American Political Mind* (New York: McGraw Hill, 1949); and A. J. Beitzinger, *A History of American Political Thought* (New York: Dodd, Mead, and Co., 1972).

The text of this book was set in a type called Times Roman,
designed by Stanley Morison for the *London Times*, and first
introduced by that newspaper in 1932. The *Times* was seeking
a typeface that would be condensed enough to accommodate
a substantial number of words per column without sacrificing
readability and still have an attractive, contemporary appearance.
It is one of the most popular typefaces in use for book work
throughout the world and quite justifies the claim made for it
of being the most important type design of the twentieth century.
Stanley Morison has been a strong forming influence, as typo-
graphical advisor to the English Monotype Corporation, as
director of two distinguished English publishing houses, and as
a writer of sensibility, erudition, and keen practical sense.

This book is printed on paper that is acid-free and meets
the requirements of the American National Standard
for Permanence of Paper for
Printed Library Materials, Z39.84, 1984. ∞

Editorial services by BooksCraft, Inc., Indianapolis, Indiana
Typography by Weimer Graphics, Inc., Indianapolis, Indiana
Printed and bound by Worzalla Publishing Company, Stevens Point, Wisconsin